The Great Valley Road of Virginia

THE GREAT

Shenandoah Landscapes from Prehistory to the Present

VALLEY ROAD

Edited by Warren R. Hofstra and Karl Raitz

OF VIRGINIA

UNIVERSITY OF VIRGINIA PRESS | CHARLOTTESVILLE AND LONDON

University of Virginia Press
© 2010 by the Rector and Visitors of
the University of Virginia

First published 2010

9 8 7 6 5 4 3 2 1

Library of Congress Cataloging-in-Publication Data
The great Valley Road of Virginia : Shenandoah
landscapes from prehistory to the present / edited by
Warren Hofstra and Karl Raitz.
   p. cm.
Includes bibliographical references and index.
ISBN 978-0-8139-2885-2 (cloth : alk. paper)
   1. Shenandoah River Valley (Va. and W. Va.) —
History, Local.   2. United States Highway 11 —
History.   3. Landscape — Shenandoah River Valley
(Va. and W. Va.) — History.   4. Transportation
— Shenandoah Rivery Valley (Va. and W. Va.) —
History.   5. Roads — Shenandoah River Valley (Va.
and W. Va.) — History.   I. Hofstra, Warren R.,
1947–   II. Raitz, Karl B.
F232.S5G74   2010
975.5'9 — dc22   2009035815

This book is published in association with the
Center for American Places, Santa Fe, New Mexico,
and Staunton, Virginia (www.americanplaces.org).

Contents

Acknowledgments

The work of numerous people has eased the journey of producing this volume, and we are indebted to all of them. Its first stage was achieved with a conference held at Shenandoah University in Winchester, Virginia, on June 4–5, 2004. Sponsored by the Shenandoah University History Center and the institution's Community History Project, this event obligated the time, toil, and skill of many individuals, most notably William Austin, program director for the History Center; Patricia Zontine, program coordinator; Sandy Snyder, administrative assistant; and Bonnie Miller, housekeeper. All four continued to work together in their varied specialties to help transform a popular public event into this volume. A grant from the United States Small Business Administration (award #SBAHQ-02-1-0012) made the History Center and this collaboration possible.

Among our greatest obligations are those owed to this book's contributing authors. For the small compensation of an academic's honorarium, they time and time again exerted extra effort to meet and exceed high expectations both for the conference presentations and the manuscripts that followed. What success this volume achieves will be a testimony to the unbuttoned hard work, high professionalism, and good cheer of Jim Bryant, Ken Keller, Gerry Kiefer, Gabrielle Lanier, Ann McCleary, and Mike McConnell. Complementing and expanding upon their efforts are Scott Jost's photographs. They dramatically bring the story of the Valley Road into the present moment and lend this volume a contemporary impact that text alone cannot achieve. Pitching in at the conference and at odd times with advice and support were session chairs Ann Denkler and Tracy Fitzsimmons, both of Shenandoah University; Carter L. Hudgins, of the University of Mary Washington; and Pam Simpson, of Washington and Lee University. The renowned folklorist of the Shenandoah Valley, the late John L. Heatwole, of Blue Ridge Community College, provided the keynote address for the conference banquet. Sharing insights on road preservation and prodding a nascent highway preservation movement for U.S. 11 into action were panelists Dan Marriott, of the National Trust for Historic Preservation; Daniel M. Rice, of the Ohio & Erie Canal Corridor Coalition; and Phil Baker, representing the Virginia Department of

Transportation. Tracy Fitzsimmons, now president of Shenandoah University, has continued to provide the essential vision and leadership that nurtures projects such as this one into fruition at America's independent colleges.

This book, however, would never have proceeded beyond the conference stage without the inspired leadership of George Thompson, founder and director of the Center for American Places, our copublisher. It was in conversations and several notable road trips along Virginia's portion of Route 11 that this volume took shape and substance. At all phases in its development, George's firm hand on the publishing process and his vision for what Center books can contribute to the intellectual and aesthetic life of our society made light the burden of editing and revising. Also assisting with honest advice, insightful critique, and many good suggestions that measurably improved the manuscript were Randy Jones, of the Virginia Department of Historic Resources, and Kevin Patrick, from Indiana University of Pennsylvania. The maps and other original images that so improve this volume are the result of the design and cartographic skills of Richard Gilbreath, director of the Gyula Pauer Cartography Laboratory at the University of Kentucky, and geographic information system specialist Jeff Levy. Butch Fravel, himself of Newtown, now Stephens City, generously provided the drawing of a Newtown freight wagon of his own drafting. Bringing the book to life was the accomplishment of the University of Virginia Press, where press director Penny Kaiserlian, managing editor Ellen Satrom, project editor Mark Mones, acquisitions assistant Angie Hogan, and copy editor Susan Murray gave the volume their unflagging support and unstinting effort. But in the largest sense, the debt that only this volume itself can repay once it sets off on its own journey is to the many men and women who love old roads and who would take along just such a reading companion on some journey down U.S. 11, knowing and enjoying the route a little better for it.

The Great Valley Road of Virginia

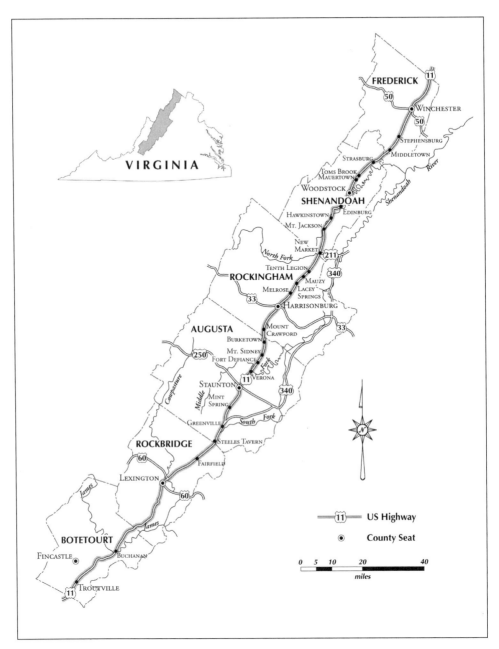

The Valley Road. (Gyula Pauer Cartography Lab, University of Kentucky)

Introduction

The Valley Road in Time and Space

WARREN R. HOFSTRA AND KARL RAITZ

Look at a satellite photograph or detailed landform map of North America, and the Great Valley of the Appalachians stands out as one of the most prominent geographic features on the continent. From New England to the southern Appalachians, this valley forms a great topographic crescent that visually overwhelms notable coastal features such as Cape Cod or the Chesapeake Bay (see fig. I.1). Not visible from the altitude of a satellite, however, is the Valley Road, which in various segments runs along most of this expansive inland trough. It is the road that is the subject of this book, as is its role in shaping the landscape of one of the most renowned segments of the Great Valley: the Shenandoah Valley.

Accounts of the first European settlements in Virginia's Shenandoah Valley in the 1720s and early 1730s often credit its ridge and valley geography with channeling population flows from the mid-Atlantic into the uplands of the southern backcountry. Landforms, by this account, directed migration much like canals or river levies control water flow. But people do not move in fluid motion, taking the course of least physical resistance in the flood tide of migration. Many factors—land markets, economic opportunities, political incentives, diplomatic initiatives, kinship, and friendship, to name a few—govern the routes of human movement. As lines on a map, the roads that facilitate this movement represent vectors resolving many forces at work in the natural and cultural worlds. Taken together, these forces create what we call landscape.

While this book is about the Valley Road, it is also about the Shenandoah Valley's landscape. Because landscape provides a way of discussing how people impress their culture on the environment in which they work and build a way of life, included in the story are the men and women of the Shenandoah Valley and the lifeways they created. The elements of any traditional landscape are familiar to all its creators, users, and visitors: farms with their fields, houses, barns, fences, and mills; towns with stores, build-

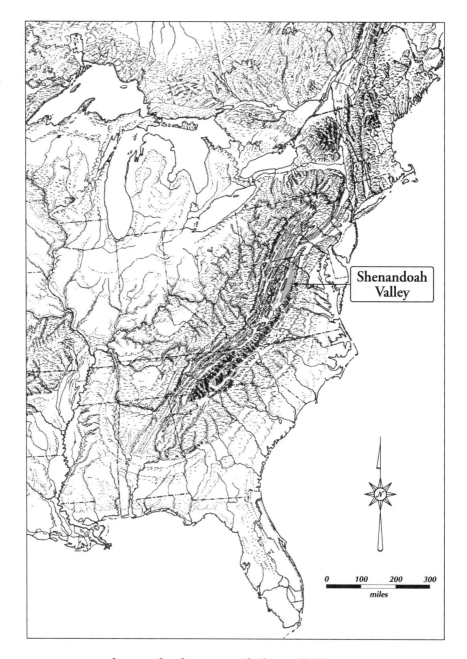

Shenandoah
Valley

ings, signs, markets, and industries; and, above all, the routeways that link
landscape elements one with another: streets, roads, highways, and byways. Behind and sustaining this visible fabric, however, are the oft unseen
webs of technological development, social relations, economic activity,
political structure, and mentality or ways of thinking about the material
world that affect how people organize landscape elements on the ground.
Governing spatial arrangements among a cluster of houses or farms in a
rural landscape, for instance, might be family ties among siblings or cous-

ins who inherited a common tract of land. Stream patterns would certainly determine the location of gristmills, but so would access by farmers who needed grain ground for market or family use. Town development and hierarchical relations among towns of varying size, commercial importance, and economic function are likewise expressions of a range of individual decisions and anonymous market forces adjusting to topography and environment. Roads allow landscape elements to work together. They are the web of accessibility that enables the organism to function. To study roads, therefore, is to study the organic culture of a people.

If understanding the Valley Road provides a window into the interior life of a people and the culture that sustains them on the land, then roads are also the key to comprehending change and the changes that transform culture. New ideas, new goods, and new people all travel on roads. Beginning in the mid-nineteenth century, canals, railroads, and the telegraph competed with roads in the commerce of change. But in the final analysis, roads have proved more enduring as agents of change than the plethora of new communications technologies that dominated life in the twentieth century.

All this is claiming a lot for roads, for the Valley Road, for the Shenandoah Valley, and for an understanding of its people. Most wayfarers would hardly consider any of these ideas even if they traveled exclusively to see the land and landscape. And students of the landscape would never limit their study to roads alone. But some roads are foundational roads whose formative stories weave in and out of the mainstream narrative of national and regional history. Such a road is the Valley Road. There are, of course, many others: the Wilderness Road, the National Road, the Natchez Trace, the Santa Fe Trail, the Oregon Trail, and Route 66, to name a few. The western trails, however, survive only in memory and in a few ruts incised into the land here and there. The Natchez Trace exists solely as a unit of the national park system, and Route 66, a twentieth-century creation, has been superseded by interstate highways.

The Valley Road, however, began in unrecorded time as a path that Native Americans followed as they moved across the interior of North America in pursuit of game, trade, or enemies. Europeans adopted it as they moved into upland frontiers in the eighteenth century. The strategic needs of European empires engaged in global conflicts drew these pioneers from the mid-Atlantic colonies into the southern backcountry, as did their individual desires for the economic independence of land ownership. The vector of these movements and their causes was the Great Wagon Road that, by the time of the American Revolution, extended from

Philadelphia to Georgia, much of it following the Great Valley. Thus by the end of the colonial period the road had not only shaped the cultural geography of native North America but also defined the first interior frontier for Europeans and established a long-distance linkage for trade and travel rivaled in length and significance only by the Camino Real connecting Santa Fe to the capital of New Spain at Mexico City.

By the end of the eighteenth century, the Philadelphia Wagon Road, as it was also known, not only drew the Shenandoah Valley into the culture area of Pennsylvania but also provided access to international markets for perhaps the most dynamic commodity in Atlantic commerce: wheat. The Shenandoah Valley quickly developed into one of the leading flour-producing regions in North America. In a state otherwise known for tobacco and slavery, the Valley became the source of sectional controversy long before the Civil War fractured the nation. Although railroads took over the job of carrying Valley flour to market during the last third of the nineteenth century, the staple economy of the region continued to outproduce that of other noted American granaries, including the Great Plains. At the same time, the wealth that flour returned to the Valley's farmers and its dispersal through a complex service economy to a broad middle class combined to create a rich material culture and a highly improved landscape. As artists and photographers popularized romantic views of this landscape before and then as a result of the Civil War, Americans came to know the region for its fabled beauty and sublime vistas. Thus one of the big stories tapped by the Valley Road in the twentieth century has been the development of the automobile, of tourism, and of a new roadside of vacation attractions, travel facilities, and mass marketing. As the road brought further commercialization and economic development throughout the course of the century, threats to the preservation of the Valley landscape have become the source of national attention and nostalgia for its pristine beauty.

If landscape represents the spatial organization and material expression of a people's way of life period by period, then landscape history is the intellectual stratigraphy of these periods layered one upon another. And cultural change is visible in the cut a road makes in the topography of time. But the elements of landscape are often enfolded back upon themselves time and time again so that a late eighteenth-century tavern might serve as a used-car dealership in the twentieth century and stand between a contemporary franchise restaurant and a 1920s bungalow refashioned as a real estate office. A discerning eye is needed to distinguish one from the other and envision historic landscapes as they merged across time. It is the purpose of this book to draw attention to these distinctions for the reader and equip anyone traveling U.S. 11 today with the insights to read down through the horizons of cultural layering for a better appreciation of the Shenandoah Valley's complex history.

Each chapter author examines a stratum of landscape history beginning with the earliest period of Native American settlement. Michael McConnell reviews the long era when native peoples used the corridor created by the Great Valley through the Appalachians. Since "Shenandoah" is an Indian word of uncertain origin that appears as "Cenuntua" on the earliest European map of the region, Native Americans no doubt distinguished the Shenandoah Valley from other Great Valley segments.[1] Archaeological evidence clearly indicates a continued Indian presence over the long course of nine millennia before Europeans arrived. McConnell chronicles the extended development of increasingly stable cultural adaptations eventuating in agricultural villages and, of course, interconnecting webs of paths and routes. Large numbers of transient sites, the archaeological presence of trade goods from throughout eastern North America, and well-known patterns of long-distance warfare all signal that the Valley served as a region of travel and transition for the continent's first inhabitants.

Warren Hofstra's chapter intersects McConnell's during the first half century of European settlement, when large numbers of migrants moving southwest from Pennsylvania took advantage of the routeway Native Americans had created and transformed the woodlands environment into an improved landscape of farms, fields, mills, and towns, all interconnected by a dense road network with the Great Wagon Road as its spine. Picking up at the late eighteenth century, Gabrielle Lanier takes the story of landscape and road development to the second quarter of the nineteenth century. During this period the Shenandoah Valley developed rapidly as both a primary avenue for migration to the trans-Appalachian West and as one of the most productive grain-growing regions of North America. As Lanier demonstrates, Virginia's emphasis on developing a western route to the Ohio to rival the Erie Canal and the network of interconnecting waterways and roadways including the Allegheny Portage Railroad linking Philadelphia to Pittsburgh stymied efforts to improve the Valley Road, which directed the commerce of grains and goods to northern cities.

The story of the Valley Turnpike is Ken Keller's to tell. He discusses the economic and political forces behind the move to transform the old wagon road into a modern turnpike and the impact one of the finest roads in nineteenth-century Virginia had on the Valley's economy and landscape. Geraldine Wojno Kiefer and James Bryant separately position the Valley Turnpike in the American Civil War through a gallery of wartime and postwar images. Not only did the road serve as the strategic anchor for both Union and Confederate armies, but partisans and combatants on both sides cast views of it that served to shape the memory of the conflict and create iconic images of a region deeply divided, not the least by a road that penetrated far into both northern and southern territory. Ann McCleary treats turnpike towns in a separate chapter. She makes the case that the commerce giving economic life to towns was road dependent and that the geography of urban places along the road created, in turn, a unique town and country landscape. In the final chapter, Karl Raitz reviews the twentieth century, when the Valley Turnpike became Lee Highway and then U.S. 11, one of the first great federal highways that joined others such as U.S. 30, the Lincoln Highway, in drawing the nation together and creating unprecedented opportunities for trade, tourism, and memorialization in the automobile era. Earlier in the volume in a chapter on the natural environment, Raitz demonstrates how the region's topography and geologic structure shaped the road, its placement, and the cultural landscape it created.

If each of these chapters represents a stratigraphic layer in the Shenandoah Valley's landscape and cultural history, then running through them are thematic veins that bond the sequence together. These are the book's big ideas that move it beyond a road history into a study that in turns is an environmental and geographical history, an ethnohistory, a social history, an art history, a political history, an intellectual history, and, in the largest sense, a cultural history. Interconnecting themes explain why a chronicle of the road and its landscape during one period may evoke ideas relevant to other periods. Where these themes penetrate beyond the region, they account for why developments in state and national history must be brought to bear on unraveling the larger meaning of local stories. Since the road was constructed of materials at hand, its route aligned by the regional geology that yielded these materials, and so much of its commerce comprised of the goods native soils and minerals produced, the environment composes an important theme of this book. That nature and natural forces not only constrain but also constitute culture is a given in modern social, political, as well as landscape histories. Any road, and certainly the Valley Road, represents a resolution of complex negotiations between nature and culture. Early nineteenth-century travelers condemned the road as one of America's most miserable routes, largely because it perforce followed the Valley's limestone beds whose rough, upturned edges presented

Fig. 1.2. An eighteenth-century stone tavern stood beside the Valley Road near Greenville. An Interstate 81 and U.S. 11 interchange here has prompted the construction of a new motel that uses the old tavern as an office, with symmetrical new motel-room wings appended to each side. A plastic backlit stilt sign is turned toward the interchange, beckoning to weary interstate travelers. A faux-colonial street lamp stands near the tavern's front door, perhaps intended to illuminate the roads that splice together here in a confused skein of the very old and the very new. (Scott Jost 2006)

an unyielding surface to unsprung, iron-wheeled wagons and coaches. This selfsame limestone, however, supplied the material that, when used in a broken-stone macadam surface a century later, had travelers praising the road as the "best thoroughfare in the South."[2] Influence on and by the environment as a theme of this volume was not always so obvious, but the role the road played in forest clearance, soil erosion, groundwater drainage, and the carriage of commodities such as fertilizer, insecticides, and agricultural machinery rendered its environmental impact profound and enduring.

Perhaps the deepest and broadest theme of this volume is that of landscape, insofar as landscape encodes the subtle discourse of nature and culture. In this formulation, road and landscape are indissoluble. To some degree, landscape is a function of the uses to which the road has been put throughout each phase in its long history. Conversely, the landscape has defined and shaped these uses. Thus road and landscape evolved in a dynamic synergy. Landscape is the road, the roadside, and the countryside, including the pattern of towns and villages — it is the material culture that makes place out of the road's geographic space. Embedded within the material culture are the immaterial relations of people making a living on the land, living together within communities, and ordering their social, economic, and political lives according to deep ways of thinking — or mental maps — that are both determinative and derivative of cultural forms. Breaking the landscape code — understanding these forms — permits insights not only into how people organize life collectively but also into the origins and development of their lifeways. The Valley Road therefore presents a metaphorical route into the history of the Shenandoah Valley and the forces of historic change that give its landscape structure, meaning, and significance.

The elements of landscape and the culture of common beliefs and practices sustaining it constitute one of the most powerful sources by which a people define themselves — regional identity. This book is therefore as much about the Valley region as it is about the Valley Road — a region with one of the strongest geographic identities in America. Say you are from the Shenandoah Valley or planning to visit the Valley, and most people will nod in understanding. The evocative and ever-popular song "Oh, Shenandoah" is partly responsible for the near universal recognition the region enjoys. So are famous Civil War battles fought here in a horrific conflict that famously pitted brother against brother, battles that still have potent meaning to many Valley families.[3]

The roots of the region's distinctive identity can be traced to the era of the American Revolution, when European writers and philosophers visited the Valley to see how a society of freehold farmers, whose land provided for domestic comfort and economic competence, lived as independent citizens of a republic, not subjects of a king. Beholden to no one, they could vote freely or seek the privileges of public office without patronage or influence — or so the ideology of the new republic held. "They are ignorant of want, and acquainted with but few vices," one of these travelers commented. "Their inexperience of the elegancies of life precludes any regret that they possess not the means of enjoying them: but they possess what many princes would give half their dominions for, health, content, and tranquility of mind."[4]

Landscape elements provide one of the most useful tools in the geographer's workshop for constructing regions and understanding regional identity. The Pennsylvania barn, for instance, with an overhanging forebay and ramp to the threshing floor, links the Shenandoah Valley to the agricultural region of central and southeastern Pennsylvania that gave birth to this archetypal architectural form. The barn is an agricultural machine for stabling livestock on the lowest floor and storing fodder above, employing gravity to move feed from loft to manger. Similarly the dense pattern of market towns arrayed in a functional hierarchy from crossroad hamlets to regional commercial centers sets the Valley off from the Tidewater and Piedmont. Prior to the twentieth century, eastern Virginia was town poor by comparison and lacking in market centers outside of the minimal services provided by county seats. In these cases and

Fig. I.3. Haun's 1920s prefranchise, house-and-canopy-style gas station near Tenth Legion stood on the east side of U.S. 11 surrounded by a large roadside parking area with sufficient space to accommodate both automobiles and trucks. Gas pumps were located on a concrete island under the canopy. Haun's could not compete with large gas station/convenience stores; its sign suggests that the business closed when gasoline prices were about one dollar per gallon. Sam's Small Engine Repair occupies the building, now separated from the rest of the site by antitheft fences and gates. The enclosures give the illusion of isolation relative to the broad expanse of U.S. 11 asphalt. A frustrated customer contemplates two signs: one reads "Open Monday," the other, "Open Tuesday." (Scott Jost 2006)

many others, the Valley Road played a defining role in the regional diffusion and distribution of landscape elements. It was down the road that Pennsylvania migrants carried the idea of the Pennsylvania barn from its American cultural hearth. And major market centers such as Winchester, Harrisonburg, Staunton, and Lexington developed where primary east–west routes intersected the Valley Road. Thus to study the road — as the authors of this volume do — is to study the region and the landscape that associates it with some adjacent regions and distinguishes it from others.

In the conflation of road and region, these authors, however, do not confine their interpretations to the Shenandoah Valley alone. All of them find that a large scale of analysis is required to understand the Valley Road's history and its resonate landscape. The story of the Valley Road therefore extends well beyond the Valley itself. In Michael McConnell's reckoning, for example, the settlements and migrations of native peoples in the Valley cannot be described apart from the movement of people and goods for reasons of trade, diplomacy, sociability, and warfare throughout the entire eastern half of North America. During the colonial period, which Hofstra treats, the movement of Europeans into the Shenandoah Valley was only one phase of a migration that created a distinctive southern backcountry frontier of small farms, diversified agriculture, and market towns stretching from central Pennsylvania to the Georgia uplands. The notable world of fecund wheat farms that nineteenth-century Shenandoah Valley farmers created was fueled by a demand for flour throughout the Atlantic economy — a case that Lanier and Keller make in their chapters. After the turnpike period and during the twentieth century, as grain production declined in importance, the Valley economy became more diversified, according to Karl Raitz. Farmers broadened their activities to include commercial livestock raising, chicken farming, and fruit production. Light industries depended on commercial flows that were national or international in scope and on workers who came from throughout Latin America and the Caribbean. Meanwhile, tourists came to the Valley from across the United States and the world beyond.

The questions we ask about the Valley often invoke answers that range far beyond the immediate Valley region. They link the Valley's history to many of the major themes shaping mainstream narratives of American history. Accounts of indigenous cultures, the frontier experience, internal improvements, and Jacksonian democracy all come to bear on the Valley, as do the grand strategy of the Civil War, the development of national and global markets in industrial America, and the emergence of an urban nation in the twentieth century.

Because the Shenandoah Valley must be interpreted or understood in the context of historical developments or cultural forces at work on a much larger scale than the region itself, the Valley Road has provided the means for dynamic interaction among many different peoples. Thus cultural encounter constitutes another theme widely treated by this volume's authors. The Native American world was hardly one of timeless cultures in a static geography. Indian peoples, goods, and innovations were in constant motion in a continental process of encounter and change. If this process were to define a cultural horizon, then it would extend at least to the American Revolution and involve immigrants from the north of Ireland, central Germany, other northern European regions, along with West Africans and African Americans in a culture defined by migration and accommodation. During the three or four decades following the Revolution, when the Valley Road provided a primary route west to burgeoning frontiers in Tennessee, Kentucky, and along the Ohio River, every day would have brought encounters among the varied peoples living and traveling in the Valley. After this traffic diverted to the National Road and other improved western routes by the 1820s, the Valley may have slipped from a backcountry into something of a backwater, but the Civil War brought many new faces to the region, as did the twentieth-century tourist trade.

Part of the Valley's attraction to outsiders, especially to modern city dwellers, was the self-made — even homemade — quality of its landscape. This was a vernacular world of folk craft and home manufacture, and each of the authors in this volume describes the landscape as one people made for themselves. "Vernacular" would undoubtedly be the appropriate term to characterize the organic and irregular roads built under county court procedures in the colonial era and the variegated roadsides created before the implementation of zoning or the onslaught of franchise businesses. Certainly republican-minded travelers in the late eighteenth century wanted to experience the lifeways of a people who by their own labor on their own land created a world of their own making. The vernacular as self-creation by need or impulse, not by plan or design, often worked in tension with what might be called official, or formal, culture. The rebuilding of the Valley Road in the turnpike era according to the macadam system specified in state laws or its reengineering as a federal highway during the 1930s certainly reflected the latter, as do the ubiquitous designs of Howard Johnson's, McDonald's, Sheetz, Triple J, Red Roof Inns, Shell, and the like today. That the vernacular theme cannot be considered apart from engineered landscapes and commercial designs is a reminder that the vernacular can never be an exclusive category and that every structure and all landscapes interweave the extralocal with the local, intention with spontaneity, and art with artifice.

Even if the view from the road represents an organic response to tradition and the cultural performance of ordinary people, it was never an expression of the immutability of folk culture. Change was a constant in the life of the landscape, and the Valley Road has been both agent and measure of change. Today's travelers often want to fix roadside scenes in static, gauzy images of remnant landscapes from the age of republican simplicity or the era of high farming. Preservationists regularly work to salvage and perpetuate these landscapes without understanding the long-lost cultural forces that once sustained and altered them. But the story of the road, and our book about it, is more an account of continual adjustment and change, not of fixed or static images.

Change has often been the product of economic development, technological innovation, trade, and industry. Historical change, we have already suggested, is experienced today as levels evident in the material culture of the road corresponding with the major periods of its history — or, for our purposes, with the separate chapters of this book. The road's story, however, can be much messier and more contradictory, competitive, or contentious than this formulation permits. By necessity this story embraces the noisy world of commerce, of people on the move or on the make, of the rough places at country taverns or big-box warehouses, of wagoners and truckers, of highwaymen, ruffians, and road hogs. The volatility of contemporary road rage is as much a part of the story as is the passivity of historic road lore. Change, and its attendant conflicts, was pervasive.

Many of the interconnecting themes in this volume concern cultural values embedded in the road and its surroundings. Roadside democracy may be one of the most apparent, if not the most obvious. Economic opportunism, unfettered quests for better lives, lofty aspirations for civic improvement, and ambitious ventures into the public space of desire, want, and need all have bombarded the traveler with diverse, sometimes dissonant, images. The creative roadside of adaptive reuse, the persuasive roadside of competitive advertising, the idiosyncratic roadside of assertive self-expression, the referential roadside of social convention, or the disciplined roadside of applied engineering, community zoning, and corporate conformity can all be found along the Valley Road. The theme of democracy, therefore, also includes related themes of individualism and identity. The democratic quality of road culture has been both producer and product of individual expressions of various roadside activities. In these expressions, diverse peoples also sought to define their identities. Just as this theme embraces the democratic qualities of the road, so it also includes what was undemocratic, exclusionary, and sometimes blatantly racist in its landscape.

The road also encodes civic values about public and private space. The Valley's earliest roads, and certainly the Great Wagon Road, were simply rights of way guaranteeing public access across the otherwise exclusive space of private property. Roads, moreover, served the public sphere by conveying the mail, the people's commerce and commodities, and the ideas contained within newspapers, books, correspondence, and human minds. Beyond the road was private space, but the degree to which property holders segregated domestic life and their land from public use varied in time and place as the notion of the commons gradually dropped from popular consciousness. Early fence laws, for instance, required landowners to fence in fields and farmsteads, leaving livestock to graze on an extensive open range irrespective of property boundaries. Only in the age of high farming and rural capitalism during the nineteenth century did the familiar landscape of fence-lined roads emerge in response to new laws requiring landowners to fence cattle in.

The roadside represents liminal space where public and private behaviors interacted in dynamic, evocative ways. In the eighteenth and early nineteenth centuries, people often built houses immediately at the roadway's edge with front doors opening directly from the dust and mud of streets or highways onto central halls, regarded by many architectural historians as an ambiguous space mediating between a public arena open to all visitors and the private confines of domestic life. The rational designs of classical symmetry of this period can likewise be interpreted as a public expression of exterior architectural order. In town as well as country, householders balanced window bays around doorways to create rhythmic façades in an outside-in concept of privileging the public view from the road. By contrast, the irregularity and setbacks of modern ranch houses and split-levels reflect contemporary desires to conceive domestic space from the inside out, giving primacy to the private environs of family life over any need for public demonstrations of control or rationality. Roadside commercial establishments were undeniably public, but many — at least until the mid-twentieth century — nonetheless provided private residences for their managers or owners. Thus the perspectives on the Valley Road taken by the authors in this volume probe many fascinating relationships in the juxtaposition of the public world of transportation, commerce, and communication with the private world of work and family.

Democracy inevitably entails diversity, and diversity surfaces in every chapter in this volume as a characteristic of the Valley Road and its landscapes. Once regarded as a threat to democracy, diversity throughout the twentieth century has increasingly come to be thought of not only as inevitable in an open society but also as the strength of its political fabric. By contrast, nineteenth-century landscapes tended to appear less variegated. The number of house types, barn forms, and building categories, for example, was limited by a few closely related architectural styles. Commercial establishments such as stores or artisan shops and even public buildings took the same shape and appearance as domestic structures. Stylistic change was correspondingly slow. The one-room-deep Georgian I-house, with two stories and a balanced façade, was as common at the end of the century as it was at the beginning, even though it was joined by the American foursquare house and Victorian structures as well as by examples of other European revival styles. The twentieth-century roadside, however, often gave way to a seeming lack of stylistic consistency with the emergence of new architectural forms associated with automotive culture and a plethora of ahistorical modernist impulses.

Introducing all these themes to readers constitutes one of the purposes of this book, as is encouraging visitors to look carefully at the Valley Road and learn how to read its landscape. But do not assume the road as vantage point and landscape as object. Because landscape serves as a metaphor for discussing the history and geography of a region's culture and the road is the progenitor of the landscape sustaining its complex of social, economic, political, and intellectual arrangements over long periods of time, the route through the countryside is also the vehicle for understanding it. Traveling the road is a true journey of discovery.

Notes

1. Franz Louis Michel's Map of the Shenandoah Valley, 1707, CO 4/1316, f. 79, Colonial Office Papers, Public Record Office, London.

2. *Staunton Daily News,* July 25, 1917.

3. For an example of Hollywood's depiction of the effects of the Civil War on the region, consider Universal Studio's *Shenandoah* with Jimmy Stewart (1965).

4. Andrew Burnaby, *Travels through the Middle Settlements in North America in the Years 1759 and 1760,* 3rd ed. (London: T. Payne, 1798; repr., New York: Augustus M. Kelley, 1970), 73–74.

The Lay of the Land

KARL RAITZ

Great Valley

Most valleys in western Virginia's Ridge and Valley country are short, narrow lowlands pinched off at one end by converging parallel ridges, restricting access and effectively isolating inhabitants. The Shenandoah Valley, named for largest river that flows northeasterly along the Valley floor, is conspicuously different. The Valley is long, expansively open, and has functioned rather like a great aortic thoroughfare, inviting and directing human movement on a grand scale. The Shenandoah is the middle section of the Great Valley that extends more than one thousand miles from Quebec's St. Lawrence Valley in the north to Alabama's Appalachian or Coosa Valley in the south. Residents reckon the Shenandoah's portion of the Great Valley at about 180 miles in length; its breadth varies from a few miles to nearly thirty.

Ten rectangular counties extend along the Valley floor from the Potomac River in the north to Natural Bridge at the Valley's south end, placed comfortably together in northeast to southwest alignment, so that when depicted on a map they resemble stepping-stones laid along a Bunyanesque pathway. Traveling the Valley Road south from Williamsport, Maryland, one intersects the Valley counties in turn — Berkeley and Jefferson in West Virginia, followed by Clarke, Frederick, Warren, Page, Shenandoah, Rockingham, Augusta, and Rockbridge in the Virginia section. The Shenandoah River and its two major tributaries, the North Fork and South Fork, drain the north section. A small southern section in Rockbridge County drains south and east into the James River (see fig. 1.1).

In prehistory, Indian paths followed the Great Valley floor. Colonial-era explorers, hunters, and settlers traveled a similar route. Had eighteenth-century topographic engineers wished to select a low-gradient roadway to serve as a convenient inland thoroughfare across the American territory east of the Appalachian crest, they could have made no better choice than

Fig. 1.1. Topography
and drainage of
the Shenandoah
Valley. (Gyula
Pauer Cartography
Lab, University of
Kentucky)

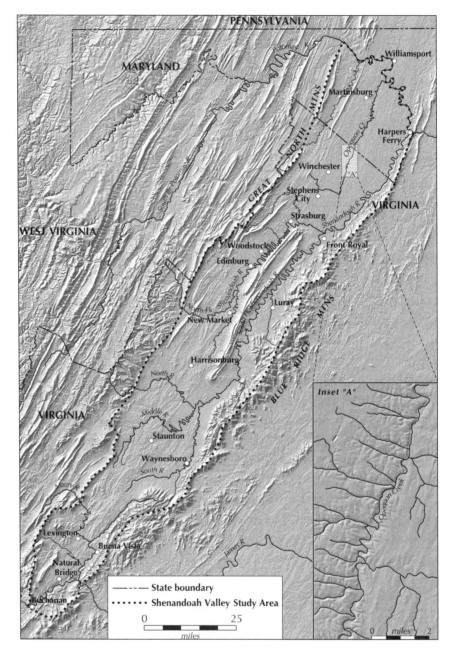

to align their road with the Indians' Valley trail. As colonial commerce
developed and seaboard cities became established, the Valley provided a
broad, low-gradient avenue from the hinterlands of New York City, Philadelphia, and Baltimore in the Northeast, to the rural frontier country
near Cumberland Gap, east Tennessee, and the Carolinas in the Southwest. If travelers headed toward the Ohio Valley frontier country were
naively inclined toward attempting a direct westerly trajectory, they met

a formidable barrier just west of the Shenandoah Valley, the notorious Ridge and Valley country — sometimes termed the "Endless Mountains" in Pennsylvania just to the north. Demarcating the Valley's western margin, North Mountain and Little North Mountain are long, linear ridges that announced the topographic grotesqueries that early travelers would encounter if they ventured directly west. Rather, the steep and formidable ridge ensemble effectively forced sensible people to turn aside and make a long detour southwest, following the Shenandoah Valley's gentle gradients toward Cumberland Gap.

The Valley's topographic attraction for eighteenth-century wagon and coach routes is still apparent today to anyone traveling its length along U.S. Highway 11 or Interstate Highway 81. Crossing the Potomac River at Williamsport, Maryland, and heading south toward Winchester, Harrisonburg, and Lexington on the interstate, one becomes aware only with some effort that they are entering one of America's most important natural transportation corridors. The bordering mountains that channel Shenandoah Valley roads and traffic lie low on the southeast and northwest horizons. The highway surface ahead rises and falls almost imperceptibly. One motors innocently along, watching local economies appear and retreat from one interchange to the next. Black and white Holstein dairy cows graze pastures; veal calves reside in igloo-shaped plastic shelters beside oversize Pennsylvania bank barns; apple trees shower white blossom petals on a thousand orchard floors in late spring and in late summer provide Winchester with one of its traditional industries, fruit processing and storage; domestic turkeys stuffed into truck-borne crates strew white feathers along road shoulders on their way to avian abattoirs; big-box stores, drive-in banks, comfort-food restaurants, franchise gas stations, auto sales lots, and truck warehouse terminals extend the boundaries of each large town toward the nearest interstate interchange. Outsized construction equipment pulverizes red-brown clay soil into powdery dust that breezes and air eddies from passing traffic swirl into the air as contractors race to install concrete water mains, sewer pipes, and electrical service ahead of new roadside business and subdivision developments. Much of the activity one observes on either side of the highway can be attributed, at least in part, to the valley character of this place, be it historical migration patterns, fertile limestone soils, or contemporary accessibility along the Valley corridor.

The Valley floor's inherent natural qualities — low-gradient and broad, fertile, well-watered lands — are no less attractive to farmers and businesspeople now than they were some 250 years ago, when settlers from southeastern Pennsylvania, Maryland, and eastern Virginia began to establish a presence here. Cross-country roads, be they frontier trails or modern interstates, are the product of the technology available to construct them, whatever the era. A road's most important qualities remain a resilient surface; a straight, direct route that represents the shortest possible distance between origin and destination; a low gradient that does not demand extraordinary energy costs; and ease of crossing natural obstacles — bridging streams or crossing hill ranges at convenient gaps. Road grades greater than 10 percent were generally too steep for horse-drawn wagons. And stopping a heavily loaded wagon or truck on a steep hill descent is more problematic than ascending the hill initially.

All of these desirable roadway characteristics accrue within the Shenandoah Valley and extend well beyond into the adjoining Great Valley sections to the northeast and southwest. This was the route of choice for many Pennsylvania and Virginia migrants bound for the North Carolina piedmont and Yadkin Valley country beginning in the mid-1700s.[1] Their most economical route choice was to follow the Valley Road from Martinsburg to Winchester, Strasburg, Woodstock, New Market, Harrisonburg, and Staunton. From there they could head southwest to Roanoke, where they crossed the Blue Ridge along the Roanoke River and continued south toward the Salem settlements.[2] Others traveling west toward the Ohio River valley and Kentucky's fabled Bluegrass plains could follow the Shenandoah toward southwest Virginia, where they intersected the Wilderness Road near Cumberland Gap. Today's interstate drivers can retrace the pioneer track toward Kentucky by way of Interstate Highway 81 and a new $270 million tunnel under Cumberland Mountain and the famous gap that eighteenth-century travelers found the only practicable southern gateway to the trans-Appalachian West. Neither the eighteenth-century Wilderness Road nor the twentieth-century tunnel under the great gap would have been a compelling route had both not been directly accessible to the Great Valley or its central section, the Shenandoah.

The Valley's form and orientation presented a tactical advantage to the South during the Civil War. "Since its course is southwesterly," the Civil War historian George Pond observed, "a Confederate army moving northward through it would at the same time draw nearer Washington, whereas a Union advance southward would diverge from the straight course to Richmond."[3] From the rise of land near Belle Grove Plantation and U.S. Highway 11, just south of Middletown, Virginia, one may look out across the Valley panorama and mentally reconstruct another dimension of the Shenandoah Valley's character important to Civil War strategists, its natural fertility and its role as "Breadbasket to the Confederacy." In the autumn of 1864, two decisive battles occurred nearby that compromised the Shenandoah's role as commissary to the Confederate armies and no doubt hastened the war's end. Commemorative plaques line U.S. 11 from Middletown south to Fishers Hill near Strasburg, and collectively they offer cryptic summaries of the September 22 Battle of Fishers Hill and the October 19 Battle of Cedar Creek. Confederate General Jubal Early's defeat at Fishers Hill by Philip Sheridan's Union troops opened the Valley's heart to the Union army. Sheridan's cavalry fired barns, mills, and crops throughout this area, an action so pervasive in its reach and effective in its destruction of productive capacity that Valley residents referred to it as "The Burning." Sheridan's victory at Cedar Creek on October 19 ended Confederate control over the Shenandoah Valley and thereby affirmed the South's loss of both a war supply center and the strategic routeway north toward Washington, D.C.[4]

Foundations

Today, the Cedar Creek Battlefield and Belle Grove Plantation offer an elevated vantage point from which one can view the interdigitation of the Valley's physical and cultural landscapes. The Belle Grove house itself offers an example of how the land's inherent qualities offered options and opportunities for clever and productive utilization. The house was constructed in 1797 from limestone quarried nearby. Consider the prospect at sunrise on a midsummer morning. From the low rise just to the east, one can look east and see the sun emerging from behind the Blue Ridge in the distance. Turning around to westward, translucent green grasslands recede to a distant horizon outlined by coniferous and deciduous treetops silhouetted along Little North Mountain. Before 1910, by which time loggers had thoroughly cut over the mountains for tan bark and timber logs, the cooler, higher slopes would have entertained old-growth forests of white pines, Canadian hemlocks, and other plants typically found much farther north in New England or Canada. But today, few remnants of this ancient forest remain except in remote side valleys such as Ramsey's Draft west of Staunton.[5]

Area maps and signs list old place-names — many of them carried forward by Anglo settlers from the region's original Algonquian speakers — that evoke Valley character: Conococheague (long [stream?]), Massanutten (big mountain), Opequon (white pool-stream), Shenandoah (spruce [stream?]).[6] Other names, no doubt sobriquets assigned by early settlers, tempt one's historical imagination to reconstruct eighteenth-century environments: Big Hellgate Creek, Buena Vista, Cave Ridge, Cedar Run, Dry Branch, Dry Fork, Dry River, Fairfield, Falling Springs, Forestville, Long Glade Creek, Pine Run, Redbud Run, Rockbridge Baths, Round Hill, Sparkling Springs, Spring Hill, Spring Run, Stony Run, Timber Ridge, Timberville, Warm Run.

Driving south from Belle Grove on back roads toward Woodstock, one encounters a richly agrarian countryside. The Valley's farms seem so comfortably fit into the land surface that they appear organic, as though the buildings and field fences sprouted and grew from the ground. But there is discomfiture here, and it lurks just underfoot within the region's sedimentary bedrock, a foundation so folded and broken by ancient continental collision that many rock formations pitch sharply upward to stand nearly on end, at right angles to their original sedimentary bedding planes. On every side, one detects clues hinting at a profound geological calamity below the surface. Normally recumbent shales stand erect to flank a long road cut below Fishers Hill on U.S. Highway 11 south of Strasburg. In pastures from Frederick County south to Buchanan, roughly aligned eoliths of dove gray limestone erupt upward through the short grass like Siegfried Line dragon's teeth, as though commemorating the primordial violence that thrust them forth (see fig. 1.2).

Two bordering ramparts, Blue Ridge on the east, Little North Mountain on the west, demarcate the Shenandoah Valley's structural and functional boundaries but also suggest that Valley history and geographic character have been defined by more than the fertile fields of its rock-rippled floor. The resilient, confining walls that delineate the Valley also influence life along its length. Movement into the Valley from the east or west was funneled through a few gaps in the bordering ridges. Movement along the Valley has been necessarily linear, and regional crossroads are few, generally confined to those places where regional trails crossed gaps in the Blue Ridge or Little North Mountain and intersected Valley thoroughfares. Trail crossings became the nexus of local and regional traffic and fostered markets, trade, and eventually a town or even county seat at those favored intersections. For travelers and migrants, the Valley's salient character was that of Edenic corridor through otherwise rugged and contentious topography. The English wayfarer Archdeacon Andrew Burnaby traveled from Tidewater Williamsburg to the Blue Ridge in 1760 to see the Valley, and his commentary on the experience attests to the Valley's qualities: "When I got to the top [of the Blue Ridge at Ashby's Gap] I was inexpressibly delighted with the scene which opened before me. Immediately under the mountain . . . was a most beautiful river: beyond this an extensive plain

diversified with every pleasing object that nature can exhibit; and at a distance of fifty miles another ridge of still more lofty mountains called the Great or North Ridge, which enclosed and terminated the whole."[7] For those who occupied the Valley floor and turned its natural fertility into a cornucopia of agricultural produce and its ores and minerals into iron goods and other needful products, the Valley offered compelling environmental circumstances not found east of the Blue Ridge or west of Little North Mountain.

Appreciating the Valley's physical character as a basis for human occupancy — eighteenth-century settlement, nineteenth-century farming, twentieth-century industry and transportation — requires only a regional perspective and sufficient patience to conceive of landforms evolving on a geologic time scale. Virginia's landforms, as is the case with neighboring states to the north and south, align into five distinctive belts that trend northeast-southwest. From the Chesapeake Bay westward, the belts, in turn, are the Coastal Plain, Piedmont, Blue Ridge, Ridge and Valley (in which the Shenandoah is the broadest valley), and the Appalachian Plateau (see fig. 1.3).[8]

Nearly 500 million years ago, the rocks that now comprise the Shenandoah Valley floor lithified from Cambrian and Ordovician tidal flat

Fig. 1.2. Near-vertical limestone outcrops in a Rockbridge County pasture near Natural Bridge Station. (Scott Jost 2004)

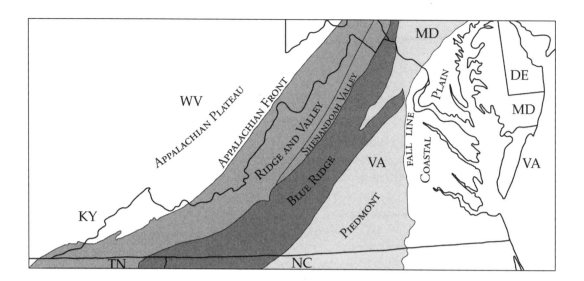

Fig. 1.3.
Virginia's topographic regions.
(Gyula Pauer Cartography Lab, University of Kentucky)

sediments into vast, horizontally bedded sequences of limestones and dolomites. Subsequent collision with an offshore land mass in the late Ordovician and early Silurian period, or roughly 400 million years ago, created a mountain range where the Piedmont now lies, and a basin atop the Shenandoah Ordovician limestones. Sediments eroded from the mountain range and washed west into the basin; under the compressive weight of more overlying sediments, the muds transformed into shales, sands became sandstones and quartzites, and calcium carbonate deposits formed more limestones.

This sequence was followed by another continental impact, this one with Africa, between 320 and 230 million years ago.[9] Though the collision speed would likely have been measurable in inches per year, the cumulative effect was cataclysmic for existing rock formations, rather like placing one's foot on one end of a large throw rug and pushing it across a polished wood floor. Just as the rug breaks friction with the floor and slides into looping folds in response to the directional pressure exerted by the foot, Piedmont and Ridge and Valley rocks reacted to the continental collision by shearing away from basement rocks, breaking into megasections, and folding into great loops, some of which skidded up and over rocks to the west. Collision pressures forced some Precambrian granites and Cambrian sandstones into a tall A-shaped fold, or anticline, so pronounced that it almost folded over upon itself. As subsequent erosion peeled away weaker overlying rocks, the spectacular Blue Ridge emerged from the fold's core to become the Valley's eastern delimiting boundary. The complex layerings of horizontal-lying limestones, shales, and sandstones to the west buckled and folded into vertical pleats as sharply creased as those on a closed accordion. Subsequent erosion reduced this surface differentially; the softer limestones and shales became valleys, and the hardest sandstones and quartzites emerged as ridges. In some sections, the Shenandoah Valley harbors comparatively low-amplitude hills and ridges. In other sections, the Valley floor is almost planar, tempting one to assume the Valley is underlain by horizontal-lying sedimentary rocks. But finding level rock beds here is difficult. Most stand at steep angles, the product of ancient compressions that folded some upward into anticlinal folds and others downward into V-shaped synclinal troughs that align tangent to the direction of compression.

The more resistant members within the folded subsurface strata present themselves in low whale-back hills along some Valley floor sections (see fig. 1.4). By comparison, Massanutten Mountain is the most prominent fold feature to erupt from the Valley floor. It is the bottom section of a large syncline exposed by eons of erosion. Extending from Harrisonburg in the south fifty miles north to Strasburg, this great canoe-shaped ridge partitions the middle Valley into east and west sections, and its bulk narrows the Valley floor considerably (see fig. 1.5). From Massanutten eastward to the Blue Ridge lies the Page or Luray Valley, which is drained by the Shenandoah River's South Fork. Between Luray and Front Royal, Page Valley wedges into a one-mile-wide narrows. Residents refer to the broader valley west of Massanutten as the Shenandoah or Strasburg Valley; its five-mile breadth is drained by the North Fork (see fig. 1.6). Although Massanutten's east and west flanks are girded by stout, down-warped quartzites, its core is soft Devonian shale that has eroded away to form a deep trough, thereby creating the mountain's distinctive canoe-like shape, and a rare topographic sequence — a valley within a mountain within a valley.

Although the Blue Ridge and Little North Mountain are outwardly similar in form, a traverse of their flanks reveals that they are substantively different. The ancient Blue Ridge rises to nearly 3,000 feet above sea level, its crest looming some 2,300 feet above the Valley floor. The ridge has a granite massif at its core. Viewed from the Valley side, the ridge's northwest flank presents a solid shoulder of rugged Paleozoic sedimentary quartzite rocks. Just above the quartzites lies a basalt lava flow long since metamorphosed into a stout greenstone. Finally, near the crest, granites cap the ridge and extend down the east side toward the Piedmont.[10] As a collection, few other rock types offer the strength and resistance to erosion as does this sequence that armors the Blue Ridge.[11] The only chinks that compromise its resilience are a few faults or points of structural weakness, and at each such

Fig. 1.4. (*Top*)
Rolling limestone
farmland east of
U.S. 11 between
Natural Bridge
and Lexington in
Rockbridge County.
(Scott Jost 2004)

Fig. 1.5. (*Bottom*)
The south nose
of Massanutten
Mountain rises in
the distance, as
seen from a low
ridge west of Har-
risonburg in Rock-
ingham County.
(Scott Jost 2003)

Fig. 1.6. The North Fork of the Shenandoah River on Massanutten's west flank at Red Bank, north of Mount Jackson. The river is shallow along much of its length. Where the stream channel erodes into the bedrock at right angles to the bedding plane, two types of rapids form. Above the 1930s concrete bridge railing, a bedrock-ledge rapid is visible in the middle distance. Farther downsteam, an extended reach of rapids tumbles across what is termed a cobble rock garden. (Scott Jost 2003)

place low gaps in the ridge have eroded to sufficient depth along cracks and fissures that they offered comparatively easy passage across the ridge.[12]

Near the Blue Ridge's western base, iron and manganese ore deposits lie concentrated in a long, narrow strip in association with quartzite and dolomite rocks. Commercial mines probed for these ores along a zone from Front Royal south to Staunton and Waynesboro, the earliest in 1838. A manganese mine near Waynesboro produced over 160,000 tons of ore between 1867 and 1917 and ranked as the largest-producing mine in the United States.[13] Smaller mines tapped commercially valuable iron and manganese deposits on the northwest flank of Massanutten Mountain near Strasburg and west of Little North Mountain, as did numerous smaller sites in the south Valley.

At the Valley's western margin, Little North Mountain juts from the Valley floor at a near-vertical angle, a bulwarklike 1,800- to 2,500-foot anticline of sharply folded sedimentary Tuscarora quartzite. At the mountain's eastern foot lies an enfeebled brown shale, the Martinsburg, easily erodible, the stuff of active stream incision and valley making, and resem-

TABLE 1.1 Geological epochs, formations, and rock types

Geological epoch	Formation	Rock type
Silurian	Tuscarora	Quartzite
Ordovician	Martinsburg	Shale
	Edinburg	Limestone-siltstone-shale
	Lincolnshire	Limestone-chert
	New Market	Limestone
	Bellefonte	Limestone-dolomite-chert
	Nittany	Limestone-dolomite
	Chepultepec	Limestone
Cambrian	Conococheague	Limestone-dolomite-sandstone
	Eldbrook	Limestone-dolomite-chert

bling not at all the resilient quartzites and dolomites across the Valley at the base of the Blue Ridge.

Were the Valley's sedimentary rocks simply stacked vertically, layer upon layer as originally laid down, the sequence from the youngest on the top to the oldest at the bottom would have been straightforward (see table 1.1).

Given the Valley's tortured geological past, this simple vertical profile is nowhere on exhibit. Rather, on the contemporary surface one finds rocks layered into unexpected juxtapositions by up-warping anticlines, down-warping synclines, fractures, faults, and other forms of large-scale crustal violence. The Silurian-age Tuscarora quartzites, the backbone of Little North Mountain and a major ridge-maker in the Ridge and Valley country west of the Shenandoah, is principally quartz particles welded together by silica, yielding a rock so stout and resistant to erosion that on a scale of hardness it ranks a seven of ten. Only topaz, corundum, and diamond are harder.

Were the Valley's foundation rocks bedded in their original sequence, likely only one or two formations would extend the entire breadth of the Valley floor. Instead, one finds the full sequence with the oldest rocks generally appearing at the Valley's edges, transitioning to younger strata near the center. Therefore the sequence of rocks from the west edge to the center of the Valley floor is oldest to youngest; from the Valley center east, the sequence reappears in reverse order, from youngest to oldest, as one moves to the base of the Blue Ridge. This order is precisely what one would expect to find crossing a synclinal trough.[14] Barring displacements by large faults, this generalized rock formation sequence occurs in the northern or lower Valley section and will differ somewhat from that found in the mid- or southern Valley sections.

At the foot of Little North Mountain near Winchester, at about one thousand feet above sea level, the rock outcrop sequence begins with the Ordovician-age Martinsburg shale followed by the comparatively ancient Cambrian Elbrook limestone — a fault here displaces the entire remainder of the Ordovician limestone sequence (see fig. 1.7). Southeast-dipping beds of Conococheague and Elbrook limestones then alternate with one another, with Apple Pie Ridge representing the third swell in the Elbrook. Again, to the east, the Conococheague makes a last appearance before dipping below the out-of-sequence and reversed order Ordovician limestones and dolomites: Chepultepec, Nittany, Bellefonte, New Market, Lincolnshire, and Edinburg. The city of Winchester and the Valley Road lie atop the Nittany and Bellefonte limestones. East of Winchester, the Martinsburg brown shale emerges from the depths (again), and remains at the surface for about four miles to Opequon Creek. Beyond the Opequon to the foot of the Blue Ridge, the rocks are again primarily limestones and become sequentially older, almost a mirror image of the sequence west of Winchester — Edinburg, Lincolnshire, Chepultepec, Conococheague, and Elbrook. Though the general valley slope across these rocks is nearly imperceptible, the elevation at the base of the Blue Ridge is five hundred feet, which, given the five-hundred-foot drop across the Valley from Little North Mountain, suggests that streams should flow rather lustily down slope across this varied surface from west to east.

Rock character has consequences, and rock sequence mixes those consequences in patchy and unexpected ways across the Valley landscape. Quartzites are so resistant to erosive forces that they form ridges; useful minerals are associated with some rocks but not others; some limestones break down to form fertile soils; other limestones are susceptible to solution by rainwater and may form sinkholes and caves; and shales often form agriculturally uninviting soils and are so easily eroded that they tend to collect and entrain streams for long distances. And, as agricultural technology advanced, the marginal lands — rough and stone-outcropped limestones or indifferent shales — were further devalued by mechanization. Cyrus McCormick invented and refined his reaper at the McCormick farm near Steeles Tavern, midway between Staunton and Lexington, in the 1830s and 1840s. But the machine's mechanical advantages were best applied to fecund midwestern lands of rich, deep soils and gentle slopes, where its quantum efficiencies could be realized and its price amortized over a substantial acreage. Thus, by the 1880s, there were few reapers to be found on the Valley's poorer lands, where most of the grain continued to be cut by hand.[15] Human activity patterns along the Valley — be they

Fig. 1.7. Lower Valley floor cross-section. (After Charles Butts and Raymond S. Edmundson, *Geological Map of Frederick County, Virginia,* compiled from manuscript maps by Charles Butts and Raymond S. Edmundson, 1936–40 [Washington, D.C.: Williams and Heintz Map Corp. for Commonwealth of Virginia, 1963]; Gyula Pauer Cartography Lab, University of Kentucky)

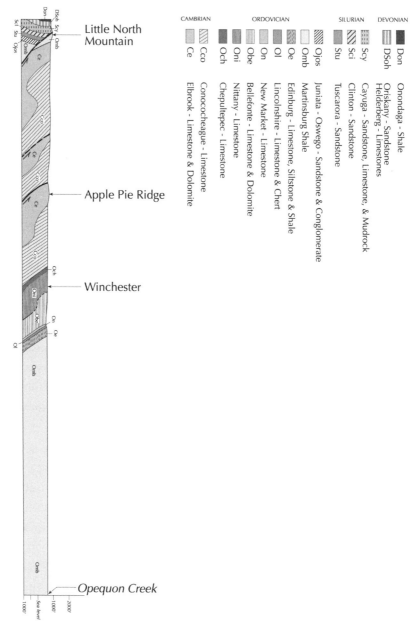

Little North Mountain

Apple Pie Ridge

Winchester

Opequon Creek

1000'   Sea level   1000'   2000'

Rock Formations

CAMBRIAN
- Ce — Elbrook - Limestone & Dolomite
- Cco — Conococheague - Limestone

ORDOVICIAN
- Och — Chepultepec - Limestone
- Oni — Nittany - Limestone
- Obe — Bellefonte - Limestone & Dolomite
- On — New Market - Limestone
- Ol — Lincolnshire - Limestone & Chert
- Oe — Edinburg - Limestone, Siltstone & Shale
- Omb — Martinsburg Shale
- Ojos — Juniata - Oswego - Sandstone & Conglomerate

SILURIAN
- Stu — Tuscarora - Sandstone
- Sci — Clinton - Sandstone
- Scy — Cayuga - Sandstone, Limestone, & Mudrock

DEVONIAN
- DSoh — Oriskany - Sandstone / Helderberg - Limestones
- Don — Onondaga - Shale

historic or contemporary — often represent considered adjustments to differing opportunities and options offered by the rocks, soils, and waters that people encountered.

Moving Water

Shenandoah Valley settlement and land use patterns are often directly or indirectly related to the behavior of surface and subsurface water-drainage systems. The most direct access into the Valley, either across the Blue

Ridge on the east or Little North Mountain on the west, has necessarily been via stream-cut gaps. The region's two major streams, the Potomac River in the north and the James River in the south, must crosscut the Blue Ridge to gain the Piedmont to the east. Following an irregular though predominantly southeasterly flow toward base level in Chesapeake Bay, the Potomac rises within the Ridge and Valley country south of Cumberland, Maryland. From there, it flows east and south transversely across the prevailing topographic trend, repeatedly crosscutting through stout quartzite ridges before reaching the Shenandoah Valley floor through a water gap in North Mountain roughly midway between Hagerstown, Maryland, and Martinsburg, West Virginia. Once into the Valley, the Potomac casts broad meander loops across the Valley floor as it angles sharply south-southeast toward Harpers Ferry, where it bisects the Blue Ridge.

Roughly 180 miles southwest of Harpers Ferry, the James River rises near Clifton Forge and flows around the south end of North Mountain toward Buchanan at the west base of the Blue Ridge. Here the James turns northeast, following the ridge about twenty-five miles to Glasgow, where it finally turns east, cutting a 1,800-foot-deep notch through the Blue Ridge at Balcony Falls on its way across the Piedmont toward Richmond and the Chesapeake (see fig. 1.8). The points at which the James and Potomac successfully incised water gaps across the Valley's delimiting ridges are likely sections of weakness along ancient faults or other points of rock vulnerability.[16]

Several smaller, higher gaps crease the Blue Ridge crest. They are the product of ancient erosion by several eastward-flowing streams, the Rappahannock and Rapidan rivers and Goose and Rockfish creeks among them. Incising drainage channels into the formidable Blue Ridge and Piedmont basement rocks was a sluggish process for these low-energy streams. Meanwhile, just to the west and north, the Shenandoah's South Fork was actively cutting its channel into the softer limestones and shales at the edge of the Blue Ridge anticline. The yielding rock permitted the river to deepen its bed and extend it southward. Thusly privileged, the South Fork beheaded the eastward-flowing streams, diverting their captured flow northward. In this way, South Fork stream piracy converted several cross-ridge stream channels into dry ravines that gradually emerged as crest line gaps or passes as regional erosion continued, exposing the bulky Blue Ridge in high relief.[17] Because these gaps do not today entertain streams, they are called wind gaps. While shallow compared to the much deeper water gaps cut by the James and Potomac, wind gaps reduced the elevation travelers had to climb to cross the ridge into the Val-

Fig. 1.8. Near Glasgow in Rockbridge County, the confluence of the Maury and James rivers is west of the Blue Ridge near Balcony Falls. (Scott Jost 2004)

ley and thus became the focus of mid-eighteenth-century Valley trails and roads that connected eastward with Piedmont and Coastal Plain market towns. Given the manner in which the physics of weight, inertia, and friction worked upon wagons drawn by harnessed horses, experienced nineteenth-century road engineers such as Claudius Crozet were especially keen to survey low-angle road routes across the Blue Ridge by way of the lowest gaps because a freight wagon would impose at least one hundred pounds more load per horse should the road angle increase from 4 to 5 degrees.[18]

Although the Valley Road provided farms, mills, and ironworks access northward to Philadelphia markets, the wagon hauls and livestock drives were long, time-consuming, and very expensive. Eastern Virginia markets in Fredericksburg, Alexandria, and the Tidewater ports along the lower James and Rappahannock rivers were closer and therefore attractive alternatives for Valley merchants and farmers could they be made accessible. In the 1760s and 1770s, Valley residents actively petitioned the state assembly to clear roads across the Blue Ridge gaps to shorten the distance petitioners were "obliged to carry their commodities to market."[19] The result was dramatic. Wheat buyers from Alexandria made their way to the lower Valley's limestone lands and successfully diverted to Potomac Tidewater much of the dray wagon traffic that had formally made the much longer trip north along the wagon road to Philadelphia.[20] Twentieth-century improvements to several old trans-ridge market trails have turned them into state and federal highways. In rough order from north to south, the larger wind gaps that today host highway crossings include Snickers, Ashby, Manassas, Chester, and Compton. Then Thornton Gap, Fishers, Swift Run, and Rockfish Gap. Finally, U.S. Highway 60 crosses the ridge through Indian Gap at Buena Vista, a few miles north of the point where the James River flows through the Blue Ridge across Balcony Falls.

Flowing athwart North Mountain and the Blue Ridge, the Potomac and James rivers neatly bracket the Shenandoah Valley into a linear rect-

Fig. 1.9. Closely guarded by a split-rail fence, the entrenched old road across Snickers Gap leads down the west shoulder of the Blue Ridge toward the Shenandoah Valley, ca. 1880s. (Library of Congress, Washington, D.C., LC-J698-61182)

angle. Each river provides a base level or low point toward which Valley streams flow, giving the greater Shenandoah Valley two distinct drainage basins. The northern basin accounts for approximately seven-eighths of the Valley's total length from the Potomac River south to Natural Bridge. It drains northeast by way of the Shenandoah River's North and South Forks, which merge at Front Royal and flow north as a combined stream toward the Potomac. At Bolivar, the Shenandoah joins the Potomac just before flowing through the Blue Ridge at Harpers Ferry. The northern Valley's low point is about 260 feet above sea level. Immediately across the Valley, Apple Pie Ridge on the Valley's west side is about 790 feet. But the Valley floor also rises steadily to the south so that Staunton, near Middle River and the Shenandoah River headwaters, stands at about 1,570 feet. Therefore, the northern Valley floor tilts rather dramatically down slope to the north and east, giving the advantage of gravity and gradient to streams flowing along the Valley's east side, closest to base level. Utilizing this topographic largesse, the South Fork became the north Valley's master trunk stream, the collector of streams that originate above it to the west and south.

South of Staunton, a drainage divide marks the transition where the Maury River and its tributaries capture south Valley runoff. If the south Valley has a corollary master stream to the Shenandoah's South Fork, it is the Maury. From a point near Buena Vista, the Maury collects short tributaries as it flows south and east toward the low point at the Blue Ridge base. Here it joins the James River just above Balcony Falls, the dramatic passage through the Blue Ridge where the river plummets two hundred feet in just four miles. Headwaters elevations south of Staunton exceed 1,900 feet, whereas the elevation at Balcony Falls where drainage exits the south Valley is about 790 feet (see fig. 1.10). Thus the south Valley drains vigorously south and east toward the James, the regional trunk stream that trends eastward across the Piedmont and Coastal Plain where it flows into Chesapeake Bay at Norfolk.

The working world of eighteenth- or nineteenth-century farmers, "mechanics" (millwrights, carpenters, blacksmiths, masons, and other skilled tradespeople), or Main Street merchants was largely dependent upon hand-tool and waterpower technologies. Farmers required access to flowing springs or perennial streams as potable water sources for their farm households and livestock. Because the only reliable source of stationary motive power was an all-season stream with gradient sufficient to provide the head pressure required to turn a waterwheel, millwrights sought sites for grist and fulling mills, sawmills, and iron furnace blast workings along

well-graded streams where dams and water-delivery races provided sufficient fall.[21] Consistently flowing, all-season streams attracted millwrights
who built mills and associated structures.

In each Valley section, regional bedrock configuration (or structure)
and rock-layer character (or lithology) strongly affect the directional flow
of surface and subsurface water. Bedrock tends to guide stream courses in
two ways. First, streams will tend to follow the directional trend or strike
of weak rocks such as shales where they intersect the surface. And second,
if a bedrock formation is systematically broken along joints or fractures,
streams will tend to erode their channels along the joint pattern.

Fig. 1.10. The Maury
River north of
Lexington in Rock-
bridge County.
A swayback tree
leans out over the
river channel. Local
swimmers have
nailed board steps
to the tree. (Scott
Jost 2003)

Valley limestones are generally harder and more resistant to erosion than shales. Some limestones contain beds of exceptionally robust chert and thus are even more resilient against the erosive effects of running water.[22] Despite these qualities, the Valley's carbonate rocks are susceptible to gradual chemical weathering by mildly acidic rain water, a process that widens cracks and bedding joints and eventually—over long periods of geologic time—forms a surface pockmarked by shallow sinks and underground caverns and caves. Clay-based shales, on the other hand, especially those stacked into the Martinsburg formation, lack inherent bonding strength and, being much less competent than the limestones, erode readily toward base level, forming low-angle surfaces along which streams move assuredly down gradient.

When streams flow off limestone onto the Martinsburg shale, they behave very differently and so create on the shale dissimilar drainage network patterns and channel alignments that would affect land use decisions by eighteenth- and nineteenth-century Valley residents and transients. Although tight, steep-angled folds interdigitate the Martinsburg shale and its companion limestones, the Valley floor's topographic surface is strongly differentiated by bedrock character because the shale exhibits two formative characteristics that the nearby limestones do not share; a northwest–southeast–oriented fracture and joint system, and a lack of soluble carbonate ingredients.[23] Surface streams flow across limestone surfaces, given their relative hardness, at somewhat steeper gradients than on the softer shales.[24] Further, limestone's solubility promotes enlargement of joints and cracks that allow some precipitation to flow away via subterranean drainage ways rather than surface streams. Water thus diverted underground reduces the frequency or density of surface streams and even leaves some sections bereft of surface streams over broad areas.

The shale is not subject to underground solution channel development, but its system of joints and fractures strongly influences the direction and pattern of surface stream flow. The Opequon Creek drainage in the north Valley provides a spectacular example of stream realignments that occur as surface drainage moves from limestone to shale. The Opequon drains about 344 square miles in the north Valley and rises on Conococheague limestones south of Winchester. The creek flows east to the Martinsburg shale east of Winchester, where it then turns smartly down valley and hews resolutely along the shale toward the Potomac north of Martinsburg, West Virginia. Flowing on the shale belt's eastern edge, the Opequon gathers numerous short tributaries flowing out of the shale from the west, many less than a mile apart. Immediately across the Opequon to the east, the surface is underlain by the Chambersburg and New Market limestones. Here few streams flow on the surface toward the Opequon. Instead, the limestone drainage is predominantly through underground channels, and only a low-density, course-textured stream valley pattern has developed on the surface.[25] In dramatic contrast, across the Opequon to the west, streams have cut a fine-textured, high-density surface drainage network into the shale, and active stream erosion here has produced a land of rather steep slopes compared to the limestone surface just to the east. These shale lands, therefore, are ill-suited for open field agriculture, and much ground remains in riparian forest or pasture, although it is increasingly attractive as homesites for exurban commuters or people building weekend retreats. To the east, farmers have cleared the trees from most of the limestone soils, and the preferred agrarian land uses are grains and row crop cultivation, and livestock production.

The contrasting natural fertility and drainage characteristics of limestone and shale and the differential in surface stream density across contrasting bedrock formations influenced many aspects of eighteenth-century life in the Valley, including agricultural production, milling industry development, road placement, and town location. Farmers much preferred to cultivate limestone lands where available and affordable. And, because some limestone sections were largely bereft of surface streams, millers often sought mill sites on the shale where stream densities were higher and seasonal water flow was more reliable (see fig. 1.11).[26] Extant milling technology could be adapted to a variety of stream and slope conditions if milldams were properly supported by stout abutments, although limestone, given its bulk, weight, and resilience, was often the building material of choice, even in the shale zones.[27] Roads laid out across limestone, in turn, would have required fewer stream crossings and less concern to locate low-angle fords and narrow bridging points, while potentially serving a somewhat higher density of farms and towns. From near Mauzy south to Mount Sidney, an old Indian trail followed fine-grained limestones — especially the Edinburg and Conococheague formations — skirting the dissected shale to the east and the cherty limestone's choppy topography to the west.[28] The considered relationship between transport routes and bedrock provided context for the location of Winchester in 1744, one of the north Valley's first town settlements. James Wood laid out the first Winchester lots near where one of the few surface streams on the Ordovician limestones, Town Creek, crossed the Great Valley Road.[29] Consid-

Fig. 1.11. Kline's Mill on Kline's Mill Road north of Middletown in Frederick County. The log mill was powered by West Run near the point where the stream entered the Martinsburg shale. Though in relict condition, the mill still contains machinery designed by Oliver Evans. (Scott Jost 2004)

ered more grandly, along the extended Valley Road section from the Potomac River south to Staunton, the road detours from the limestone onto the shale at only three places: North of Martinsburg near the Potomac River, south of Strasburg at Fishers Hill, and at Harrisonburg.[30]

The Virginia road engineer Claudius Crozet took pains to explain and publicize the basic requirements for high-quality road construction, including the need for a hard-packed stone surface. From the 1820s and 1830s onward, Virginia's main turnpikes were generally hard surfaced with broken stone according to either McAdam or Telford road-design principles, although most lesser roads remained little more than earth tracks. The Telford plan required a durable foundation of hand-placed vertical stones upon which smaller stones would be packed to form the load-bearing road surface. The simpler and less expensive McAdam plan did not utilize foundation stones but employed layers of tightly packed smaller stones. Whichever technique was employed, the critical logistical problem for road construction crews was locating a convenient supply of resilient yet readily workable stone. The Piedmont's metamorphic rocks were extremely difficult to quarry and resistant to breakage into the small sizes required for roadwork. The Valley's Ordovician limestones, on the other hand, were nearly ideal for use as road metal, given their natural horizontal bedding planes and vertical joints. And, because the cost of moving stone any appreciable distance by wagon was prohibitive, road engineers were perforce obligated to obtain stone from near-road ledges and quarries. While many Virginia turnpikes were comparatively rough, the Valley Road's resilient stone surface accommodated horse-drawn wagons of five to six tons, in large part because of the almost ubiquitous availability of limestone bedrock for surfacing stone the full length of the Valley.[31]

Although farmers and road builders avoided the Valley shales when they could, streams had an affinity for them. On the Martinsburg formation, the most facile places for streams to gradually plow out flow channels is along fractures and linear joints. So enabled, the larger streams on the Martinsburg shale exhibit a proclivity to channel themselves into trough-like topographic belts that extend nearly the entire length of the Valley.[32] The shale's joint system trends northwest–southeast, athwart the general northeast stream-flow gradient. Once on the shale, streams tend to turn abruptly northwest and flow for a considerable distance along a given joint alignment before turning 180 degrees to intersect another lateral crack trending southeast. A stream on the shale might repeat this pattern again and again, creating a long, looping meander belt along the shale bed. Stream meander reach — the straight channel distance between the tight bends on either end of a loop — on the shales tends to be twice as long as meanders cut into adjacent thick-bedded limestones.[33] Opequon Creek eroded looping meanders near Martinsburg, West Virginia, in the northern Valley. Christians Creek and Middle River eroded others in Augusta County, near Staunton in the south Valley.

The north Valley's trunk stream, the Shenandoah's South Fork, flows across the Martinsburg formation from south of Luray to Front Royal, incising a broad, joint-controlled meander belt the full distance. The North Fork has cut the Valley's most spectacular meanders into the Martinsburg rocks near the village of Toms Brook, between Edinburg and Strasburg. Here, as the river courses along the shale, its bed follows an extended meander belt for forty-four miles, a channel more than three times as long as the direct, as-the-crow-flies down-valley distance.[34] Long known as the Seven Bends, this section of the North Fork loops into tight one- to two-mile-long meanders, though the lateral distance between channels is less than a half-mile (see fig. 1.12). And once the North Fork enters the Martinsburg's province there is no turning back; the river follows the shale faithfully until it rounds Massanutten Mountain's north nose and plunges directly toward Front Royal, where it joins the South Fork to form the Shenandoah's main channel.

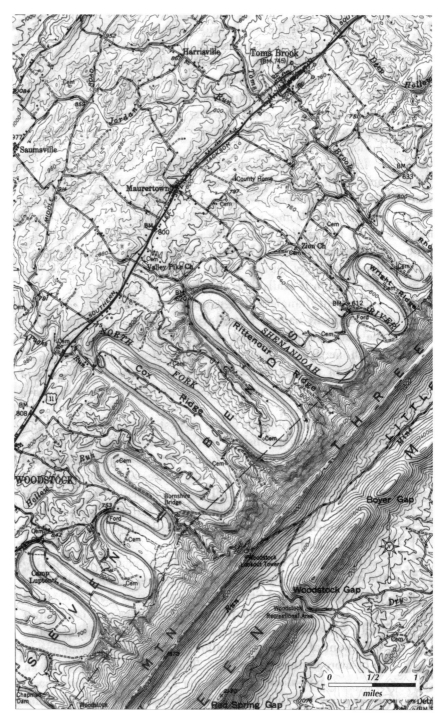

Fig. 1.12. The Seven Bends. (Modified from the Strasburg Quadrangle, 1:62,500 [contour interval 40 feet, supplementary contours 20 feet], Washington, D.C.: United States Geological Survey, 1950)

Caves, Caverns, and Underground Streams

A signal characteristic of carbonate rocks such as the limestones and dolomites that floor the Valley is that they are susceptible to chemical erosion
through contact with surface streams, underground drainage flows, and
groundwater. As rainwater falls through the atmosphere, it may absorb
small quantities of carbon dioxide, forming a mild carbonic acid. In the
ground, water can acquire acidity through absorption of carbon dioxide
from limestone soils. Rainwater and groundwater so fortified can dissolve
carbonate rocks, given sufficient time. Water percolating into limestone
bedrock moves along natural bedding cracks and the joints produced by
breakage or faults, slowly enlarging slim cracks into channels small and
large, producing what is termed a karst limestone landscape. Moving
groundwater takes up calcium carbonate and calcium sulfate and often
later deposits these minerals as calcite formations. Some carbonate rocks
are especially soluble and, given adequate precipitation, may form surface
sinkholes with broad, shallow basins that may collect water after a rain,
but will usually drain underground. Sink development is enhanced by extreme fluctuations in groundwater levels. When the water table drops, because of seasonal drought, for example, sinkhole soils may lose their shear
strength and collapse into voids in the limestone below, thereby enlarging
sinkhole diameter at the surface.[35]

The Valley's most extensive karst landscape lies in the upper Valley limestones between Harrisonburg and Staunton on the South Fork
headwaters, although solution features can also be found farther north.
Sinks tend to cluster along the larger streams where the volume of groundwater flow is greater and the gradient along which ground water flows is
steeper.[36] Some underground drainage ways in the upper Valley formed
springs that emerge onto the surface to feed streams such as Quick Spring,
which forms Falling Spring Creek north of Staunton.[37] Drainage basins
on limestone with surface sinkholes and underground water flow often
exhibit a much lower surface stream density than do stream basins on
shale.[38]

The groundwater-limestone solution process opened some fissures
into large underground passages or caves, and the larger ones with direct openings to the surface have been developed as "natural curiosities"
and tourist destinations for two centuries or more. Although one might
reason that because caves are "below ground," they necessarily formed
in low valleys, this is decidedly not the case in the Shenandoah Valley.
Most karst caves here open into hillsides. Grand Caverns near Grottoes,

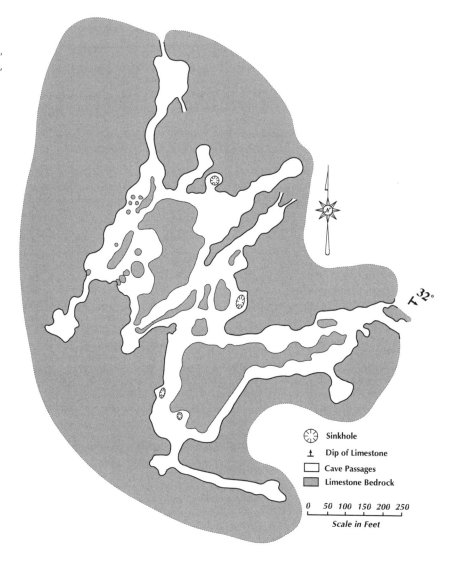

Fig. 1.13. Luray Caverns. (After William M. McGill, *Caverns of Virginia,* bulletin 35, educational series 1 [University, Va.: Virginia Geological Survey, 1933]; Gyula Pauer Cartography Lab, University of Kentucky)

Sinkhole

Dip of Limestone

Cave Passages

Limestone Bedrock

0   50 100 150 200 250

Scale in Feet

for example, opens into Cave Hill. Similarly, Luray Caverns opens into a rise named Cave Hill that stands some 250 feet higher than the town of Luray, about one mile to the southeast.[39] Most major caverns occur close to the Massanutten syncline. Endless Caverns, Melrose Caverns, and Shenandoah Caverns lie on Massanutten's west side, adjacent to the Valley Road between Harrisonburg and Mount Jackson. Luray Caverns, the most extensive of Virginia's developed caves, formed in the Nittany dolomite east of Massanutten near South Fork in the broadest section of Page Valley (see fig. 1.13).[40]

Calcium minerals taken up by groundwater as it moves across carbonate stone may be deposited elsewhere as stalactites, stalagmites, and extensive flowstone formations. The English traveler Isaac Weld visited a cave near Staunton in the 1790s — likely present-day Grand Caverns.[41] He explored one chamber that was sixty feet long, thirty feet across, and fifty feet high. "The petrifactions [mineral deposits] formed by the water dropping from above," he said, "are most beautiful, and hang down from the ceiling in the form of elegant drapery, the folds of which are similar to what those of large blankets or carpets would be if suspended by one corner in a lofty room."[42]

About fourteen miles south of Lexington, the Valley's south end is demarcated by Natural Bridge and Natural Bridge Caverns. Standing about 200 feet above Cedar Creek, Natural Bridge is a large limestone arch that spans some 90 feet and varies from 50 to 150 feet wide. Thomas Jefferson was so captivated by the formation that in 1773 he petitioned King George III for a land grant that included it. The Cedar Creek valley and Natural Bridge were produced, Jefferson thought, "by some great convulsion," and were, he wrote, "the most sublime of nature's works."[43] "It is impossible for the emotions arising from the sublime to be felt beyond what they are here; so beautiful an arch, so elevated, so light, and springing as it were up to heaven! the rapture of the spectator is really indescribable."[44] Cedar Creek valley is deeply incised into the limestones that comprise this section, and Natural Bridge provided "a public and commodious passage over a valley which cannot be crossed elsewhere for a considerable distance."[45] Today, U.S. Highway 11 crosses Cedar Creek atop Natural Bridge.

Rock and Soil

In 1670, the German fur trader John Lederer traveled inland from eastern Virginia to explore the land and seek out trading prospects. He and his companions "crossed the Blue Ridge easily at Manassas Gap, then descended into broad savannas, flowery meads, where herds of red deer were feeding. The grass which spring [sic] from the limestone soil was so high that they could tie it across their saddles. Since Indians burned this land over every autumn to make their game preserve, it was only lightly wooded with occasional groves of oak or maple."[46] Early travel accounts such as Lederer's suggest that most Valley occupants, be they Native Americans or the early Anglo settlers, were keenly aware of the Shenandoah's natural qualities, especially its superior limestone-derived soils. Contemporary soil science catalogs the Valley limestone soils as members of the alfisol group whose character includes a relatively high proportion of base minerals — calcium, magnesium, sodium, and potassium. Unlike many acidic Coastal Plain and Piedmont soils to the east, high-base alfisols were chemically neutral and could sustain relatively high vegetative production yields for prolonged periods. As Lederer observed, the Valley limestones fostered high-quality natural pasturelands from which farmers produced meat, dairy, and leather products, and when tilled, created fields that could be planted in grains and fiber crops, a production diversity not found in the cotton or tobacco monoculture commonly practiced on the Piedmont uplands or the Coastal Plain. Alfisols, and the highly productive agriculture they engendered, provided the basis for the Valley's reputation as Virginia's granary.[47]

Eighteenth-century settlers entered the Valley from two directions. Some arrived from long-established, English-origin settlements in eastern Virginia's plantation country. Others, primarily Palatinate Germans and Ulster Scots from southeastern Pennsylvania and the adjoining Maryland Panhandle, followed the Great Valley southwest into the Shenandoah country. By the eve of the Revolution, a mix of other European settlers had arrived and settled along the Valley floor: Swiss, Dutch, Swedes, Welsh, and Irish. The latter came in relatively large numbers as indentured servants.[48] Farmers produced a variety of crops for both commercial sale and for self-sufficiency: hemp, wheat, corn, flax, barley, oats, and rye. Hemp, considered a strategic naval supply by England, was the primary "money crop." Hemp production was stimulated by "bounty" payments from the British Parliament and the Virginia Burgesses. By the early 1770s, Augusta, Botetourt, and Frederick counties were producing more than 300,000 pounds of hemp annually.[49] Wheat, the traditional frontier crop across eastern America, ranked second to hemp, and by the eve of the Revolution, wheat farmers supported scores of flour mills across the Valley. By the mid-1770s, north Valley farmers were exporting quantities of flour and wheat, albeit by wagon along rather wretched roads. Pasture grasses proliferated on Valley farms and, together with feed grains, supported livestock production, especially cattle, horses, and hogs. Farmers could market beef and pork to nearby coastal cities — Philadelphia, Baltimore, Alexandria, and Richmond — either by droving animals overland or slaughtering them in the Valley and shipping dried, smoked, or salted meats.[50]

The basic requirements of productive agriculture, be it during the initial settlement period or today, are a humid climate and reasonably fertile soils. The Valley receives thirty-four to thirty-eight inches of precipitation annually, almost 60 percent of which falls during the growing season, April 1 through September 30. The engineer and geographer Charles Varle traveled through the northern Valley in 1810 and readily identified differences in soils and farm productivity. He observed that three different "slips" of land comprised the Valley floor. The first, about six miles wide, extended west from the base of the Blue Ridge to Front Royal and was "very superior quality . . . limestone land." A second "slip" of "slate" land lay west of Front Royal, which, while of lesser quality, responded well to attempts by farmers to increase its productivity. "The plaister of Paris [gypsum] work miracles on this soil," Varle noted. The third Valley floor parcel ran from Winchester and Middletown west to the base of Little North Mountain and was "a strong lime-stone land, excellent for the production of all kinds of grain."[51] Mr. Varle's "slate land" was the Martinsburg shale.

By the eve of the Civil War, the Valley's limestone farmlands were, as George Pond saw them, "Beautiful to look upon . . . rich in its well-filled barns, its cattle, its busy mills, the Valley furnished from its abundant crops much of the subsistence of Lee's army. When Confederate forces occupied it, their horses fattened on its forage, and in quitting it to invade the North, the commissaries filled their wagons from its storehouses and farms."[52] In his 1885 essay titled *The Physiography of Augusta, County, Virginia,* the teacher and Civil War engineer and topographer Jed Hotchkiss observed that the Valley lands underlain by limestone were "by far, the most valuable and attractive portion of the county . . . , a natural blue-grass country the larger portion of which is the best of plow-land or pasture-land; land good for wheat or corn, or for other grains, favorable for the raising of fruit, and that naturally clothes itself with parklike forests chiefly of hardwoods."[53] Crop yields on Valley farms were roughly twice that of the state as a whole.[54] Shale lands, on the other hand, were not nearly so desirable, in Hotchkiss's estimation. The south Valley shale surfaces were "much broken into steep-sided ravines and sharply-rounded hills with numerous narrow stream-valleys and plateaulike divides; portions of it furnish good soils for small grains and fruits," he allowed, whereas "other portions are poor."[55] Yet, clay soils derived from limestone were not without problems. Dry weather, especially in late summer and autumn, could turn clay soils to dust. Hotchkiss noted in his Civil War journal that during the drought of 1862 huge clouds of dust billowed up and blew down the Valley Turnpike, making life almost unbearable and travel next to impossible.[56]

The Frederick County soil survey published in 1987 essentially confirms the nineteenth-century observations made by Varle and Hotchkiss. "The prime farmland in the county," the surveyors note, "is mainly in the limestone region of the valley belt, east of Little North Mountain and west of Stephenson, Winchester, and Middletown."[57] These same soils, primarily the Frederick-Poplimento series, have weathered from lower Ordovician and Cambrian limestones and extend southwest along the Valley floor into

Shenandoah, Rockingham, and Augusta counties. The region's rainfall is sufficient to leach from the soils water-soluble minerals, leaving behind nonsoluble materials such as iron oxides that turn the soils a reddish hue. If solution removes calcium and carbonate materials more rapidly than they are naturally replenished, soils can turn acidic. Shale soils, on the other hand, unless they are limed — plaster of paris was used in Varle's time — and fertilized, are best used to support pasture grass or trees.

Navigating the Valley

Evaluating the Valley's evolution as a travel and movement corridor necessarily requires two perspectives: intravalley, or regional, and extravalley, or national. Regionally, the early nineteenth-century Valley residents, and those in adjoining sections of the Piedmont and the Appalachian Plateau, clearly recognized that the Valley's northeast to southwest alignment and low-gradient floor strongly affected the direction and volume of travel. While the Valley Road was the main route through the Valley, one could also travel long distances on two or three parallel routes such as the Middle Road that ran three to four miles west of the Valley Road linking Winchester and Harrisonburg. Smaller cross-valley roads developed linking mill settlements to stream crossings, farms, and the main trunk roads so that few farms were more than a mile or so from a road, however awkward and uninviting their winter mud and summer ruts might be for travelers.

Nationally, East Coast merchants and politicians, especially from Philadelphia, Baltimore, and Richmond, were buoyed by the success of the National Road in linking Baltimore to the Ohio River valley by about 1818. But they were also fearful of the possible monopoly on trade with the western interior that the Erie Canal imparted to New York City after that routeway opened in 1825. Consequently, a diverse group of development-minded individuals began to plan the financing and construction of trans-Appalachian roads, canals, and railroads that would link their coastal cities to the rapidly developing West. While trade with the Valley was sufficient to provide profitable commercial exchange with coastal populations, for coastal merchants the lucrative potential gains that awaited them beyond the Appalachian crest were almost beyond imagination. Yet, this national view had to acknowledge the substantial topographic barriers that engineers and laborers would have to surmount to reach the Ohio Valley — the Valley's bordering ridges, the phalanx of ridges west of North Mountain, and the formidable labyrinth of the Appalachian Plateau.

Eighteenth- and early nineteenth-century transportation was primarily water oriented. American settlements clung to coastal port sites and spread inland via navigable rivers. Roads into the interior were merely paths with little formal engineering or construction, often impaired by rocks, stumps, and ruts, and nearly impassable when wet from rain or melting snow. Consequently, overland wagon transportation was mechanically difficult, time consuming, and extremely expensive. During the first two decades of the nineteenth century, wagon freight charges could exceed fifteen cents per ton-mile on the best roads. Consequently, farmers rarely shipped farm products more than one hundred miles for beyond that distance freight charges could exceed the market price that might be obtained in Philadelphia, Baltimore, or the Virginia port towns.[58] By the turn of the twentieth century, overland roads were little improved. Consequently, the cost of moving grain five miles by wagon from farm granary to a railroad freight depot or steamboat wharf was about the same as moving the same volume of goods by ship from an Atlantic coast port to England's Liverpool.[59]

The rivers that crosscut the Shenandoah Valley, the Potomac and James, were relatively shallow, and where they encountered especially resistant rocks, rapids and falls interrupted navigation for long sections. Within the Valley, the Shenandoah River and its major branches also flowed in shallow beds, and although advisors to George Washington claimed that the trunk stream could be improved for navigation, the upturned limestone and shale strata in the channel created numerous shallows and rapids, hazards as formidable as marlinspikes to those foolhardy enough to venture the river in a boat with a draft any deeper than a canoe.[60] Necessarily, the Valley's early transportation connections to the coastal settlements were overland and, consequently, slow and expensive.

The Valley's inherent fertility and productivity, on the its corridor character on the other, were the basis for the d two types of trails or roads early on, emigrant roads and tr The Valley Road — also known as the Philadelphia Wag the Valley Turnpike — functioned in both capacities. By l delphia and the German settlements of southeastern Pennsylvania with Cumberland Gap and the North Carolina piedmont, the Valley route allowed emigrants to travel to both destinations. Drovers utilized the route to herd cattle and hogs to East Coast market towns. The Valley Road and other trade routes linking to coastal markets and ports would have also entertained large wagons heavily loaded with Valley produce, the traffic necessitating some measure of road construction and frequent repair. But in lieu of either road-maintenance funds or knowledgeable engineers and road-repair crews, roads, once established, soon deteriorated and were often in poor condition. In 1786, an Italian count visited Staunton and Winchester. His carriage "found the going so rough on 'the Great Road' between these two principal Valley towns, that it 'broke into a hundred pieces and at the first smithy [he] determined to abandon the vehicle and proceed on horseback.'"[62]

The road connecting Alexandria on the Potomac to Valley towns Berryville and Winchester by way of Snickers Gap across the Blue Ridge was among the most heavily traveled trade routes. Because Virginia did not have a sufficient treasury to underwrite road construction or repair, the government adopted the Act of 1785, which appointed nine commissioners and instructed them to "erect, or cause to be set up and erected, one or more gates or turnpikes across the roads . . . leading into the town of Alexandria from Snigger's [Snickers] Gap."[63] Tolls collected at turnpike stations were then applied to road construction and repair. The Alexandria Road, now State Route 7, thus became America's first toll road, and Virginia's legislation was widely copied by other states, thereby introducing the century-long turnpike era to American overland road travel. Despite the appeal that passable roads had for people living away from navigable water, Virginia's roads in 1907, three hundred years after the founding of Jamestown, were little improved over their colonial antecedents.[64]

Regional crossroads where the Valley Road intersected east–west roads linking seaboard market towns and mountain settlements in the Alleghenies were likely locations for town development. Harrisonburg grew up at the junction of the Valley Road and the turnpike that crossed the Blue Ridge at Swift Run Gap, a route that continued west into the Ridge and Valley by way of Dry River Gap. Several roads converged upon Winchester including the Berryville Turnpike, which traversed the Blue Ridge by way of Snickers Gap and then linked to Alexandria. In the south central Valley, Staunton — initially an outfitting post for emigrants headed southwest toward Cumberland Gap — also became the focus of east–west roads linking the Piedmont to the Valley by way of Rock Fish Gap.[65] Other towns grew up as Valley Road service centers with taverns and other facilities for stagecoach travelers and cargo wagon teamsters. Roadside accommodations added to road travel costs, which remained very high, especially compared to commodity transport via canal or riverboat.

While falls and rapids made the Potomac and the James uninviting avenues for in-channel river navigation, the river-cut gaps through the Blue Ridge at Harpers Ferry and Balcony Falls did provide potential gateways into the Valley for roads, canals, or railroads. George Washington introduced a bill in the Virginia House of Burgesses in 1774 advocating improvement of navigation on the Potomac and James rivers.[66] Eventually, a plan to construct a canal, the C&O, from Washington, D.C., to Cumberland, Maryland, along the Potomac gained sufficient political support and financial backing — $1 million in federal appropriations — so that construction began in 1828.[67]

During this same time, America's nascent railroad technology was fitfully cycling from innovation, to construction and testing, to failure — followed by more innovation. Nevertheless, railroads were sufficiently attractive to invite investment and construction in direct competition with canals. Baltimore entrepreneurs underwrote the construction of the Baltimore and Ohio (B&O) Railroad to link their city to the Ohio Valley at Wheeling, West Virginia, by way of the Potomac Gap at Harpers Ferry. Construction on the B&O Railroad began the same day as on the C&O Canal, and rail bed and track construction proceeded much more rapidly than canal excavation. Though the railroad originated in Baltimore, its route trended southwest to the Monocacy River valley and beyond to the Potomac. Canal and railroad ran in tandem along the Potomac from Point of Rocks through the Blue Ridge. The B&O bridged the Potomac at Harpers Ferry in 1837. Other railroads that attempted to gain the Valley by way of more southerly routes did not enjoy the topographic indulgence of a water-level gap in the Blue Ridge as the B&O did at Harpers Ferry, unless by way of the Balcony Falls route along the James River. Instead, the Virginia Central Railroad linked Richmond and Charlottesville to Staunton by way of a 4,300-foot tunnel through the ridge under Rockfish Gap. The project was completed and opened for traffic in the late 1850s and impressed observers as "a formidable work."[68]

Canal construction across the Shenandoah Valley was relatively benign compared to the problems encountered both downstream and upstream. The canal required seventeen locks from Harpers Ferry across the Valley floor west to North Mountain. Near mid-Valley, at the point where the Valley Road crossed the river, the canal town of Williamsport grew up around a complex of canal basins, a lock, and a spectacular limestone aqueduct over Conococheague Creek, a Potomac tributary.[69] The canal finally reached the foot of the Appalachian Plateau at Cumberland, Maryland, its terminus, in 1850. The B&O Railroad had arrived eight years earlier and continued west toward Wheeling and the Ohio River valley. Although the railroad's presence offered stiff competition for canal boats, slack water canal transport efficiencies dropped the price of shipping goods by 90 percent or more, and the canal functioned as a major intraregional carrier.[70] Williamsport had functioned as a river port for

Valley products and produce before the canal arrived in 1834. Once linked to the canal, it became an active boomtown as a transshipment point for western coal, and corn, wheat, flour, and other farm products. Moreover, the canal proved an attractive location for manufacturers — mills, foundries, and textile operations — where they might purchase from the canal rights to water that could be diverted to power their mills. Canal operations also required local support industries. The four hundred canal boats that moved along the canal were in need of periodic repair just as their crews needed access to comestibles and other supplies. The two thousand tow mules consumed considerable quantities of hay, corn, and oats annually. As the canal's central place, the Valley town of Williamsport became a commissariat for canal provender.[71]

Businesspeople in Richmond, Virginia, also looked to canal transportation to gain for themselves a competitive link to the West. Their avenue was the James River, which rose in the upper Shenandoah Valley. To arrange financing and initiate construction on river channel improvements and canal construction, the Virginia General Assembly authorized the formation of the James River Company in 1785, naming George Washington titular president.[72] Encouraged by the completion of a short canal around the falls at Richmond in 1789, upcountry farmers, millers, and distillers sent their products on river flatboats down the James to Tidewater markets.[73] Managing the hazards of flatboat navigation at Balcony Falls and other roily river rapids during low water was a rather grave experience because the rocks and rough water routinely claimed boats, freight, and lives. Nonetheless, downriver freight rates were often less than two cents per ton-mile as early as 1800.[74] Canals offered many potential advantages over open river navigation, including the reliability and safety of slack water travel and rate costs of one cent per ton-mile or less by the 1840s. The promise of transport surety and lower movement costs fed interests in canal investment and construction. The James River Canal opened for navigation between Richmond and Lynchburg in 1840, and an extension to Buchanan in the upper Valley was completed in 1851, bringing the canal's length, including the improved river channels for slack water navigation, to about 197 miles. Lexington also linked into the canal by way of the North, or Maury, River. The James River Canal was far enough south that it did not freeze in the winter so boats could move along its length year-round. By the eve of the Civil War in 1860, upcountry Virginia farmers exported 143,000 bushels of wheat and 423,194 barrels of flour to Richmond via the canal, helping to make the routeway the largest freight carrier in the state.[75]

The Civil War and repeated floods disrupted traffic, and regional railroads siphoned freight shipments away from the venerable canal, yet it provided an important southern outlet for Shenandoah Valley products until major floods in 1877 and 1878 damaged the canal throughout its entire length. Unable to recover financially, the James River Canal system was acquired by the Richmond and Alleghany Railroad Company in 1880, which promptly laid new tracks atop the old canal tow path from Richmond to Clifton Forge, some thirty miles above Buchanan; the canal soon lost all commercial functions. In 1888, the Chesapeake and Ohio Railway Company acquired the Richmond and Alleghany line, thereby providing a national-scale outlet to the flow of commodities from the upper Shenandoah Valley.[76]

Both canals and the railroad stimulated commerce and economic development within the Valley. Large coal shipments, for use in industry and home and commercial heating, arrived in Williamsport from Cumberland via the C&O Canal, where it could be used locally, shipped south into the Valley, or forwarded down the canal to Coastal Plain settlements.[77] The B&O Railroad, when improved with new equipment, provided economical transportation links to export lower Valley products and import manufactured goods from eastern ports. Within the Valley, Winchester's citizens planned and financed the construction of the twenty-eight-mile-long Winchester and Potomac Railroad that by 1836 linked the lower Valley with the river near Harpers Ferry. Although the B&O connected with the Winchester and Potomac line, thereby forming the first junction of two railroad companies in America, railroad investors in Baltimore were unwilling to direct the main line of the B&O southward through the Valley by way of the Winchester and Potomac tracks as the main route to the Ohio Valley. Never mind the commerce that route would have gained from Shenandoah Valley farms, mines, and forges, it was viewed as an unnecessary southerly detour of considerably longer length than the direct westerly route to Wheeling that they preferred.[78]

Though modest in scale and carrying capacity by the standards of the late nineteenth century, the early railroad markedly altered the geography and economy of Valley farming. Lower transport costs translated into greater profits for wheat and other products. Farmers were now motivated to adopt progressive farming techniques to salvage exhausted land and increase yields. By the mid-1830s, a writer in the *Farmer's Register* proclaimed that "a new day had dawned for the Valley with the completion of the railroads and that the farmers were awakening from the errors of exhausting methods and beginning new and better ways."[79] After the Civil

War, B&O management would eventually link the Valley line southward as far as Staunton, and it became known as the Valley Railroad.[80]

Coda

The Shenandoah Valley's physical attributes — climate, streams and rivers, bedrock and karst caverns, soils, and bordering ridges — have helped define its cultural character and economy for more than two centuries. Early on, the limestone lands attracted Pennsylvania German farmers and others who recognized the Valley's inherent fertility, and they turned the Valley into an agricultural cornucopia. The Valley also became one of the major routeways in the East, a two-way avenue linking the frontier with coastal port settlements and traversed by migrants as well as farm produce and manufactured goods. During the Civil War, Valley farms fed Confederate armies, and the South, buoyed by this strategic resource, would not be subdued until its Shenandoah Valley storehouse had been compromised by Union army predations.

While nineteenth-century canals and railroads offered economical alternatives to Valley road transportation, the political and technological transformation of highway construction that began in the 1920s reclaimed the Valley routeway's proprietary qualities. In 1925, the geographer J. Russell Smith lauded the Valley's good limestone-surfaced roads. The Valley had, he said, "per county or per thousand people several times as much good stone road as equally rich districts occupied by the same kind of people in the Piedmont but a few miles away."[81] The Valley Road, widened, straightened, and otherwise improved according to new federal guidelines, became U.S. Highway 11 after 1926, and for some time was known as the best automobile highway from New York to Georgia and Florida. During the interstate highway era, engineers surveyed and built a new limited-access roadway, Interstate 81, parallel to the old road. Transport technology — road, canal, railroad — has advanced in fits and starts; regional and national economic and political priorities have tacked from one heading to another. Through all of this, the Shenandoah Valley's geographic character as corridor, routeway, and farming and industrial center remains as compelling as it was two and a half centuries ago.

Notes

1. Robert W. Ramsey, *Carolina Cradle: Settlement of the Northwest Carolina Frontier, 1747–1762* (Chapel Hill: University of North Carolina Press, 1964), 34–39.

2. Freeman H. Hart, *The Valley of Virginia in the American Revolution, 1763–1789* (Chapel Hill: University of North Carolina Press, 1942), 8.

3. George E. Pond, *The Shenandoah Valley in 1864* (New York: Scribner's, 1885), 1–2. Cf. Ellen Churchill Semple, *American History and Its Geographic Conditions* (Boston: Houghton Mifflin, 1903), 294–300.

4. Jeffry D. Wert, "Jubal A. Early and Confederate Leadership," in Gary W. Gallagher, ed. *Struggle for the Shenandoah: Essays on the 1864 Valley Campaign*, 27–39 (Kent, Ohio: Kent State University Press, 1991).

5. Robert H. Mohlenbrock, "This Land: Ramsey's Draft, Virginia," *Natural History* 94, no. 11 (1985): 76–78.

6. George R. Stewart, *American Place-Names* (New York: Oxford University Press, 1970).

7. Fairfax Harrison, *Landmarks of Old Prince William: A Study of Origins in Northern Virginia*, vol. 2 (Richmond: Old Dominion Press, 1924), 472.

8. John T. Hack, *Physiographic Divisions and Differential Uplift in the Piedmont and Blue Ridge*, Geological Survey Professional Paper 1265 (Washington, D.C.: U.S. Government Printing Office, 1982), map.

9. Harold A. Winters et al., *Battling the Elements: Weather and Terrain in the Conduct of War* (Baltimore: Johns Hopkins University Press, 1998), 117–18.

10. Hack, *Physiographic Divisions*, 26.

11. H. H. Mills, "The Endogenic Imprint on Landscape in the Valley and Ridge Province," in William L. Graf, ed., *Geomorphic Systems of North America* (Boulder, Colo.: Geological Society of America, 1987), 9.

12. Ibid., 8.

13. John T. Hack, *Geomorphology of the Shenandoah Valley Virginia and West Virginia and Origin of the Residual Ore Deposits*, Geological Survey Professional Paper 484 (Washington, D.C.: U.S. Government Printing Office, 1965), 60. See also Philip B. King, "The Floor of the Shenandoah Valley," *American Journal of Science* 247, no. 2 (1949): 73–93.

14. Charles Butts, *Geology of the Appalachian Valley in Virginia*, Bulletin 52 (University, Va.: Virginia Geological Survey, 1940), 9.

15. G. Terry Sharrer, *A Kind of Fate: Agricultural Change in Virginia, 1861–1920* (Ames: Iowa State University Press, 2000), 69, 85.

16. Mills, "Endogenic Imprint," 9; Hack, *Geomorphology of the Shenandoah Valley*, 60.

17. William D. Thornbury, *Principles of Geomorphology* (New York: Wiley, 1954), 150–52.

18. Robert F. Hunter, "Turnpike Construction in Antebellum Virginia," *Technology and Culture* 4, no. 2 (1963): 189.

19. Hart, *The Valley of Virginia*, 20–21.

20. Harrison, *Landmarks of Old Prince William*, 407. See also Warren R. Hofstra and Robert D. Mitchell, "Town and Country in Backcountry Virginia: Winchester and the Shenandoah Valley, 1730–1800," *Journal of Southern History* 59, no. 4 (1993): 640–41.

21. Edmund P. Tompkins, *Rockbridge County, Virginia: An Informal History* (Richmond, Va.: Whittet and Shepperson, 1952), 84.

22. John T. Hack and Robert S. Young, *Intrenched Meanders of the North Fork of the Shenandoah River,* Virginia Geological Survey Professional Paper 354-A (Washington, D.C.: U.S. Government Printing Office, 1959), 7.

23. Ibid., 4.

24. Mills, "Endogenic Imprint," 9.

25. Ronald C. Page, A. E. Burford, and A. C. Donaldson, *Geology of the Martinsburg Quadrangle, West Virginia, 1:24,000* (Morgantown: West Virginia Geological and Economic Survey, 1964).

26. Warren R. Hofstra and Clarence R. Geier, "Farm to Mill to Market: Historical Archaeology of an Emerging Grain Economy in the Shenandoah Valley of Virginia," in Kenneth E. Koons and Warren R. Hofstra, eds., *After the Backcountry: Rural Life in the Great Valley of Virginia, 1800–1900* (Knoxville: University of Tennessee Press, 2000), 58.

27. James Leffel & Co., *The Construction of Mill Dams* (Springfield, Ohio: James Leffel & Co., 1874), 121–22.

28. Aaron Cross, "Prehistoric Origins of an Interstate Highway," typescript (Charlottesville, Va., 2004), 9; E. K. Rader and T. M. Gathright II, *Geologic Map of the Front Royal 30 × 60 Minute Quadrangle: Portions of Clarke, Page, Rockingham, Shenandoah, and Warren Counties Virginia,* Publication 162 (Charlottesville, Va.: Department of Mines, Minerals and Energy, 2001).

29. Robert D. Mitchell and Warren R. Hofstra, "How Do Settlement Systems Evolve? The Virginia Backcountry during the Eighteenth Century," *Journal of Historical Geography* 21, no. 2 (1995): 135.

30. Hack, "Generalized Geologic Map of the Shenandoah Valley Virginia and West Virginia," plate 1, 1:250,000, in Hack, *Geomorphology of the Shenandoah Valley.*

31. Hunter, "Turnpike Construction in Antebellum Virginia," 200.

32. Hack, *Geomorphology of the Shenandoah Valley,* 28.

33. Mills, "Endogenic Imprint," 10.

34. Hack and Young, *Intrenched Meanders,* 1.

35. David A. Hubbard Jr., *Selected Karst Features of the Northern Valley and Ridge Province Virginia,* Publication 44 (annotated map), Department of Conservation and Economic Development, Division of Mineral Resources (Richmond: Commonwealth of Virginia, 1983).

36. Hack, *Geomorphology of the Shenandoah Valley,* 59 and plate 3.

37. Frank Reeves, *Thermal Springs of Virginia,* Bulletin 36 (University, Va.: Virginia Geological Survey, 1932).

38. Hack, *Geomorphology of the Shenandoah Valley,* 60.

39. Butts, *Geology of the Appalachian Valley in Virginia,* 445.

40. William M. McGill, *Caverns of Virginia,* Bulletin 35, Educational Series 1 (University, Va.: Virginia Geological Survey, 1933).

41. Thomas Jefferson, *Notes on the State of Virginia* (published as part of vol. 8 of *The Writings of Thomas Jefferson,* ed. H. A. Washington) (New York: H. W. Derby, 1861; repr., New York: Harper and Row, 1964), 19.

42. Isaac Weld, *Travels through the States of North America and the Provinces of*

Upper and Lower Canada, during the Years 1795, 1796, 1797, 4th ed., vol. 1 (London: John Stockdale, 1807; repr., New York: Johnson Reprint Corp., 1968), 228–29.

43. Jefferson, *Notes on the State of Virginia,* 21.

44. Ibid.

45. Ibid., 22.

46. Julia Davis, *The Shenandoah* (New York: Farrar and Rinehart, 1945), 24–25.

47. Douglas Helms, "Soil and Southern History," *Agricultural History* 74 (2000): 730.

48. Hart, *The Valley of Virginia,* 7. See also John W. Wayland, *The German Element of the Shenandoah Valley of Virginia* (Charlottesville, Va.: self-published; Michie Co. Printers, 1907), 20–31.

49. Hart, *The Valley of Virginia,* 8.

50. Ibid., 10–12.

51. Charles Varle, *Topographical Description of the Counties of Frederick, Berkeley & Jefferson, situated in the State of Virginia in which the author has described the natural curiosities of those counties* . . . (Winchester, Va.: W. Heiskell, 1810), 11–12. See also Avery O. Craven, "Soil Exhaustion as a Factor in the Agricultural History of Virginia and Maryland, 1606–1860," special issue, *University of Illinois Studies in the Social Sciences* 13, no. 1 (1926; repr., Gloucester, Mass.: Peter Smith, 1965), 94; and Sharrer, *A Kind of Fate,* xxii.

52. Pond, *The Shenandoah Valley in 1864,* 2.

53. Jed Hotchkiss, *Historical Atlas of Augusta County, Virginia* (Chicago: Waterman, Watkins and Company, 1885), 31.

54. Sharrer, *A Kind of Fate,* 89.

55. Ibid.

56. William J. Miller, *Mapping for Stonewall: The Civil War Service of Jed Hotchkiss* (Washington, D.C.: Elliott and Clark, 1993), 92; Archie P. McDonald, *Make Me a Map of the Valley: The Civil War Journal of Stonewall Jackson's Topographer* (Dallas: Southern Methodist University Press, 1973), 90.

57. Robert L. Holmes and David L. Wagner, *Soil Survey of Frederick County, Virginia* (Washington, D.C.: U.S. Department of Agriculture and Soil Conservation Service, 1987), 4.

58. Carville Earle, "Regional Economic Development West of the Appalachians, 1815–1860," in Robert Mitchell and Paul Groves, eds., *North America: The Historical Geography of a Changing Continent* (Totowa, N.J.: Rowman and Littlefield, 1987), 175.

59. United States Department of Agriculture, Office of Public Road Inquiries, *Proceedings — The Jefferson Memorial and Interstate Good Roads Convention* (April 2, 3, and 4, Charlottesville, Va.), Bulletin no. 25 (Washington, D.C.: U.S. Government Printing Office, 1902), 57.

60. Hart, *The Valley of Virginia,* 56.

61. James E. Vance Jr., *Capturing the Horizon: The Historical Geography of Transportation since the Transportation Revolution of the Sixteenth Century* (New York: Harper and Row, 1986), 168–69.

62. Hart, *The Valley of Virginia,* 166.

63. Frederic J. Wood, *The Turnpikes of New England and Evolution of Same through New England, Virginia, and Maryland* (Boston: Marshall Jones, 1919), 7.

64. Sharrer, *A Kind of Fate,* 199.

65. Archer Butler Hulbert, *Soil: Its Influence on the History of the United States* (New Haven: Yale University Press, 1930), 173.

66. Henry S. Drago, *Canal Days in America* (New York: Bramhall House, 1972), 47.

67. Carter Goodrich, *Government Promotion of American Canals and Railroads, 1800–1890* (New York: Columbia University Press, 1960), 41; Ulrich B. Phillips, *A History of Transportation in the Eastern Cotton Belt* (New York: Columbia University Press, 1908), 15.

68. Israel D. Andrews, *Trade and Commerce of the British North American Colonies and upon the Trade of the Great Lakes and Rivers,* 32nd Cong., 1st sess., Doc. No. 112 (Washington, D.C.: Robert Armstrong, Printer, 1853), 324.

69. National Park Service, *Chesapeake and Ohio Canal: A Guide to the Chesapeake and Ohio Canal National Historic Park, Maryland, District of Columbia, and West Virginia,* Handbook 142 (Washington, D.C.: U.S. Department of the Interior, 1991), 96–97.

70. Carter Goodrich, ed., *Canals and American Economic Development* (New York: Columbia University Press, 1961), 228.

71. National Park Service, *Chesapeake and Ohio Canal,* 64–65.

72. Wayland F. Dunaway, *History of the James River and Kanawha Company* (New York: privately printed, 1922), 26–30.

73. Drago, *Canal Days in America,* 76.

74. Earle, "Regional Economic Development West of the Appalachians," 175.

75. Dunaway, *History of the James River and Kanawha Company,* 165, 184.

76. Ibid., 239–40.

77. Caroline E. MacGill, *History of Transportation in the United States before 1860* (Washington, D.C.: Carnegie Institution, 1917), 268–69.

78. Edward Hungerford, *The Story of the Baltimore & Ohio Railroad, 1827–1927,* vol. 1 (New York: G. P. Putnam's Sons, 1928), 148–49.

79. Quoted in Craven, *Soil Exhaustion as a Factor in the Agricultural History of Virginia and Maryland,* 134.

80. Hungerford, *The Story of the Baltimore & Ohio Railroad,* 2:117–18.

81. J. Russell Smith, *North America* (New York: Harcourt, Brace, 1925), 199.

Before the Great Road

Indian Travelers on the Great Warriors' Path

MICHAEL McCONNELL

The Great Warriors' Path, as the principal footpath through the Shenandoah Valley was once known, conjures up complex images. The name suggests less a thoroughfare than a path to a battleground: Indian warriors — perhaps Cherokees or Iroquois — launching attacks against hapless settlers. It hints at a popular understanding of "frontiers" as places marked by violence between natives and newcomers, part of an inevitable process whereby Indian country became the United States.

A different reading of events along the Path suggests a more complex story. Around the beginning of the eighteenth century, native fighting men *did* use the Path in raids against enemies who were more often Indian than colonist. But before the Warriors' Path assumed its brief, popular association with warfare, we find another rich history. That precolonial past is best viewed through a wide lens: much of what occurred in the Valley and along the Path before the eighteenth century was influenced by encounters between peoples throughout much of eastern North America that, in turn, led to profound changes in the cultural landscape of the Valley. It is a past filled with migrating peoples, agricultural villagers, diplomats, and refugees, as well as warriors.

Paths: Networks through Indian Country

The popular imagination raises images of a narrow tract through dense woods, inviting only to those who know the path, forbidding to those who do not. This impression is reinforced by seventeenth- and, especially, eighteenth-century cartographers whose task it was to translate reports from traders, explorers, and others into two-dimensional impressions of a three-dimensional world. Paths became thin lines on maps, running from village to village, from portage to mountain pass, snaking their way through a real or imagined wilderness.[1]

Colonial maps and written descriptions often portray paths in rather

Fig. 2.1. The Augusta Stone Presbyterian Church, dating to 1747–49, may be the oldest Presbyterian church in Virginia and is said to have served as a fort, offering early settlers protection from Indian attack. (Scott Jost 2000)

sterile terms: tracks that connect this place to that. If we could imagine what the Path and Valley looked like at any time in their precolonial past, the impression would be one of activity, the movement of groups and individuals, regulated by the seasons and the rhythms of intersocietal relations, all leaving some mark, however temporary, along the way. Indian travelers would know they were on the path by the unmistakable signs of those who had gone before: abandoned campfires, the remains of a meal, perhaps a totemic symbol or other mark left on a tree to mark the passing of some person or group.

Travel was also heavier than images of narrow paths might suggest. Most journeys would have been undertaken by groups, not solitary individuals. War parties would have included varying numbers of mostly young men. Diplomatic missions or trading ventures would have included women and children, likely members of close kin groups, while the periodic movements of whole villages, in search of better farmland, cleaner surroundings, or shelter from enemies, would have involved scores or even hundreds of people and their portable belongings. The important point, though, is that the network of paths through the Valley would have been in constant use for centuries before the arrival of newcomers from Europe and West Africa.[2]

Some paths *were* narrow tracks, especially through forests or along

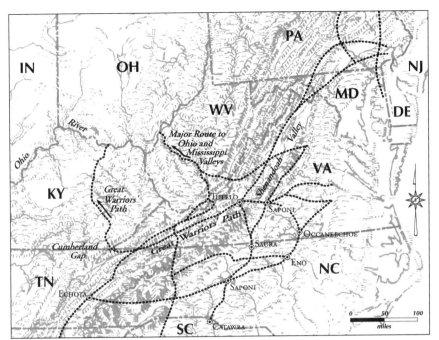

Fig. 2.2. Major Indian trails of the Chesapeake hinterland. (After Helen Rountree, *Powhatan Foreign Policy* [Charlottesville: University Press of Virginia, 1993]; Gyula Pauer Cartography Lab, University of Kentucky)

ridgelines. Popular trails would be readily identifiable as narrow, well-worn tracks running through wooded land (see fig. 2.2). In open country, however, the path might be harder to identify.[3] It might be more useful, though, to imagine the paths that ran through the Valley less as specific places than as itineraries that would carry knowledgeable travelers to their desired destinations. Routes would vary with the seasons, compensating for swollen rivers, tree falls, or swampy ground. Paths might follow, for instance, high ground between streams that tended to flood during heavy rains. Then, too, travelers might have to chart their own way around obstacles. John Lawson, moving through western Carolina, was forced to take lengthy detours when rain rendered the usual paths impassable.[4] Moreover, travelers would need to locate food and freshwater; routes could shift, then, to take advantage of local resources. Finally, as native populations moved, so did the paths; long-used routes might simply be abandoned once villagers relocated to better sources of firewood or to sites less exposed to enemies.[5]

The notion of itineraries is useful in one other way. Colonial travelers often narrated their journeys along Indian paths in terms of significant points along the route: mile markers of a sort that helped them find their way out and back. So, for example, people moving along these paths spoke of "sleeping places" — possibly caves, hollow logs, or cliff overhangs — or "Indian bridges," perhaps a single log spanning a swift-running creek.[6]

Fig. 2.3. (*Right and facing page*) Indian Trail Road (present-day Route 717) at Mauzy in Rockingham County follows a ridge crest along the Valley floor. (Scott Jost 2004)

Routes could be marked in other ways. Christopher Gist, sent to view lands in the Ohio Valley for the Ohio Company of Virginia, came upon "a large Warriors Camp" identified by the "Picture or Arms" of a war leader called the Crane "painted on a Tree."[7] And, years earlier, upon reaching the crest of the Blue Ridge in 1716, the party led by Virginia governor Alexander Spotswood found trees that, according to John Fontaine, had been formerly marked "by Northern Indians." Spotswood's party wisely decided to follow this marked trail and found a safe path down into the Valley.[8]

Spotswood's experience also suggests something else about paths and the people who used them: travelers could — and did — get lost. We sometimes assume that native peoples of the Eastern Woodlands would have been at home anywhere and could easily navigate through any territory. But as Fontaine reminds us, natives — in this case northern Indians (Iroquois) heading south through Virginia, found it necessary to mark their route for future reference. Thus, it should not surprise us to learn, as we do from a colonial captive during the Seven Years' War, that natives would

sometimes stop and climb trees in order to point out the course they should take.[9]

The notion of itineraries takes us, finally, to one other important aspect of the Warriors' Path. If this route shifted over time, if there may have been at any given moment *several* paths running north and south through the Valley, there were also other routes that intersected the Warriors' Path, producing a latticework arrangement of trails not unlike what we see today with the interstate highway, state roads, and local byways. Spotswood's party in the early eighteenth century followed one such path in order to find its way over the Blue Ridge. This was just one of many local subsystems of spreading prongs and feeder routes, trails that would have linked the Valley to the Tidewater, the Smoky Mountains of North Carolina, the Ohio Valley, and regions beyond. The Great Warriors' Path, then, was less an isolated route than the main artery of a dense communication system. This system, in turn, reminds us that the native peoples who inhabited the Valley, or moved through it at any time in the past, were themselves never isolated, but were active participants in dynamic regional relations that helped shape their spiritual and material lives. In the long precolonial history of the Valley, this network would have been alive with the movement of peoples. And, of course, this network of paths would ultimately facilitate the meeting of natives and colonists.[10]

Paths and Peoples: The Valley before Virginia

Who, then, designed and used the Valley routeway system? Certainly parts of it were very old by the time Europeans learned of it. Native peoples began to exploit the Valley and the surrounding area even as the last great glaciers began their slow retreat to the Arctic beginning about ten thousand years ago. By about 6,500 years ago, the climate and landforms began to take on their modern characteristics, with mixed forests along the Blue Ridge and the Allegheny Plateau to the west, a mixture of meadows and occasional marshes on the Valley floor. In the process, small bands of migratory hunters began to exploit local ecosystems for wild plants, fish, and birds as well as game, transforming the Valley into a patchwork of discrete landscapes. It was probably then that the system of paths began to take shape. Developed by pioneering native groups, these paths facilitated movement into and through the Valley.[11]

Native populations continued to grow throughout the region during what archaeologists term the Archaic and Woodland periods of cultural development. Extensive use of seasonally abundant foods permitted more people to live in a given area and semi-permanent villages began to appear. After AD 900, native life in the Valley and the surrounding region took on an important new dimension with the adoption of domesticated plants, notably corn, beans, and squash. Arriving from the southwest, where they were being adopted by natives in the Mississippi Valley and elsewhere, corn and beans, first domesticated in Mexico, provided predictable, renewable food supplies. Yet, rather than viewing the arrival of these plants as some sort of agricultural revolution, we might better imagine that native peoples simply added these new foods to an already complex diet. These new sources of nutrition did, however, contribute to rising populations and, perhaps, marginally longer life expectancies. They also contributed to changes in local landscapes as villagers began to clear and maintain planting fields. In understanding the human history of the Valley before Jamestown, the importance of agriculture lies in a growing number of sedentary village communities, the remains of which offer insight into social and cultural development that, in turn, suggests how the Great Path and its tributaries were used.[12]

Agricultural villages composed of clusters or lines of circular dwellings appeared along secondary streams.[13] Determining the numbers of people living in these settlements, however, is difficult. For example, the Opequon Creek drainage holds the remains of more than two hundred native sites occupied from the Archaic to Middle Woodland eras.[14] Yet, not all sites from any particular period were occupied at the same time; some were permanent settlements, and others the remains of camps of transient hunters. The latest effort to reconstruct the native population of the larger region from the Arkansas River to the upper Potomac, including Kentucky, West Virginia, and western Virginia, concludes that "This was by far the least populous area in the entire South" and places the maximum population at no more than 8,500 people, a number that continued to fall in the seventeenth and eighteenth centuries because of the combined effects of disease, warfare, and expanding colonial settlement.[15]

Villages also were likely to be fortified with palisades after about AD 1450. This would suggest that a rising incidence of intergroup warfare, noticeable throughout much of the Northeast, was affecting those living in the Valley as well. Local hostilities may have been triggered, in part, by the shifts in long-term climate known as the Little Ice Age that began in the thirteenth century.[16] As cooler weather cut into growing seasons, villagers may have expanded their hunting and foraging activities — while running into neighbors jealous of those same resources. Evidence of warfare has been uncovered on at least one site: Rapidan Mounds, where archaeologists found human skulls mutilated and crushed by heavy blows.[17]

Climate change, hostilities, and reasons yet unidentified also produced migrations into and within the Valley. One such event saw the incursion of people from the northwest about AD 1400, mingling with, perhaps replacing, the local population, though not necessarily altering the appearance of village landscapes.[18] A century earlier, similar events took place as villagers in the Valley were replaced by peoples moving north — most likely along the Great Warriors' Path.[19] Meanwhile, villages relocated in the face of depleted soil and firewood. Such relocations were a routine part of native life throughout much of eastern America; colonial travelers would later refer to abandoned native towns as "old fields," which were readily distinguished by the rich second growth they supported.[20]

The peoples that lived along the Path did enjoy contact with people over a very broad area, as confirmed by material evidence. Copper, a highly valued substance throughout the native East, found its way into the Valley through contacts with peoples in the Ohio Valley to the west who, in turn, obtained it from trading partners nearer the source in the

Great Lakes basin. From the Shenandoah Valley, some copper made its way east to the Tidewater.[21] This trade may be an indication of a much more complex network of exchange that predated the arrival of corn and beans to the Valley. From 400 BC to AD 400, Hopewell Culture villagers in southern Ohio, for example, developed a wide-ranging interaction sphere in high-value materials such as copper, obsidian, and mica.[22]

Trading systems of this kind were common throughout North America, a reminder that native peoples did not live in isolation.[23] Indeed, evidence suggests that natives in the Valley continued to maintain indirect contact with distant peoples. In southwestern Virginia, archaeologists have found European-manufactured brass disc pendants of a sort widely popular in the interior Southeast between 1580 and 1650.[24] At roughly the same time, marine shell and objects made from scraps of European copper and brass, such as pendants, projectile points, and metal tubular beads, were finding their way into towns as far away as western Pennsylvania, central New York, and southern Ontario. While there is no certainty on this point, some of these objects may have passed through the network of trails that marked the Valley.[25] What does seem certain is that in the centuries before Jamestown, the Valley was a busy place. Moreover, the *lateral* paths that connected the region to the Allegheny Plateau to the west and the Tidewater to the east may have witnessed more traffic than the better-known north-to-south Great Warriors' Path.

We know far less about who engaged in settlement, trade, and intrusion than what they did. By the time colonists set foot in the Valley, most of its native inhabitants had long since departed. The names by which we identify these societies — the Luray, or Mason Island, peoples who once lived at sites now called Bowman, Cabin Run, or Perkins Point — reflect archaeologists' need to label the remains they find and place them in some sort of temporal and spatial order. What these villagers called themselves, what language(s) they spoke, are now lost.

Pathways to Encounters:
The Sixteenth and Seventeenth Centuries

We might assume that curious colonists would have asked about who lived beyond the next ridgeline or watershed. And we would not be completely wrong: English colonists at Jamestown almost immediately began assembling what information they could about their Powhatan neighbors and other peoples known to be living farther away. Yet intersocietal hostilities between Indian peoples, not to mention the conflict-laden relations between natives and newcomers, meant that what knowledge was collected by Tidewater settlers was, at best, incomplete, even when the formidable differences in languages could be overcome.

We know, for example, that the Powhatan chiefdom was in a chronic state of warfare with people called Monacans living along the Blue Ridge, with access to copper being one of the issues. The English soon learned of another people well to the west known to Tidewater natives as the Massawomecks and thought to live on the shores of a great western sea. The Monacans were a Siouan-speaking people, and the Massawomecks were in all likelihood the Seneca Iroquois.[26] What peoples lived within the Shenandoah Valley between these formidable peoples is much less clear. What seems indisputable, however, is that the arrival of Europeans led to what one historian has aptly called a collision of histories with profound consequences for natives, including those in the Valley.[27]

The appearance of Europeans — and Africans — produced a diffusion effect roughly akin to that of a stone dropped into a pool of water. The resulting waves carried new European technology and artifacts as well as diseases that spread outward, encompassing an ever larger area. This diffusion did not occur with the symmetry of waves, however; newcomers often triggered wholly unplanned, unpredictable consequences. Explorers and traders who began to arrive in the early sixteenth century brought with them an array of their material goods, especially edged tools and weapons, that would greatly alter Indian lives. And the visitors themselves were strange peoples, in exotic attire, with bizarre habits that would not fit easily into the natives' own worldviews.[28] Of course, this was a process of *mutual* discovery that had French, English, Basques, and others scrambling to make sense of people and lands not accounted for by *their* religion or science.[29]

Permanent colonial settlements appeared from Quebec to Charleston during the seventeenth century. Though they were small communities, they perched on the edge of Indian America and had a profound effect upon both the landscape and native peoples. Casual trade for furs and hides increasingly grew into a transatlantic business for many of these newcomers, further ensuring the flow of manufactured goods into Indian towns. Agriculture, too, became a basis for colonists' livelihoods, and in some regions, like the Chesapeake and coastal Carolina, trade involved natives themselves as labor-starved landowners encouraged one tribe to war against enemies, with enslaved captives as the proceeds.[30] But it was the colonists who arguably had the greatest long-term impact on native peoples. New towns, inhabited by children as well as adults, became breeding grounds for Old World crowd diseases, especially smallpox. As this and other illnesses swept through native America following well-traveled paths, including those in the Valley, populations plummeted, survivors took to these same routes as they fled disease epicenters, and much of the East's social landscape was radically altered as a result. Though these developments took place far from the Valley, they nonetheless had a substantial effect on natives living there. Regional trade routes that circulated European goods also became the routes for the diffusion of new diseases. Thus, the seventeenth century saw cycles of warfare and sickness that had a profound impact on the Valley's people.[31]

This transformation of Indian country and culture took place beyond the view and understanding of the colonists themselves. A point worth remembering about the precolonial history of the Valley is that by the time the settlers arrived, the region's peoples had already experienced the forceful impact of colonial newcomers far to the east and south.[32] And, in the absence of interested, literate observers, much of what happened to the Valley's native peoples will remain beyond our understanding. Nevertheless, certain features do stand out. First was the wide-ranging movement of peoples away from epidemics. Evidence from elsewhere suggests that people in many areas moved to escape. The St. Lawrence Valley, for example, was populated by Iroquoian-speaking villagers in the 1530s when Jacques Cartier met them; two generations later, these villages had disappeared, victims of disease as well as increasing intertribal warfare, with remnant populations merging with culturally similar peoples in New York or Ontario.[33]

Encounters: The Valley's Transformation

In the interior Southeast, epidemics contributed to the collapse of complex societies based on hierarchies of power; what greeted the English and French in the late seventeenth century were not the large chiefdoms seen by Hernando de Soto more than a century earlier, but clusters of small, largely independent, agricultural villages. In the process, regions once heavily populated were all but emptied as surviving peoples recombined and resettled as far as possible from the perceived centers of alien diseases.[34]

Next, warfare accelerated the seventeenth-century movements of peoples. Diseases created power vacuums as local populations declined, making intrusion into valuable hunting or farming areas easier for aggressive neighbors not yet adversely affected by smallpox and other pathogens. More important, given the nature of native societies, was the social and psychological trauma that came with unexplained, catastrophic losses of kin. Normally, deaths could be made good by the ritual offering of symbolically important goods, such as shell beads, by exacting revenge on those thought responsible for the loss, or through the adoption of captives taken from enemy peoples, who thereby served to reanimate the dead. Revenge attacks and captive taking were part of what has been called the "mourning war," and closely identified with the Iroquois in the area of modern New York State.[35]

The mounting casualties brought on by disease and attacks by enemies frequently better-armed with European weapons had a cumulative and ultimately catastrophic effect. The upward spiral of losses and retaliation led to ever more warfare, an escalation best exemplified by the so-called "Iroquois Wars," or "Beaver Wars," that engulfed much of northeastern America in the seventeenth century. From the late 1640s through the 1660s, the Five Nations systematically dispersed most of their near neighbors, sometimes incorporating whole villages of captives or refugees into their own society. Many others died, and still others fled in all directions, as far east as Quebec, and as far west as Green Bay, Wisconsin.[36]

Though these conflicts occurred outside the Shenandoah Valley, local natives would have felt their effects as refugees followed the Great Warriors' Path and its tributaries to havens beyond the reach of the Iroquois. The Eries, whose homeland lay along the south shore of Lake Erie in New York and Pennsylvania, may have been the Richahecrians known to mid-seventeenth-century Virginians. By the late seventeenth century, newly arrived colonists in Charleston, South Carolina, were trading with natives they knew as Westos, people now thought to be remnant Eries who had fled farther south.[37] People from southwestern Pennsylvania, known as the Monongahela Culture, may have headed toward the Shenandoah Valley as they, too, were dispersed in the 1630s.[38] And, as late as the 1680s, French missionaries learned that other bands of Eries living near Virginia had surrendered to the Five Nations and returned to New York.[39]

Finally, the appearance of permanent colonial settlements led to trade with neighboring Indian peoples and prompted more distant natives to move closer to colonies that had become the sources of valued, even necessary, goods ranging from tools and weapons to cloth and kettles. Trade, then, added yet another dimension to the widespread arrangement of peoples and landscapes in the East, including the Valley.[40] By the late seventeenth century, most, if not all, of the Valley's inhabitants were swept out of the region by a combination of disease, warfare, and migrations. In the process, local villagers might have joined neighbors to forge new collective identities.[41] Thus travel on the Path would have been dominated

Fig. 2.4. The Seven Bends section of the North Fork of the Shenandoah River north of Woodstock, as seen from atop the Blue Ridge looking west into the Valley. With the exception of meandering streams, the low-amplitude topography along the Valley floor provided an inviting routeway for Indian movements. (Scott Jost 2004)

by refugees taking advantage of the network of trails to move in all directions away from epidemics or enemies and toward sources of European goods. By the time Europeans began to enter the Valley to take up farms, they found no one against whom they had to contend for land or other resources.

The Warriors' Path: Natives and Empires

What, then, of the Great Warriors' Path? There is precious little to suggest that the Path was a major north–south avenue for warfare at any time before the eighteenth century. Instead, the Path was transformed into a warriors' road by events far outside the Valley that, as in the past, continued to shape life within the region. At the beginning of the eighteenth century, the Five Nations Iroquois had exhausted themselves — and others — by their long, increasingly costly wars against native enemies in the Great Lakes basin and against the French, who were allies and trading partners of the western nations. In a series of negotiations designed to extricate themselves from these conflicts, Iroquois diplomats made peace with the French and their western allies and pledged neutrality in the ongoing imperial conflict between the English and French.[42]

The simultaneous treaties concluded at Montreal and Albany in 1701 marked the end of two generations of attack and retaliation that had done so much to alter the human landscape in and around the Shenandoah Valley. The end of large-scale warfare coupled with the decline in the scope and devastation of epidemic diseases meant that the need for mourning war raids was greatly reduced. Reduced, but not eliminated. Since the dead still had to be replaced, literally or symbolically, Iroquois warriors began to look south — not west — to more distant and therefore somewhat less threatening enemies: the natives of the southern interior, Catawbas and Cherokees. It was undoubtedly during the early years of the eighteenth century, then, that the trails through the Valley became the Great Warriors' Path.[43]

In launching mourning war raids against southern Indians, Five Nations warriors found in the Valley an ideal route. Largely devoid of people, but full of game to sustain raiding parties, the Path and its tributaries had become a warriors' road — one of many throughout eastern North America.[44] The distinction accorded this particular route as the Great Warriors' Path probably had more to do with the Iroquois' reputation among westering colonists than its role as the premier warpath in the east.[45]

Activities along the Great Warriors' Path are reflected in observations by colonists. John Lawson, traveling through the Carolina interior at the beginning of the eighteenth century, learned that Seneca warriors "were abroad in that Country." The Iroquois, whom the westward Indians dreaded, did not have things all their own way, however. Lawson also learned that Saponis from southwestern Virginia had taken five of them captive.[46] The Saponis' small triumph is a reminder that raiding parties headed north as well as south. Catawbas, in particular, launched retaliatory attacks against their Iroquois foe.[47] A generation later, Pennsylvania's Conrad Weiser encountered an Iroquois warrior, Anontagketa, on his way home from a failed raid against the Catawbas.[48] Yet, the Path also saw the passage of diplomats from the Five Nations and southern Indians who were trying to arrange truces or prisoner exchanges. And, the Path continued to host refugees. Iroquoian-speaking Tuscaroras began moving north from their homeland in western Carolina in the wake of war with colonists in 1711. Within a decade, some two thousand Tuscaroras moved through the Shenandoah Valley to new towns in New York, where they were adopted as the sixth nation of the Iroquois League.[49]

As happens all too frequently, other peoples found themselves caught up in this low-level warfare. Saponis and other natives began gathering at the Virginia trading post of Fort Christianna in Bedford County. The fort and armed Virginians seemed to offer some measure of security on

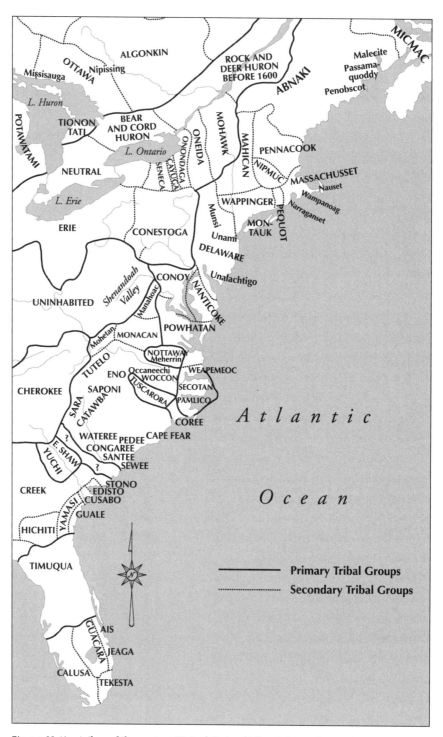

Fig. 2.5. Native tribes of the eastern United States. (After A. L. Kroeber, *Cultural and Natural Areas of Native North America* [Berkeley and Los Angeles: University of California Press, 1963]; Gyula Pauer Cartography Lab, University of Kentucky)

what was becoming a dangerous frontier. Nevertheless, in 1717, Indians encamped near the fort were set upon by Iroquois raiders bent on attacking some of their Catawba enemies living at the post.[50] Such experiences may have been more common than we know and helped convince whoever was still living in the Valley to depart rather than risk becoming casualties in someone else's war.

More important for the later history of the Valley and the Great Warriors' Path, however, was that, in one scholar's words, "colonists and traders frequently got caught in the native crossfire."[51] Such a problem is a reminder that, just as in the past, the region continued to develop, often through the influence of outside forces. In this case, those forces appeared in the shape of German and Ulster immigrants looking for land, and speculators eager to further their efforts. By the 1730s, the Valley was already beginning to serve not only as a new home for some Europeans, but as a highway for others. And, when the Great Warriors' Path began to be called the "Great Wagon Road," the possibilities for intercultural violence increased.

The problem of who would control traffic through the Valley surfaced quite early. With western Pennsylvania and northern Virginia empty of people because of the Iroquois Wars, the Six Nations enjoyed unfettered access to the Shenandoah Valley, which they claimed as their own. Nevertheless, Iroquois warriors traveling through the region began to collide with colonists moving west. Indeed, by 1722 the Valley's future had already become the central issue in discussions between colonies and the Iroquois. At Albany that year, New York, which had strong ties to the Mohawks, hosted a conference between Virginians and Iroquois that tried to solve the problems arising from warriors traveling on paths being used by increasing numbers of colonists.[52] The issue was not native animus toward settlers, but rather the unpredictable outcomes of encounters as each group eyed the other with a combination of curiosity and wariness. Warriors would occasionally help themselves to cattle or horses if no deer could be found in the woods; colonists were inclined to see any Indians as potentially dangerous. When hunting became poaching, misunderstanding could — and did — turn violent, with natives as well as colonists falling victim. Such "unfortunate accidents," as New York's governor termed these encounters, could escalate into major warfare as both sides thought of retaliation.[53]

The result of the meeting, the 1722 Treaty at Albany, seemed to solve the problem. Simply put, the Iroquois would agree to keep to the west of the Blue Ridge and out of the way of oncoming settlers.[54] But problems continued to arise, especially when colonists began to spill over the mountains and appropriate lands along the Path. What both sides feared — the collision of warriors and farmers — occurred in 1742, when a band of Six Nations' warriors traveling south got into a fight with colonists over livestock the Indians were supposed to have killed.[55] This violence raised the need for further negotiations, prompting yet another council, this time in Lancaster, Pennsylvania, in 1744, which was now linked to Virginia's land claims in the Valley as well as to efforts aimed at reducing intercultural violence.[56]

The Lancaster Treaty of June 1744 addressed the problems created by intercultural use of the Valley in two ways. First, the Six Nations agreed to accept payment for their claims to the lands west of the Blue Ridge, thus clearing the way for further Virginia settlement. Second, Iroquois rights to use the Warriors' Path were confirmed. Henceforth warriors were to be given safe conduct passes that could be carried through the Valley, from one justice of the peace to another, thus giving them written proof of friendship and official protection.[57]

Natives and colonists continued to collide in the Valley, though native war parties did begin to shift their routes westward. George Washington "met ... with 20 Warriors who were going to the Southward to war" while traveling through the Ohio country in 1753.[58] Nearly two decades later, while viewing lands in the Ohio Valley, Washington again met Six Nations warriors bound for the Cherokee towns.[59] In both cases, the natives were traveling well beyond the Valley, moving south by way of Kentucky. By then, however, the Shenandoah Valley had already been incorporated into the expanding economy and society of eastern Virginia as settlers moved into the region at a rate of from one to two thousand a year during the decades of the 1740s through the 1770s.[60]

By the time Washington delivered his government's ultimatum to the French forces in the Ohio country in 1753, the heyday of the Great Warriors' Path was over and, with it, that of the native cultural landscapes that had defined the Valley for so long. Now there was the Great Wagon Road; instead of native hunters, farmers, warriors, and diplomats, the Valley played host to British American settlers, some of whom stayed while others moved farther south to the Carolinas and Georgia.

Appropriately, perhaps, the disappearance of the Great Warriors' Path coincided with the creation of *other* warpaths: Braddock's Road in 1755 and the Forbes's Road in 1758. The movement of British-provincial armies during the Seven Years' War into the lands north and west of the Valley helped lay the foundation for new settlements in the Ohio country while stimulating local economies that further accelerated the transformation of the Shenandoah Valley from Indian country to the backcountry of British America. One small measure of that transformation lay in the words used to describe the Indian warpath. Seeking the best route west across the Appalachians, scouts from General John Forbes's army in 1758 noted in their journals that they had crossed the "old warriors' path."[61] Like "old towns" or "old fields," "old path" speaks of a trail no longer used.

Conclusion

Three features of the Valley's and the road's history emerge from a look into the region's precolonial past. First, the existence of dense networks of paths leading into and through the Valley meant that much of the region's human history would be shaped by outside influence. Trade, warfare, and migrations all linked the Valley's native peoples to Hopewell and Monongahela peoples and Iroquois to the north, as well as with Indians in the interior Southeast and in Tidewater Virginia. Though our knowledge about Indian occupation of the Valley and their travel via the paths continues to grow, one thing is clear: people living here were not isolated. Second, within the extended period of native occupation, the Great Warriors' Path represents a rather brief episode — some four or five decades at best. Finally, there is the issue of movement, voluntary or forced, seasonal or permanent. The history of native paths through the Valley is one rooted in motion, not stasis: villages and whole peoples come and go and, as we approach the seventeenth and eighteenth centuries, that long-standing characteristic of life in the Valley only intensifies. Native travel along the Great Warriors' Path, then, serves to anticipate the world that would come with the Great Road and that is with us still.

Notes

1. One of the best examples of this sort of representation can be found in Lewis Evans's "A General Map of the Middle British Colonies in America" (1755; reprinted in Lawrence Henry Gipson, *Lewis Evans* [Philadelphia: Historical Society of Pennsylvania], 231).

2. Helen C. Rountree, "The Powhatans and Other Woodland Indians as Travelers," in Rountree, ed., *Powhatan Foreign Relations, 1500–1722* (Charlottesville: University Press of Virginia, 1993), 21–52; Nancy Shoemaker, *A Strange Likeness: Becoming Red and White in Eighteenth-Century North America* (New York: Oxford University Press, 2004), 23–24; John Lawson, *A New Voyage to Carolina,* ed. Hugh Talmage Lefler (Chapel Hill: University of North Carolina Press, 1967), 213–14.

3. See Rountree, *Powhatan Foreign Relations,* 38.

4. Paul A. W. Wallace, ed., *Conrad Weiser: Friend of Colonist and Mohawk* (Phil-

adelphia: University of Pennsylvania Press, 1945), 155 (swollen streams); Lawson, *A New Voyage to Carolina*, 23. See also James H. Merrell, *Into the American Woods: Negotiators on the Pennsylvania Frontier* (New York: Norton, 1998), 130–31.

5. Rountree, "The Powhatans and Other Woodland Indians as Travelers," 35–37; Helen Hornbeck Tanner, "The Land and Water Communication Systems of the Southeastern Indians," in Peter H. Wood, Gregory A. Waselkov, and M. Thomas Hatley, eds., *Powhatan's Mantle: Indians in the Colonial Southeast* (Lincoln: University of Nebraska Press, 1989), 6–9; Paul A. W. Wallace, *Indian Paths of Pennsylvania* (Harrisburg: Pennsylvania Historical and Museum Commission, 1965), 180.

6. These examples are drawn from Michael N. McConnell, *A Country Between: The Upper Ohio Valley and Its Peoples, 1724–1774* (Lincoln: University of Nebraska Press, 1992), 33. The Virginian Christopher Gist, during his travels to the Ohio country in 1751, reported that he spent a night in a cave (see Lois Mulkearn, ed., *George Mercer Papers Relating to the Ohio Company of Virginia* [Pittsburgh: University of Pittsburgh Press, 1954], 38).

7. "Christopher Gist's First and Second Journals, September 11, 1750–March 29, 1752," in Mulkearn, ed., *George Mercer Papers*, 28.

8. Edward Porter Alexander, ed., *The Journal of John Fontaine: An Irish Huguenot Son in Spain and Virginia, 1710–1719* (Charlottesville: University Press of Virginia, 1972), 105–6.

9. "A Narrative of the Captivity of John M. Cullough, Esq.," in Wilcomb E. Washburn, ed., *Narratives of North American Indian Captivities* (New York: Garland, 1976), 58:88; but see Lawson, *A New Voyage to Carolina*, for John Lawson's opinion that natives "are expert Travellers" who could orient themselves by the use of moss growing on trees (213). Early colonial settlers in the Valley appear to have adopted and extended this dense network of native paths in developing their own social landscape (see Warren Hofstra, *The Planting of New Virginia: Settlement and Landscape in the Shenandoah Valley* [Baltimore: Johns Hopkins University Press, 2004], 33, 158–59).

10. Quotes from Tanner, "Land and Water Communication Systems," 6, 9. On the lack of isolation between native peoples in precolonial America, see Neal Salisbury, "The Indians' Old World: Native Americans and the Coming of Europeans," *William and Mary Quarterly*, 3rd ser., 53 (1996): 435–58.

11. On the physical characteristics of the Valley, see Robert D. Mitchell, *Commercialism and Frontier* (Charlottesville: University Press of Virginia, 1977), 23.

12. On the development of agriculture in eastern North America, see Bruce D. Smith, *The Emergence of Agriculture* (New York: Scientific American Library, 1998), 183–201; Bruce D. Smith, "Seed Plant Domestication in Eastern North America," in Douglas Price and Anne Birgitte Gebauer, eds., *Last Hunters, First Farmers: New Perspectives on the Prehistorical Transition to Agriculture* (Santa Fe, N.M.: SAR Press, 1995), 193–213.

13. William M. Gardner, *Lost Arrowheads and Broken Pottery: Traces of Indians in the Shenandoah Valley* (Manassas, Va.: Thunderbird, 1986), 80, 83; Hofstra, *The Planting of New Virginia*, 104–7.

14. Clarence R. Geier and Warren R. Hofstra, "Native American Settlement in the Middle and Upper Drainages of Opequon Creek, Frederick County, Virginia," *Quarterly Bulletin of the Archaeological Society of Virginia* 54 (1999): 154–65.

15. Peter H. Wood, "The Changing Population of the Colonial South: An Overview by Race and Region, 1685–1790," in Wood, Waselkov, and Hatley, eds., *Powhatan's Mantle,* 39, 84 (quote). By way of comparison, the upper Ohio Valley of western Pennsylvania and northeastern Ohio was gradually reoccupied by natives beginning in the 1720s. By 1731, the population stood at roughly 1,300; by 1750, this number may have tripled (see McConnell, *A Country Between,* 22–23).

16. On the likely impact of the Little Ice Age in Virginia, see Stephen R. Potter, *Commoners, Tribute, and Chiefs: The Development of Algonquian Culture in the Potomac Valley* (Charlottesville: University Press of Virginia, 1993), 154.

17. This discussion is based on Jeffrey L. Hantman, "Monacan Archaeology of the Virginia Interior," in David Brose, C. Wesley Cowan, and Robert Mainfort, eds., *Societies in Eclipse: Archaeology of the Eastern Woodlands Indians, AD 1400–1700* (Washington, D.C.: Smithsonian Institution Press, 2001), 107–24; Potter, *Commoners, Tribute, and Chiefs,* 147.

18. Mary Ellen Hodges, "The Archaeology of Native American Life in Virginia in the Context of European Contact: Review of Past Research," in Theodore R. Reinhart and Dennis J. Pogue, eds., *The Archaeology of 17th-Century Virginia* (Richmond: Archaeological Society of Virginia, 1993), 23–24; Joseph L. Benthall, *Archaeological Investigation of the Shannon Site, Montgomery County, Virginia* (Richmond: Virginia State Library, 1969), 145–46.

19. Potter, *Commoners, Tribute, and Chiefs,* 130, 137.

20. Robert D. Mitchell, "Over the Hills and Far Away: George Washington and the Changing Virginia Backcountry," in Warren R. Hofstra, ed., *George Washington and the Virginia Backcountry* (Madison, Wisc.: Madison House, 1998), 68–69.

21. Hantman, "Monacan Archaeology of the Virginia Interior," 120.

22. Lynda Norene Shaffer, *Native Americans before 1492: The Mound Building Centers of the Eastern Woodlands* (New York: M. E. Sharpe, 1992), 38–50.

23. On the widespread nature of these systems and their importance both before and after the arrival of Europeans, see Salisbury, "The Indians' Old World."

24. Gregory Waselkov, "Seventeenth-Century Trade in the Colonial Southeast," *Southeastern Archaeology* 8 (1989): 122–23.

25. James W. Bradley, *Evolution of the Onondaga Iroquois: Accommodating Change, 1500–1655* (Syracuse, N.Y.: Syracuse University Press, 1987), 89–103; James Axtell, *Natives and Newcomers: The Cultural Origins of North America* (New York: Oxford University Press, 2001), 79–103.

26. On the Monacans, see Hantman, "Powhatan's Relations with the Piedmont Monacans," in Rountree, ed., *Powhatan Foreign Relations,* 94–111; John F. Scarry and Mintcy D. Maxham, "Elite Actors in the Protohistoric: Elite Identities and Interaction with Europeans in the Apalachee and Powhatan Chiefdoms," in Cameron B. Wesson and Mark A. Rees, eds., *Between Contacts and Colonies: Archaeological Perspectives on the Protohistoric Southeast* (Tuscaloosa: University of Alabama Press, 2002), 161–63. On the identity of the Massawomecks, I have

followed James F. Pendergast, "The Massawomeck: Raiders and Traders into the Chesapeake Bay in the Seventeenth Century," *Transactions of the American Philosophical Society* 81, pt. 2 (Philadelphia: American Philosophical Society, 1991).

27. The literature on encounters between Indians and Europeans and Africans is vast, but the broad contours of this all-important aspect of early American history can be gained from Colin G. Calloway, *New Worlds for All: Indians, Europeans, and the Remaking of Early America* (Baltimore: Johns Hopkins University Press, 1997); and Daniel K. Richter, *Facing East from Indian Country: A Native History of Early America* (Cambridge: Harvard University Press, 2001). The phrase "collision of histories" comes from Edward Countryman, *America: A Collision of Histories* (New York: Hill and Wang, 1996), 3–6.

28. Richter, *Facing East from Indian Country,* chaps. 1–2; Calloway, *New Worlds for All,* chap. 1.

29. Axtell, *Natives and Newcomers,* 25–45.

30. On this issue, see Alan Gallay, *The Indian Slave Trade: The Rise of English Empire in the American South, 1670–1717* (New Haven: Yale University Press, 2002).

31. Calloway, *New Worlds for All,* chap. 2; George R. Milner, David G. Anderson, and Marvin T. Smith, "The Distribution of Eastern Woodlands Peoples at the Prehistoric and Historic Interface," in Brose, Cowan, and Maintfort, eds., *Societies in Eclipse,* 9–18.

32. Mary Ellen Hodges notes that for western Virginia, including the Valley, there is little reliable information before the eighteenth century (Hodges, "The Archaeology of Native American Life," 16–17).

33. Richter, *Facing East from Indian Country,* 33–38; Bruce G. Trigger, *Natives and Newcomers: Canada's "Heroic Age" Reconsidered* (Kingston, Ontario: McGill-Queen's University Press, 1985), chap. 3.

34. The best study of this phenomenon in the Southeast is Marvin T. Smith, *Archaeology of Aboriginal Culture Change in the Interior Southeast: Depopulation during the Early Historic Period* (Gainesville: University Press of Florida, 1987). See also James H. Merrell, "The Indians' New World: The Catawba Experience," *William and Mary Quarterly,* 3rd ser., 41 (1984): 537–65.

35. Daniel K. Richter, "War and Culture: The Iroquois Experience," *William and Mary Quarterly,* 3rd ser. 40 (1983): 528–59.

36. Richard White, *The Middle Ground: Indians, Empires, and Republics in the Great Lakes Region, 1650–1815* (New York: Cambridge University Press, 1991), 1–5.

37. Verner W. Crane, *The Southern Colonial Frontier, 1670–1732* (New York: Norton, 1981), 6, 12, 17; Smith, *Archaeology of Aboriginal Culture Change,* 132–33; Eric E. Browne, *The Westo Indians: Slave Traders of the Early Colonial South* (Tuscaloosa: University of Alabama Press, 2005). At about the same time that the Westos appeared in Carolina, another group, known locally as "Savannahs," made their appearance. These people were the Shawnees, who originated in the middle and lower Ohio Valley (see Charles Callender, "Shawnee," in Bruce G. Trigger, ed., *Northeast,* vol. 15 of *Handbook of North American Indians,* ed. William C. Sturtevant (Washington, D.C.: Smithsonian Institution Press, 1978), 630.

38. William C. Johnson, "The Protohistoric Monongahela and the Case for an

Iroquoian Connection," in Brose, Cowan, and Mainfort, eds., *Societies in Eclipse*, 67–82.

39. [Jean de Lamberville], "Relation . . ." (1682), in Reuben Gold Thwaites, ed., *The Jesuit Relations and Allied Documents*, 73 vols. (Cleveland: Burrows Brothers, 1896–1901), 62:71.

40. Hantman, "Monacan Archaeology of the Virginia Interior," 116; Hodges, "The Archaeology of Native American Life," 16–17.

41. Benthall, *Archaeological Investigation of the Shannon Site*, x, 146; Hodges, "The Archaeology of Native American Life," 23.

42. Richter, "War and Culture," 551–53. The details of these negotiations can be followed in Richter, *The Ordeal of the Longhouse: The Peoples of the Iroquois League in the Era of European Colonization* (Chapel Hill: University of North Carolina Press, 1992), chaps. 8–9.

43. Richter, "War and Culture," 557–59.

44. Evidence of the abundance of resources in the region in the early eighteenth century can be found in Alexander, *The Journal of John Fontaine*, 106.

45. Wallace, *Indian Paths of Pennsylvania*, 180. One branch of the Great Warriors' Path in Pennsylvania was known locally as the "Catawba Path," suggesting its use in north–south raids. Wallace also remarks, however, that "warrior" simply meant "men" and that these "warrior paths" served a variety of male-related activities, including hunting and diplomacy (see below).

46. Lawson, *New Voyage to Carolina*, 49, 53.

47. James H. Merrell, "Their Very Bones Shall Fight: The Catawba–Iroquois Wars," in Daniel K. Richter and James H. Merrell, eds., *Beyond the Covenant Chain: The Iroquois and Their Neighbors in Indian America, 1600–1800* (Syracuse, N.Y.: Syracuse University Press, 1987), 115.

48. Wallace, *Conrad Weiser*, 220.

49. Douglas Boyce, "As the Wind Scatters the Smoke: The Tuscaroras in the Eighteenth Century," in Richter and Merrell, eds., *Beyond the Covenant Chain*, 151–62, esp. 154–55. This migration was marked in Pennsylvania by the "Tuscarora Path," which followed the Great Valley northeast to Shamokin on the Susquehanna River (see Wallace, *Indian Paths of Pennsylvania*, 168–69).

50. Richter, *The Ordeal of the Longhouse*, 240. On Fort Christianna, see Mary C. Beaudry, *Excavations at Fort Christianna, Brunswick County, Virginia* (Williamsburg, Va.: Department of Anthropology, the College of William and Mary, 1979), 4–7.

51. Richter, *The Ordeal of the Longhouse*, 241.

52. Francis Jennings, *The Ambiguous Iroquois Empire: The Covenant Chain Confederation of Indian Tribes with English Colonists* (New York: Norton, 1984), 294–98.

53. Gov. Burnet to Board of Trade, November 21, 1722, in Edmund B. O'Callaghan and Berthold Fernow, eds., *Documents Relative to the Colonial History of the State of New York*, 15 vols. (Albany: Weed, Parsons, and Company, 1856–87), 5:655.

54. Peter Wraxall, *An Abridgement of the Indian Affairs Contained in Five Folio Volumes, Transacted in the Colony of New York from the Year 1678 to the Year 1751*, ed.

Charles H. McIlwain (Cambridge: Harvard University Press, 1915), 241 (Spotswood's definition of the new path).

55. Hofstra, *The Planting of New Virginia*, 41, 45–47.

56. Jennings, *The Ambiguous Iroquois Empire*, 354–61. Hostilities between natives and settlers continued, arguably worsening with each incident. In 1758, Cherokees traveling north to join General John Forbes's army were attacked by Virginians in Bedford County and near Fort Loudoun. The natives, as British allies, were "much irritated" and pledged not to travel that way again (see William Ramsay to Washington, October 17–19, 1758, in W. W. Abbot and Dorothy Twohig, eds., *The Papers of George Washington, Colonial Series* [Charlottesville: University Press of Virginia, 1988], 6:81; and "A Return of the Southern Indians," Winchester, Apt. 21, 1758, reel 1, #133, Headquarters Papers of John Forbes, McGregor Library, University of Virginia).

57. Hofstra, *The Planting of New Virginia*, 172–75. The treaty minutes appear in Julian P. Boyd, ed., *Indian Treaties Printed by Benjamin Franklin, 1736–1762* (Philadelphia: Historical Society of Pennsylvania, 1938), 41–80.

58. Washington quoted in William E. Myer, "Indian Trails of the Southeast," *Bureau of American Ethnology Annual Report* 42 (1927): 757. On the conflicts engendered by colonial settlement along the Warriors' Path, see Hofstra, *The Planting of New Virginia*, 41–44.

59. Myer, "Indian Trails of the Southeast," 757.

60. "Greater Virginia" comes from D. W. Meinig, *The Shaping of America*, vol. 1: *Atlantic America, 1492–1800* (New Haven: Yale University Press, 1986), 147, 153–60. Numbers of migrants are from Mitchell, *Commercialism and Frontier*, 46; and Bernard Bailyn, *Voyagers to the West: A Passage in the Peopling of America on the Eve of the Revolution* (New York: Knopf, 1987), 15. The new cultural landscape that native travelers would have encountered in the Valley has been vividly revealed in Hofstra, *The Planting of New Virginia*, 17–49.

61. Sylvester K. Stevens, Donald H. Kent, and Louis M. Waddell, et al., eds., *The Papers of Henry Bouquet*, 6 vols. (Harrisburg: Pennsylvania Historical and Museum Commission, 1951–94), 2:236.

The Colonial Road

WARREN R. HOFSTRA

No wagon road eased the route of a motley party of Europeans as they worked their way into the Shenandoah Valley during the gathering winter of late 1731. These pioneers were several months out of southeastern Pennsylvania, where most had lived before seeking land in the isolated backcountry of Virginia. At their lead was Jost Hite, a native of the Kraichgau region of south central Germany who, since coming to the New World under the succor of the English Queen Anne as a refugee in the War of the Spanish Succession (1702–13), had engaged in previous frontier ventures in New York and along Pennsylvania's Perkiomen Creek. Now Hite had orders from the Virginia government for 140,000 acres of Valley land on the condition of recruiting 140 settlers in an imperial effort to secure and expand England's North American frontiers.[1]

Later celebrated as the fabled first "sixteen families," this party of more than one hundred men, women, and children with wagons, equipage, and livestock slowly negotiated their wagons through dense forests of huge trees blanketing the Shenandoah Valley. They crossed glades of long grass and descended steep slopes to streams and bordering meadows. They were a diverse lot. Many were German, and most of these were kin to Hite. Sons John, Jacob, Isaac, and Abraham accompanied this patriarch along with his wife, Anna Maria, and daughters Mary, Magdalena, and Elizabeth. Another contingent of the sixteen traced their roots to the north of Ireland.[2]

They were not the first Europeans to come to this rich and fertile valley. Seventeenth-century explorers had viewed it, Indian traders traveled it, and smaller groups or single families had arrived during the late 1720s. Native Americans, of course, had occupied it for centuries. Hite's assemblage, however, was the first to carve a road. Their route would come to be known as "Jost Hite's Road." Maps later recorded it as the "Philadelphia Waggon Road."[3]

This band of German and Scots-Irish settlers had crossed the Potomac River at a ford approximately ten miles north of its confluence with the Shenandoah. Perhaps following an Indian path, they set out southwest with the strike of the Valley across a large ridge of limestone land, avoiding damp bottoms and the mire of marsh and mud while clinging to the dryer uplands. After twenty miles, they crossed Opequon Creek, which parallels the Shenandoah in the center of the Valley. Progressing now across the steep ravines and more sparsely forested plateaus of less-fertile shale land, they soon encountered another trail that Native Americans had long used for trade or warfare between Iroquoia in the north and the homelands of Cherokees, Catawbas, and Creeks in the south. Striking a more southerly course with shale hills on their left and another band of rolling limestone land on the right, they soon came to the strategic spot where their path crossed Opequon Creek again near its headwaters. Here Hite fixed his homestead on a five-thousand-acre tract of some of the best-watered, most productive land in the region. Others in the company of sixteen took up portions of this land or settled along the Indian route to the north and south.

In time the Valley Road, also known variously as the Great Wagon Road or the Philadelphia Wagon Road, took the central Valley course from Evan Watkins Ferry (later Williams Ferry or Williamsport) on the Potomac to the southwestern extant of Virginia settlement as it pushed progressively up the Valley. By the mid-1730s, as one resident of the area near present-day Staunton later recalled, "there was no Road for more than seventy Miles downwards, other than the narrow, almost impervious, Paths made through the lonely Forrests by Buffaloes, and Indians." But by the 1750s, the road reached the settlements forming along the Yadkin River in North Carolina. Jost Hite's Road provided an alternative route to Philadelphia connecting the lower Shenandoah Valley to settlements in south central Pennsylvania.[4]

Thus partly by dead reckoning, partly by reading the land, partly by adopting the prior cultural landscape of Indians into their own world, and partly by imposing European concepts of spatial order on the land, the men and women of Hite's generation laid down a road. The road represented a way of moving across the land that would have immense significance for their lives as it would for the future of their region. During the colonial period, the road helped define and shape the southern backcountry frontier. Arguably Anglo-America's first frontier, or inland area of expanding settlement, this backcountry forged the mold in which all subsequent frontiers were cast. Viewed from the later perspective of national history, the road would help guide the development of the United States

as it expanded from the Atlantic Ocean to the Mississippi River during the first half of the nineteenth century.

On a regional scale, the Valley Road was the key to landscape evolution in the Shenandoah Valley. Landscape entails much more than the visual appearance of the land or the simple sum of its cultural features — fields, fences, dwellings, barns, and so forth. Landscape is all these, but it also embodies the economic activities, social relations, political practices, and mental habits — the culture — of its creators. Landscape, as culture, is a system. Take one feature away, and others change. Without the Valley Road, the distinctive features of Valley life would be different. Small-farm, mixed grain–livestock agriculture, ethnic diversity, religious pluralism, a middle-class society connecting town and country depended on the road for their origins and growth. Life in the Shenandoah Valley thus reflected life in Pennsylvania far more than life in Old Virginia, where dispersed tobacco plantations, African American slavery, Anglo-American patriarchy, and Anglican conformity dominated the landscape. Coming into focus around the Valley Road in the decades immediately following the American Revolution was the developed world of family farms producing some of the finest flour in Atlantic commerce, of market towns where refinement could be purchased in the shops of merchants and artisans,

Fig. 3.1. Valley colonial roads and land settlement parcels, ca. 1730. (After a map by Galtjo Geertsema, in Cecil O'Dell, *Pioneers of Old Frederick County, Virginia* [Marceline, Mo.: Walsworth, 1995]; Gyula Pauer Cartography Lab, University of Kentucky)

Fig. 3.2. By the end of the colonial period in Virginia, the Valley Road traversed the length of the Shenandoah Valley and extended into North Carolina. Shown here is a detail from "A Map of the most Inhabited part of Virginia. . . . Drawn by Joshua Fry & Peter Jefferson in 1751." (Virginia Historical Society, Richmond, Virginia)

and of a landscape regarded as both sublime and picturesque at the same time it embodied the spirit of simplicity, enterprise, and improvement so emblematic of the young American republic. Because the road connected one of the great centers of American commerce in Philadelphia and one of the hearths of its folk, or vernacular, culture in south central Pennsylvania through the Valley to the Carolinas by mid-eighteenth century and to trans-Appalachian frontiers in Ohio, Kentucky, and Tennessee during the Age of Independence, it entered into the mainstream of American history, geography, and iconography as one of the great corridors of national development and expansion. All this, however, was too far in the future for Jost Hite and his band of sixteen families to envision. To them, the world they entered in the 1730s was "wilderness."[5]

The names of his children suggest that Jost Hite might have cast his own image in a biblical reflection of the children of Israel entering the land of Canaan. The Scots-Irish accompanying him also could have heard the sermons commonly preached in the Presbyterian pulpits of the north of

Ireland describing Ulster Protestants as God's chosen people. Hite did describe the "Countrey" of the Shenandoah Valley in 1730 as "unsettled, & a Wilderness . . . whose Surface was Rocks & Mountains." He and his company knew they were penetrating the world of Native Americans and pointed out that "it's Inhabitants [were] Wildbeasts or Hostile Indians." This was a world of dense forests dominated by old-growth oak and hickory trees. Massive pines marked poorer lands, while walnuts populated the bottoms, and chestnuts dug into the higher slopes. One early traveler in the region characterized this sylvan ensemble as "majestic woods; the whole interspersed with an infinite variety of flowering shrubs." Breaking the forest cover, however, were openings of grasslands extending from a few to several hundred acres. How much this mosaic of forest and savanna was owing to previous occupation by Indians, however, is unknown. Glades and prairies could have been the work either of Indian burnings or natural causes such as lightning strikes, fires, soil conditions, or slope, aspect, and exposure. Reminders of the Indian past, however, were numerous for the first European settlers in the Shenandoah Valley. The land was filled with the remnants of palisaded villages, burial mounds, and "old fields" once cleared for native towns.[6]

Although the Iroquois wars of the seventeenth century had left the Shenandoah Valley largely devoid of Indian inhabitants at the time Europeans first occupied it, the continual movement of Native Americans along the Valley provided abundant opportunity for cultural encounters among indigenous and immigrant peoples. The Valley Road, of course, facilitated culture-crossing experiences. Jost Hite's grandson recalled that "numerous parties of Indians, in passing and repassing, frequently called at . . . grandfather's house, on Opequon" (see fig. 3.3). There were tense times there as well as good times. Clearly the settlers' views of Indians were conditioned by circumstances. Jost Hite's reference to hostile Indians appeared in a lawsuit in which Hite's case stressed the suffering that white pioneers endured. Violence did break out into murders on both sides during the troubled years of 1738 and 1742. But with the passing of the pioneer generation, the Valley's first historians came to emphasize the nobility and peacefulness of its native inhabitants. "Tradition informs us, and the oral statements of several aged individuals of respectable character confirm the fact that the Indians and white people resided in the same neighborhood for several years after the first settlement commenced," wrote one historian. "The Indians were entirely peaceable and friendly."[7]

Native Americans certainly had cause for grievance. Shortly after the first Europeans began taking up Valley land in the early 1730s, Iroquois

Fig. 3.3. John Hite House. The remnants of the house his father, Jost Hite, built lie to the right in this photograph. (Scott Jost 2004)

leaders protested that the region belonged to them by "right of Conquest." In earlier treaties, furthermore, they had promised to keep to the west of the Blue Ridge and had moved their travels to new paths through the Shenandoah Valley. They "had not been long in the Use of this new Road," they complained, "before your People came like Flocks of Birds, and sat down on both Sides of it." The accused were, of course, Hite, the families accompanying him, and many more that followed. A large number of the earliest tracts of land they patented did line the Indians' "new Road." This was the road they transformed into the Valley Road.[8]

The relationship among the Indian path, the Valley Road, and the alignment of the earliest settlement tracts in the Shenandoah Valley raises numerous questions about the varied influences upon the location of the road. The first of these questions concerns environment and culture. Native American and European American cultures clearly intersected in the conjunction of the Indian road and the white settlements along it. Both the road and the settlements, however, also conformed to the geologic feature marking the contact between shale and limestone bedrock soils (see fig. 1.7 on p. 30). The shale-limestone boundary runs through most of these tracts and aligns as well with the Indian road and thus later to the Valley Road. Did, then, the European landscape take shape around the

Fig. 3.4. The Indian Trail Road south of Mauzy (Route 717) followed the New Market limestone outcrop. (Scott Jost 2004)

natural environments of the contact zone or around the cultural feature of the Indian road?

The shale and limestone formations of the Shenandoah Valley produce distinct topographies and biological regimes. As Hite and his company discovered when they traversed the Valley from the Potomac fords to the headwaters of the Opequon, subsurface drainage on limestone soils allows erosion to work the land into gently rounded hills and broad, shallow valleys (see fig. 3.5). The erosive force of surface runoff across more impermeable shale soils, however, excavates steep-sided, V-shaped valleys, leaving tablelike uplands (see fig. 3.6). The fertility of limestone soils, moreover, nurtures a hardwood forest at the same time that thin, rocky shale soils encourage pines. Edge habitats at the shale-limestone contact therefore would have contained the greatest biological and topographical diversity. Hunting and gathering while they traveled, Native Americans could have sought out this diversity, as might Europeans whose eye for the land was adjusted more toward its potential for mixed agriculture in which some crops, like flax, were thought to thrive in deficient soils. Sorting out the varied influences on the Valley Road might never be possible, but clearly its route cannot be taken for granted. Where the road ran represents a complex negotiation among the environment and the cultures of Indians as well as Europeans.[9]

The route of the road raises other questions posing even larger scales of analysis: Why did the first road into the Virginia frontier lead southwest from Pennsylvania instead of west from the developed centers of the colony's plantation economy throughout the Chesapeake Tidewater region or adjoining Piedmont? The question is worth asking because the resulting cultural differences distinguishing eastern from western Virginia and the associated sectional tensions shaping nineteenth-century state politics forced the separation of West Virginia from Virginia during the American Civil War along a fault line of counties paralleling the road. The story of the Valley Road is therefore a part of one of the big stories of American history that began with the clash of empires and imperial politics shaping the colonial world. In 1700, no Native American and no subject of the crowns of Spain, France, or England could have foretold that within less than a century a new nation, the United States, would control the North American interior. That the eighteenth century would be marked by conflict among European and Indian nations over this vast territory, however, would have been apparent to any prescient observer.

The pattern of imperial conflict emerged during the first decades of the eighteenth century. While England sought a foothold in the trade with inland Indians and Spain consolidated a borderland frontier of mission settlements from Florida to Texas and New Mexico, France laid the foundation of a continental empire in the Louisiana colony extending from Mobile Bay up the Mississippi to the Illinois country. Outposts along the Great Lakes at Detroit and elsewhere completed a connection between the Gulf Coast and the St. Lawrence. Meanwhile a new peace negotiated

Fig. 3.5. (*Top*) A farm field on limestone east of Opequon Creek along old U.S. 50 in Clarke County. The relict dry-laid rock fence was likely constructed of rocks cleared from the field. (Scott Jost 2004)

Fig. 3.6. (*Bottom*) Shale valley slopes near Opequon Creek along old U.S. 50 east of Winchester in Frederick County. Sour shale soils are often planted in pasture grasses, while woodland is often the predominant land use on steep slopes. (Scott Jost 2004)

by the Iroquois with England and France allowed for the resumption of wars of reprisal, or mourning wars, with Indian groups throughout the American Southeast. Resulting tensions governed the way the European conflict over the Spanish succession was fought in North America and precipitated the failure of imperial powers to resolve colonial boundaries in the Treaty of Utrecht in 1713. English fears of French encirclement then prompted London authorities to set aside a colony-by-colony approach to frontier defenses. By the early 1720s, the Board of Trade was calling for "making ourselves considerable at the two heads of your Majesty's Colonies north and south [Nova Scotia and South Carolina]; and building forts, as the French have done, in proper places on the inland frontiers." The board furthermore refused to consider the Appalachian Mountains as the "boundary of your Majesty's Empire in America. On the contrary it were to be wished that the British settlements might be extended beyond them."[10]

Extending royal imperium west of the Blue Ridge was precisely what Virginia governor William Gooch attempted in issuing land orders to Jost Hite and others like him from 1730 to 1732. These totaled close to 400,000 acres and obligated recipients to recruit settlers at the ratio of one family per one thousand acres. All that would distinguish the society of western Virginia — freehold farms, nonplantation agriculture, and cultural diversity — was, then, the intentional consequence of imperial politics. The governor knew precisely what he was doing when he responded to Jost Hite's petition that his and "divers others Families to the number of one hundred are desirous to remove from thence [Pennsylvania] & seat themselves on the back of the great Mountains" of Virginia. Within four years, Gooch could write the Board of Trade to "demonstrate to your Lordships how soon that part of Virginia on the other side of the great Mountains may be Peopled, if proper Encouragements for that Purpose were given: Most of these Petitioners are Germans and Swissers lately come into Pensilvania, where being disappointed of the quantity of land they expected . . . have chosen to fix their habitations in this uninhabited part of Virginia . . . for by this means a strong Barrier will be Settled between us and the French." In securing and defending farms held under royal patent, freeholders presumably would defend the king's dominion of Virginia.[11]

That the first and most important road into western Virginia tied the colony's frontier to Pennsylvania was owing to neither the chance coincidences of frontier expansion nor the path of least resistance provided by the geography of the Great Valley extending from New England into the southern uplands. The global politics of imperial strategy instead drew northern settlers to the banks of the Shenandoah. Thus the force of royal policy would ensure the close, functional relationship between the Valley Road and the landscape it propagated.

Under the press of imperial purpose, the Virginia government permitted settlers to spread out and select their own lands. As Jost Hite put it, "nothing but a prefference to the choice lands, would tempt men to become adventurers." Thus no official order was imposed upon the spatial arrangements of settlement: no roads were called for, nor were towns or fortifications. These would emerge in time, but from the outset the landscape of the Shenandoah Valley would be the settlers' own creation. Encoded within it were their values and aspirations. Dispersal in search of the best lands did not produce household isolation, nor did it express an all-pervading individualism. The economic competence of the household and command of family destiny were what settlers held most dear. Visiting and trading with neighbors were essential to survival as the surpluses of one family offset the shortages of another. Upon getting from farm to farm, or from farm to mills, stores, shops, and taverns rested the success of the household and the self-sufficiency of the community. Thus paths for foot travel or pack horses appeared as fast as settlers transformed wilderness into private property. Wagon roads soon followed along the most important routes. First and foremost, of course, was the Valley Road.[12]

"In every back settlement in America, the roads and paths are first marked out by blazes on the trees," observed traveler John F. D. Smyth. "A blaze is a large chip sliced off the side of a tree with an axe; it is above twelve inches in length, cut through the bark and some of the sap wood, and by its white appearance, and brightness, when fresh made, serves to direct the way in the night as well as in the day." The surveys conducted between 1732 and 1734 by Robert Brooke, the colony's surveyor for lands along the Shenandoah, record numerous informal paths and roads (see fig. 3.7). The earliest reflected personal arrangements among settlers and lacked the force of law in their establishment and use. Moravian travelers happened upon one such path along the North Branch of the Potomac during the 1740s: "The road is a single narrow path, frequently hardly recognizable. . . . A person has to be very careful lest he take a cow path." Many early paths indeed followed the routes of animals searching the land for sustenance.[13]

Transforming informal routeways into public roads was the work of county government. The statute law of the Virginia colony and many traditional provisions of the English common law governed the construction,

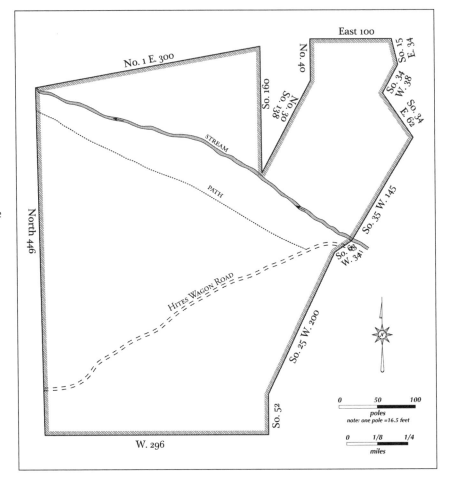

Fig. 3.7. Robert Brooke, the official surveyor for lands on Shenandoah River, often depicted roads and paths on surveys drafted between 1732 and 1734, as in this example from "Robert Brooke Survey Book, 1732–1734." (After the original held by the Virginia Historical Society, Richmond, Virginia)

maintenance, and use of public roads. Most importantly, the designation of a public road assured public access over private property. Governments did not own roadways; they only established and protected the right of all people to use them. Creating a road began with a petition to the county court from individuals intending to benefit from the ability to get from one specific place to another. If the members of the court approved the petition, they would appoint two or three prominent men — usually from among the petitioners — to "view, mark, and lay off" the route within a few months' time. On the return of an acceptable report detailing a suitable route, the court designated an overseer of the road. This individual possessed the legal power to order residents living near the road to work on it. Those who failed to serve could be fined by the courts. Courts also docked the purse of overseers for poorly constructed or maintained roads.[14]

Thus no county or colonial office or agency built roads. Roads and road networks were the piecemeal work of people meeting specific needs. No system or plan governed their efforts. Insofar as vernacular landscapes represent the unschooled work of people fashioning the world around them element by element out of necessity and according to common wants, norms, and traditions, colonial Virginia roads were vernacular expressions of popular interests.

So it was with the Valley Road. By the early 1740s, European settlement in the Shenandoah Valley had progressed for nearly a decade. The ability to travel locally from here to there, or regionally from Pennsylvania to Virginia, still depended upon the sufferance of individual landowners. Although economic competence and well-being relied on the ease of travel and transport, no one enjoyed assurance that an irate farmer might not turn or obstruct a road. And no one cleared or repaired roads voluntarily. Thus on August 27, 1741, George Hobson placed before the justices of Orange County, Virginia, a petition "in behalf of ye Inhabitants of the North side of Opecken for a road from the most convenientest fford over Sherundo at Ashbys Bent & from thence the Best way to and between the Lands of John Littler and John ffrost to the Chappell house & from thence to Evan Watkins ferry upon potomack." The segment from Littler's property to Watkins Ferry became the northern leg of the Valley Road. The gentlemen justices then ordered that "Morgan Bryan Arthur Buchannan & John ffrost or any two of them View ye sd road petd for & make report of their proceedings to ye next Court." When the trio finally returned a report to the court the following February with a detailed description of its route — "from Evan Watkins fferry by a Course of Marked trees to the head of ye ffaling Spring thence to Roger Turners thence to Edward Beasons over the Taskerora Branch thence to Joseph Evans Spring head thence to the Middle Creek thence to New Chappell," and so forth — the court ordered that the "said road be cleared . . . [by] all the tithables [taxable people] from Potomack between Opecken and the little Mountain." Thus the informal wagon route from the Opequon settlement to Pennsylvania became a public road.[15]

Other links soon appeared. In September 1741, the Orange County court had ordered that a road "be viewed marked laid of and cleared" from Alexander Ross's settlement adjoining Littler's to Jost Hite's mill (see fig. 3.1). Two years later, the public road was extended in one segment from Hite's to Jacob Funk's mill on a bend in the Shenandoah River that later became the site of Strasburg town. A second segment created at the same time assured public access up the Shenandoah Valley as far south as Ben Allen's homestead, the site of future Mount Jackson. By 1745, the Valley

Fig. 3.8. The route of the Valley Road as laid off in county court road orders in the early 1740s. (After cartography by Galtjo Geertsema, in Cecil O'Dell, *Pioneers of Old Frederick County, Virginia* [Marceline, Mo.: Walsworth, 1995]; Gyula Pauer Cartography Lab, University of Kentucky)

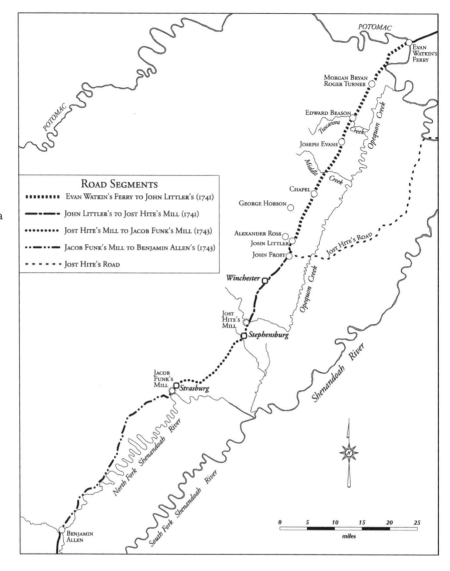

ROAD SEGMENTS
▪▪▪▪▪▪▪▪ EVAN WATKIN'S FERRY TO JOHN LITTLER'S (1741)
▬▬ ▪ ▬▬ ▪ JOHN LITTLER'S TO JOST HITE'S MILL (1741)
▪▪▪▪▪▪▪▪ JOST HITE'S MILL TO JACOB FUNK'S MILL (1743)
▪▪▬▪▪▬ JACOB FUNK'S MILL TO BENJAMIN ALLEN'S (1743)
▪ ▪ ▪ ▪ ▪ JOST HITE'S ROAD

Road reached the banks of the James River well beyond the drainage of the Shenandoah. As it penetrated farther and farther south during the 1740s, the wagon road quickly merged with expanding webs of local roads. Soon the Valley Road and its subsidiary routes created an extensive road network in the form of a trellis much like a rose espaliered against a wall with trunk and branches at right angles. Amplifying the trellis effect were major routes — many laid off in the 1740s — linking the Valley Road eastward across wind gaps in the Blue Ridge to markets and ports in eastern Virginia. Many local routes and wagonways became public roads during this same time.[16]

Thus the story of the Valley Road is a big story. Its establishment and creation as a public road cannot be understood apart from the major is-sues and conflicts governing relations among European imperial powers and Native American nations. The settlement of the Shenandoah Valley frontier in freehold farms largely by immigrants from the north of Ire-land, central Europe, and other parts of Great Britain and North America bore strategic significance beyond the ambitions of individual families for land and independence. Despite the official purposes Shenandoah Valley settlements served, English law and Virginia governance ensured that the resulting road system and the landscape it nurtured would nonetheless re-main a vernacular artifact — the creation of people meeting private needs to move about the land, to trade, and to engage in social commerce. What, then, were the consequences of employing ancient and ordinary practices to align, construct, and maintain the vital arteries of both community and imperial life?

As was evident to everyone on the colonial Virginia frontier, the roads were terrible. Built and repaired by unwilling workers, they remained un-graded, unditched, and unpaved. Rarely did counties appropriate public monies for road improvement. Travelers complained incessantly about mud, rocks, and ruts. During a winter journey, one German visitor com-mented that the "back road, which leads from Fredericktown between the South and North Mountain to Carolina, was from all accounts not to be travelled at this season of the year without great difficulty." Vari-ous obstructions compounded the problem of mud from winter rains and snows. "Rocks are very numerous," one French aristocrat grumbled dur-ing a visit more than a half century after the Valley Road became a public road. According to Moravian visitors, some roads were "frequently hardly recognizable . . . because the path is blocked with trees and overgrown with grass and weeds."[17]

Ruts from repeated wagon traffic grew so deep at times that wagon-ers had to seek alternative ways around bad patches, and roads became more like braided paths than single routeways. On their first journey from Pennsylvania to Bethabra, North Carolina, in 1753, a group of Moravians encountered an unexpected problem: their wagon did not fit existing ruts. "We held a little conference about our wagon, which is too wide, extend-ing several inches beyond the track," they wrote in their journal. In order to proceed, they "unloaded the wagon and took it to a blacksmith shop. . . . In the evening, when our wagon had been fixed, having been made three inches narrower, we packed all our belongings, to leave early next morning."[18]

Even when the weather was dry and road conditions good, travelers often lost their way. Roads built to link this place to that and serve the limited needs of local inhabitants rarely interconnected in ways apparent to long-distance travelers. Many spent most of their time wandering from one road to another despite colonial laws — often ignored — requiring signposts at intersections. Farther along in their journey, the Moravian sojourners found, for instance, that they "had to inquire for the way in one house after another, as we did not have a straight road." One traveler wandering through woods east of the Blue Ridge discerned that the "roads through them are very bad, and so many of them cross one another in different directions, that it is a matter of very great difficulty to find out the right one." Having set out on a journey early one morning, another wayfarer soon found himself wandering "a bit aimlessly." "For in these mountains where there are either too many or too few roads," he explained, "people always think they have given sufficient directions to travelers, who seldom fail to go astray."[19]

Webs of roads that confused travelers, however, worked well for inhabitants needing to get to a mill, a shop, or a nearby farm to grind some grain for daily use, to repair a wagon, or to trade spare corn, extra apples, or new linen in the reciprocations that improved life on the frontier. So well did the perplexing and convoluted array of roads work for locals that towns failed to form even at the crossroads of what one geographer has called the "dispersed general store" of early American rural neighborhoods.[20] Towns in the Shenandoah Valley came not as a product of settlement nucleation or commercial concentration but as a consequence of government action. In 1738, the Virginia House of Burgesses established the Shenandoah Valley counties of Frederick and Augusta in response to conflicts with Indians that year. Although courts did not convene until the mid-1740s, the first justices acted quickly thereafter to establish county towns: Winchester, initially called Frederick Town, in 1744 and Staunton in 1747. So important was the Valley Road to these towns that, in the case of Winchester, the road was moved more than a mile to serve as the main street in 1744. Thinking in terms of the proverbial horse and cart, it cannot thus be said that roads emerged to link towns or even that towns appeared along and because of roads. The landscape consequences of road building and the establishment of the Valley Road as a public way were, nonetheless, profound for town growth and landscape development.[21]

Just as the Valley Road linked the towns of the Shenandoah Valley to one another, the road also joined the entire region to Pennsylvania. The road, of course, would not have served so vital a purpose had the majority of Valley settlers not migrated from northern colonies. Once the Valley was settled, however, the road became the corridor over which people, goods, and ideas moved north and south. According to one eighteenth-century traveler: "When you see the Shenandoah you think you are still in Pennsylvania." The house types, barns, and town plans common in Pennsylvania came to define the Shenandoah Valley landscape. In the thinking of folklorists and geographers, Pennsylvania became a cultural hearth from which folklore, folk arts, and various aspects of the material culture of everyday life diffused most prominently up the Shenandoah Valley and then westward into the Appalachians and across the American heartland. Ethnic and religious diversity, so characteristic of life in Pennsylvania, also defined social relations and political culture in the Shenandoah Valley. "This Great Philadelphia Wagon Road became the main avenue of commerce as well as migration," asserts the geographer Donald Meinig. "It bound these remote new districts of Pennsylvania settlement to the familiar facilities on the Delaware that offered a range of services far beyond the capacity of meager tidewater ports." Thus merchants in the Shenandoah Valley, many of whom operated country stores before setting up shop in emerging towns, looked to Philadelphia for a stock in trade and the credit that could then facilitate exchange in rural Valley communities. Not surprisingly, historical geographers label the Shenandoah Valley a "socioeconomic extension of Pennsylvania."[22]

The French and Indian War, or the Seven Years' War, strengthened the commercial, landscape, and cultural connections between the Shenandoah Valley and Pennsylvania. The effect of the war on the road, however, was indirect. Most of the fighting took place to the north and west of the Shenandoah Valley. General Edward Braddock's ill-starred march to capture Fort Duquesne at the forks of the Ohio in 1755 also bypassed the Valley's foremost town, Winchester. John Forbes in the concluding campaign on the western frontier, moreover, cut a new road across central Pennsylvania that diminished the Valley's importance in the conflict. Indian raids penetrated the Valley, but the region's contribution to the conflict lay more in supply and support than in providing battlefields and strategic ground for engagement.

Because of what he termed the town's "centrical situation," George Washington selected Winchester as the garrison of his French and Indian War command, the Virginia Regiment. "For at this place do almost all the Roads centre; and secures the Great Roads of one half of our Frontiers, to the Markets of the neighbouring Colonies as well as those on Rappahannock and Potomack," he pointed out to authorities in Williamsburg. Most of the regiment's munitions and supplies would move westward from ports and markets in eastern Virginia across the Blue Ridge Mountains along roads through wind gaps. But provisioning the regiment also fell to Valley farmers, and the Valley Road served a vital role in moving local goods from farm to commissary. Building, arming, and manning the garrison, moreover, stimulated rapid economic growth in Winchester and prompted townspeople to turn with increasing fervor to the road and to Pennsylvania for goods and commerce.[23]

In 1760, toward the conclusion of the French and Indian War, one English visitor in Winchester commented upon the town's "late rapid increase, and present flourishing condition." The cause of newfound prosperity he attributed to its being the "place of general rendezvous of the Virginian troops." As a measure of the economic impact of military spending and the optimism new wealth engendered in the people, various landowners subdivided adjacent holdings and increased town lots more than sixfold. More significant for economic growth was the expansion of merchant commerce. Philadelphia played a major role in this development. English credit and American military demand combined to produce a boom in the provision trade — long a specialty of this important Atlantic port. By the late 1750s, merchant firms had acquired huge stocks of English goods on credit and were encouraging subsidiary traders to set up shop in increasingly distant locations. Thus the market area of Philadelphia trade expanded over the mid-Atlantic interior, eventually including Winchester and the Shenandoah Valley. Pennsylvanians such as Bryan Bruin and others opened stores in Winchester and brought in stocks of European goods acquired in the trading rooms of Philadelphia. When credit ran out, abundant land served as collateral on merchant debt and the lubricant of continued trade.[24]

At the conclusion of the war, with Great Britain in firm control of Fort Pitt at the forks of the Ohio and numerous outposts spread across the Ohio and Mississippi valleys, military demand for foodstuffs soared in western Pennsylvania and the Shenandoah Valley. English gold flowed into these regions in proportion to the vast stocks of flour and livestock moving west to feed soldiers. Thus the demand for store goods climbed with the means to acquire them. These goods and the groaning wagons carrying them moved along the Valley Road.[25]

The geographic pattern of economic development during the 1760s served to intensify the commercial and cultural significance of the Valley Road and its impact on the landscape. Transforming Atlantic commerce during this period was the dramatic rise in grain prices. Beginning in the 1740s, the price of wheat and flour in Philadelphia rose steadily, achieving a threefold increase by the 1770s. Behind the growing demand for this staple lay deep change in the European economy resulting from industrialization, population growth, and imperial conflict. Thus by the late 1760s, farmers could grow wheat and profit on the sale of flour from inland areas as far as seventy miles from a port. Philadelphia lay well beyond this limit for Shenandoah Valley farmers, but the seventy-mile line from the lower Valley lay directly across the newly established port of Alexandria. Flour exports from this commercial town went from practically nothing to more than 3,500 barrels in the 1760s. One resident reported that merchants were "running mad" for flour. By trading on the account of Philadelphia firms, Alexandria merchants closed the triangular connection linking the Shenandoah Valley to Philadelphia as the mid-Atlantic center for the European import trade and to regional export markets in Virginia deepwater ports. Flour profits meant English Queensware, Delft, or Chinese import porcelains on farmhouse tables in the Shenandoah Valley; bolts of Irish linens, Scottish worsteds, or plain-woven hollands on storekeepers' shelves; and a flow of newspapers and ideas at frontier taverns. How could travelers keep from thinking they were in Pennsylvania when sojourning in the Shenandoah Valley?[26]

The American Revolution did little to alter these perceptions. By the conclusion of the colonial period, the Valley Road had helped create a culture area and landscape in western Virginia strikingly different from the established patterns of Old Virginia. As previously mentioned, freehold farms, intensive grain-livestock agriculture, ethnic diversity, and religious pluralism all contrasted sharply with the culture of tobacco production, plantation life, social stratification, Anglicanism, and slavery that defined the new commonwealth's long-settled tidewater regions. Although not of Virginia, the Valley was, nonetheless, in Virginia. But as the Old Dominion's deferential systems of local government and political patriarchy overspread western regions, many farmers accumulated wealth, adapted slavery to mixed farming, and adopted a common, Anglo-American culture of genteel sophistication.[27]

Economic depression in the immediate postwar period slowed economic growth in the Shenandoah Valley, but probably less than in other areas of Virginia lacking the elastic economic base provided by grain and flour production. The 1790s, however, were not only a time of recovery but also of significant new growth both in the Valley and throughout the United States. As the economic engines of European industrialization, population growth, and imperial warfare wound up to ever-higher speeds, the United States, by capturing the Atlantic carrying trade, demanded a larger and larger share of the international market for foodstuffs. The value of U.S. exports to Europe soared. Prominent among them was flour from Pennsylvania and Virginia. By the early nineteenth century, Shenandoah Valley counties were leaders in Virginia flour production, and in 1820, Frederick County in the lower Valley was the number-one flour producer in the state.[28]

The effects of these developments on Valley roads were dramatic. East–west routes across the Blue Ridge were the primary recipients of new traffic generated by flour exports. According to one English traveler, these roads were "very bad, cut to pieces with the waggons." Efforts to improve them had begun in the 1760s, when the Virginia Assembly passed unprecedented legislation acknowledging that the "great number of waggons ... rendered [the roads] almost impassible" and allowing affected counties to impose special taxes for road repairs. The old method of maintaining roads by levying the labor of inhabitants was proving inadequate in the new age. State-chartered turnpike companies wielding revenues from stock subscriptions and employing advanced technologies for ditching, grading, and paving roads soon took over. By the first decade of the nineteenth century, many of the east–west routes across the Blue Ridge had become turnpikes, although turnpike improvements along the Valley Road would wait another thirty years. Nonetheless, the Valley Road assumed an ever more prominent role in shaping the distinctive landscape of the Shenandoah Valley.[29]

As the market for flour expanded in the late eighteenth century and farm profits kept apace, the demand for imported goods strengthened, as did the commercial connection between the Shenandoah Valley and Philadelphia. A traveler stopping in Winchester in the 1790s counted "thirty well-stocked stores, or shops" in this town of approximately two thousand inhabitants. The result of the Philadelphia connection was a material culture of refinement comparable to what passed for high style in America's foremost cultural capitals. Winchester merchants such as James and William Holiday, for instance, advertised in spring 1793 that they had "just received from PHILADELPHIA and now opened for sale ... a large and well chosen assortment of GOODS which they are enabled to sell on low terms for cash, or such country produce as answers their purpose." Shenandoah Valley merchants often made spring and fall trips to Philadelphia for the "best Goods that could be collected from the first wholesale Warehouses."[30]

Shenandoah Valley merchants also asserted that "travellers going to the back country may be supplied with almost every article on reasonable terms." In the postcolonial world, "back country" meant Kentucky, Tennessee, and Ohio. The Valley Road had long shaped the landscape of the Shenandoah Valley not only by channeling transients through it but also by opening the market for provisioning them to Valley farmers and merchants. The road was, of course, born of migration in the 1730s. As the upper Valley in the 1740s followed by the western Carolinas in the decade of the French and Indian War were progressively settled by Europeans, the road became one of the great migration routes in American history, comparable to the National Road or the Oregon Trail. The first settlements in Kentucky and the blazing of the Wilderness Road over Cumberland Gap came in the 1770s. Fertile lands in the Kentucky Bluegrass region and the Nashville Basin drew settlers like a magnet during the years following the Revolution. From the mid-Atlantic region, hosts of newcomers tramped up the Shenandoah Valley via the old Philadelphia Road on their way west. Even during ferocious Indian wars in the 1780s, the Kentucky population expanded sixfold, and in the next decade, following a tentative peace with Native Americans, Kentucky and Tennessee grew at a rate six times the national average. The four thousand or so people passing annually along the Valley Road for the new frontier struck the people of the region as truly "incredible" and "astonishing."[31]

Not only did the Valley Road forge the cultural and commercial links to Pennsylvania ever tighter and provide the thoroughfare for thousands of migrants on the western trek, but it also stimulated the development of numerous towns along its route. By the end of the eighteenth century, the Valley landscape was rich in towns, while large, dispersed, and economically autonomous plantations kept the tobacco-growing regions of Virginia poor in nucleated commercial centers. The exchanges generated by grain farmers with money to spend, by merchants with large stocks of imported, manufactured goods, and by a good road to link interior trade to the flows of Atlantic commerce ensured that towns appeared along the Valley Road at distances of a half-day's journey from farm to market. During the decades between the Seven Years' War and the conclusion of the American Revolution, new towns included Stephensburg (1758), Strasburg (1761), Woodstock (1761), Martinsburg (1778), Lexington (1778), and Harrisonburg (1780), followed by Middletown (1794) and New Market (1796) in the postwar period. Economic growth in the two decades before 1800 produced a highly improved rural landscape that supported in all more than fifteen additional towns and villages throughout the Valley. Like spokes of a wheel, roads spread from the hub of larger towns on the Valley Road to tie together numerous smaller central places and rural

Fig. 3.9. Spokelike road patterns emanate from larger towns connected linearly by the Valley Road. This detail is reprinted from Bishop James Madison, "A Map of Virginia Formed from Actual Surveys," 1807. (The Library of Virginia)

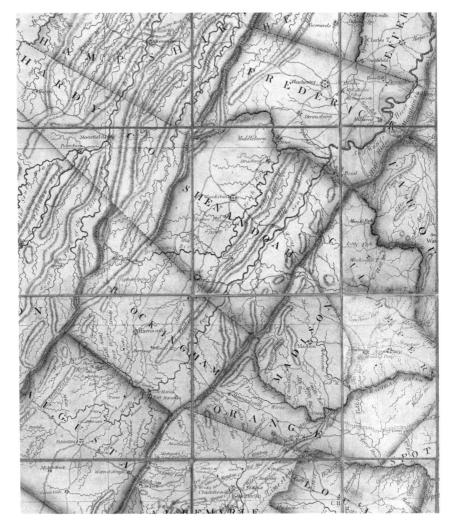

neighborhoods into economically and socially dynamic town and country relationships (see fig. 3.9).[32]

At the end of the colonial era and during the years immediately following the Revolution, scenes along the road were very different from what they had been when Jost Hite and his sixteen families picked their way among giant forest trees on their first journey into the Valley during the early 1730s. Men, women, and families riding or walking alongside wagons accompanied by livestock of every sort necessary for farm life created a living tide surging along the Valley. Because, as one traveler put it, the Valley Road was also "thick inhabited" and because the land was "good, the Country pleasant, the Houses in general large," these migrating families could count on numerous places to put up for the night or purchase provisions. And by providing for those on the move, inhabitants could likewise

Fig. 3.10. Opequon Creek east of Winchester on old U.S. 50. (Scott Jost 2004)

lead a better life. What they earned in the migrant trade, of course, only supplemented the substantial profits garnered by growing wheat, producing flour, and raising livestock. Thus, in addition to encountering numerous migrants on the road to Kentucky or Tennessee, our traveler would have passed by fields of grain, pastures and meadows, and small, rough log cabins as well as larger houses often built of Valley limestone. Descending a hill toward a creek, this traveler could count on seeing a mill and maybe stopping by a tavern to imbibe the by-products of the mill so often distilled into whiskey.[33]

Our later-day traveler would also have encountered many farmers, their families, and their workers on the quotidian journeys so vital to rural life and livelihood. Trading a little extra wheat or salt pork for a neighbor's surplus of apples or corn was as important as passing the time — literally milling around — with friends. Trips to a mill with bags of wheat loaded on wagons or packhorses, to a blacksmith for wagon repairs or shoeing a horse, or to some country shopkeeper kept the rural economy moving. So too did trips to town where produce could be sold in public markets; the services of a tailor, silversmith, clockmaker, or other artisan sought; or various goods purchased from the great array available daily in stores. Our traveler would also have passed the rigs of wagoners transporting merchant goods from Philadelphia. "It is scarcely possible to go one mile on this road without meeting numbers of waggons passing and repassing," commented one diarist. "These waggons are commonly drawn by four or five horses, four of which are yoked in pairs. The waggons are heavy, the horses small, and the driver unmerciful." Peddlers with pack or cart, lawyers riding the county court circuit, ministers commuting to a nearby chapel, or the occasional coach or chair of some prominent landowner would also attract the attention of the traveler. Post riders, scheduled stagecoaches, and turnpikes were all in the future, but at the end of the colonial period the Valley Road was, indeed, a very busy route to travel.[34]

Notes

1. For information on Hite and his winter journey to the Shenandoah Valley, see Henry Z. Jones, Ralph Conner, and Klaus Wust, *German Origins of Jost Hite: Virginia Pioneer, 1685–1761* (Edinburg, Va.: Shenandoah History, 1979); and *John Hite et al. v Lord Fairfax et al.,* Additional Manuscript 15317, British Museum, London, transcript by Hunter Branson McKay, Archives Room, Handley Regional Library, Winchester, Va. Hite's land orders appear in H. R. McIlwaine, Wilmer L. Hall, and Benjamin J. Hillman, eds., *Executive Journals of the Council of Colonial Virginia*, 6 vols. (Richmond: Virginia State Library, 1925–66), 4:253.

2. For a description of the first "sixteen families," see Thomas K. Cartmell, *Shenandoah Valley Pioneers and Their Descendants: A History of Frederick County, Virginia* (Winchester, Va.: Eddy Press, 1909; repr., Bowie, Md.: Heritage Books, 1989), 1; and Samuel Kercheval, *A History of the Valley of Virginia*, 5th ed. (Strasburg, Va.: Shenandoah Publishing House, 1973), 49.

3. A discussion of Jost Hite's Road and the Philadelphia Wagon Road appears in Cecil O'Dell, *Pioneers of Old Frederick County, Virginia* (Marceline, Mo.: Walsworth, 1995), 488–98. The "Philadelphia Waggon Road" appears on Joshua Fry and Peter Jefferson, "A Map of the most Inhabited part of Virginia containing the whole Province of Maryland with Part of Pensilvania, New Jersey and North Carolina, Drawn by Joshua Fry and Peter Jefferson in 1751," 4th State (London: Thos. Jeffries, [1755]), reproduced in Richard W. Stephenson and Marianne M. McKee, eds., *Virginia in Maps: Four Centuries of Settlement, Growth, and Development* (Richmond: Library of Virginia, 2000), 83–87.

4. Philip Vickers Fithian, *Journal, 1776–1776*, ed. Robert G. Albion and Leonidas Dodson (Princeton: Princeton University Press, 1934), 172.

5. Transcript of the Record in the case, *Jost Hite and Robert McCoy v Lord Fairfax 1749–*, folio 717, folder 100, Clark-Hite Papers, Filson Historical Society, Louisville, Ky. For a discussion of the social and economic characteristics of the Shenandoah Valley, see Charles Henry Ambler, *Sectionalism in Virginia from 1776 to 1861* (Chicago: University of Chicago Press, 1910; repr., New York: Russell and Russell, 1964); Warren R. Hofstra, *The Planting of New Virginia: Shenandoah Valley Landscapes, 1700–1800* (Baltimore: Johns Hopkins University Press, 2004); and Robert D. Mitchell, *Commercialism and Frontier: Perspectives on the Early Shenan-*

doah Valley (Charlottesville: University Press of Virginia, 1977). The diffusion of vernacular culture from Pennsylvania into the southern Appalachians and the Midwest is described in Terry G. Jordan and Matti Kaups, *The American Backwoods Frontier: An Ethnic and Ecological Interpretation* (Baltimore and London: Johns Hopkins University Press, 1989); and Henry Glassie, *Pattern in the Material Folk Culture of the Eastern United States* (Philadelphia: University of Pennsylvania Press, 1968).

6. Transcript of the Record, *Hite and McCoy v Fairfax*, folio 717, folder 100; Andrew Burnaby, *Travels through the Middle Settlements in North America in the Years 1759 and 1750*, 3rd ed. (London: T. Payne, 1798; repr., New York: Augustus M. Kelley, 1970), 74. According to one critic, Presbyterian ministers had misled their congregations with claims that "God had appoynted a country for them to dwell in . . . and desires them to depart thence, where they will be freed from the bondage of Egipt and go to the land of Cannan" (Ezekial Steward to Michael Ward, March 25, 1729, D 2092/1/3/141, Public Record Office of Northern Ireland, Belfast, as quoted in Patrick Griffin, *The People with No Name: Ireland's Ulster Scots, America's Scots Irish, and the Creation of a British Atlantic World, 1689–1764* [Princeton and Oxford: Princeton University Press, 2001], 79).

7. Kercheval, *A History of the Valley of Virginia*, 56, 53. For a discussion of the violent years of 1738 and 1742, see Hofstra, *The Planting of New Virginia*. The prehistory of the Shenandoah Valley is covered by William M. Gardner, *Lost Arrowheads & Broken Pottery: Traces of Indians in the Shenandoah Valley* ([Front Royal, Va.]: Thunderbird Museum, 1986).

8. Council held at Philadelphia, minutes, July 7, 1742, in Samuel Hazard, ed., *Minutes of the Provincial Council of Pennsylvania*, 16 vols. (Harrisburg, Pa.: Theo. Fenn, 1838–53), 4:570; and "The Treaty Held with the Indians of the Six Nations, at Lancaster in Pennsylvania, in June, 1744" (Williamsburg: William Parks, n.d.), enclosure in William Gooch to Board of Trade, Dec. 21, 1744, C.O. 5/1325, Colonial Office Papers, Public Record Office, London.

9. Charles Butts and Raymond S. Edmundson, *Geology and Mineral Resources of Frederick County*, Virginia Division of Mineral Resources Bulletin 80 (Charlottesville: Virginia Division of Mineral Resources, 1966), 5–6; Robert L. Holmes and David L. Wagner, *Soil Survey of Frederick County, Virginia* (Washington, D.C.: United States Department of Agriculture, Soil Conservation Service, 1987), 2–3.

10. Board of Trade to the king, September 8, 1721, C.O. 324/10, Colonial Office Papers. On the imperial movements of European powers and Native American responses, see Charles M. Andrews, *The Settlements*, vol. 3 of *The Colonial Period of American History* (New Haven and London: Yale University Press, 1937); Verner W. Crane, *The Southern Frontier, 1670–1732* (Durham, N.C.: Duke University Press, 1928; repr., New York and London: Norton, 1981); W. J. Eccles, *France in America* (East Lansing: Michigan State University Press, 1990); Francis Jennings, *The Ambiguous Iroquois Empire: The Covenant Chain Confederation of Indian Tribes with English Colonies from Its Beginnings to the Lancaster Treaty of 1744* (New York and London: Norton, 1984); Michael N. McConnell, *A Country Between: The Upper Ohio Valley and Its Peoples, 1724–1774* (Lincoln and London: University of Nebraska Press, 1992); James H. Merrell, *The Indians' New World: Catawbas and*

Their Neighbors from European Contact through the Era of Removal (Chapel Hill and London: University of North Carolina Press for the Institute of Early American History and Culture, 1989); Daniel K. Richter, *The Ordeal of the Longhouse: The Peoples of the Iroquois League in the Era of European Colonization* (Chapel Hill and London: University of North Carolina Press for the Institute of Early American History and Culture, 1992); Daniel H. Usner Jr., *Indians, Settlers, & Slaves in a Frontier Exchange Economy* (Chapel Hill and London: University of North Carolina Press for the Institute of Early American History and Culture, 1992); and David J. Weber, *The Spanish Frontier in North America* (New Haven and London: Yale University Press, 1992).

11. McIlwaine et al., *Executive Journals of the Council,* 4:253; William Gooch to Board of Trade, May 24, 1734, C.O. 5/1323, Colonial Office Papers. The Shenandoah Valley land orders can be found ibid., 4:223–24, 229, 249–50, 253, 270, 295.

12. Transcript of the Record, *Hite and McCoy v Fairfax,* folio 717, folder 100.

13. John F. D. Smyth, *A Tour in the United States of America,* 2 vols. (London: G. Robinson, 1784; repr., New York: New York Times and Arno Press, 1968), 1:178; William J. Hinke and Charles E. Kemper, eds., "Moravian Diaries of Travels through Virginia," *Virginia Magazine of History and Biography* (hereafter cited as *VMHB*) 12 (July 1904):79. For information about Robert Brooke and his appointment as surveyor for the Shenandoah Valley, see William P. Palmer, Sherwin McRae, Raleigh Colston, and H. W. Flourney, eds., *Calendar of Virginia State Papers and Other Manuscripts, 1652–1781,* 12 vols. (Richmond, 1875–93; repr., New York: Kraus Reprint, 1968), 1:217–18; McIlwaine et al., *Executive Journals of the Council,* 4:321; and Sarah S. Hughes, *Surveyors and Statesmen: Land Measuring in Colonial Virginia* (Richmond: Virginia Surveyors Foundation and Virginia Association of Surveyors, 1979), 98–99. See also Robert Brooke Survey Book, 1732–1734, Thornton Tayloe Perry Collection, Virginia Historical Society, Richmond.

14. For examples of major legislation on road construction, maintenance, and use, see William W. Hening, ed. *The Statutes at Large: Being a Collection of All the Laws of Virginia, from . . . 1619 . . . ,* 13 vols. (Richmond, New York, and Philadelphia, 1819–23), 3:392–95, 4:53–55, 6:64–69, 7:577–79, 10:368–69.

15. Orange County Court Orders, 2:293, 3:105, Orange County Courthouse, Orange, Va.; and Ann Brush Miller, *Orange County Road Orders, 1734–1749* (Charlottesville: Virginia Highway and Transportation Research Council, 1984), 59, 65.

16. Regarding the segments of the Valley Road established in the 1740s, see Orange County Court Orders, 3:8, 347, 348, 445; 4:331; and Miller, *Orange County Road Orders,* 60, 80, 81, 85, 86, 109–10.

17. Johann D. Schoepf, *Travels in the Confederation, 1783–1784,* 2 vols., trans. and ed. Alfred J. Morrison (Erlangen: Johann Jacob Plam, 1788; repr., New York: Bergman, 1968), 2:27; François Alexandre Frédéric, duc de La Rochefoucauld-Liancourt, *Travels through the United States of North America . . . in the Years 1795, 1796, and 1797,* 4 vols., 2nd ed., trans. H. Neuman (London: R. Phillips, 1800), 3:184; Hinke and Kemper, "Moravian Diaries of Travels," *VMHB* 12 (July 1904): 79.

18. Hinke and Kemper, "Moravian Diaries of Travels," *VMHB* 12 (October 1904): 136.

19. Ibid., 379; Isaac Weld, *Travels through the States of North America*, 2 vols. (London: John Stockdale, 1807; New York: Johnson Reprint, 1968), 1:90–91; François Jean, marquis de Chastellux, *Travels in North America in the Years 1780, 1781 and 1782*, 2 vols., trans. Howard C. Rice Jr. (Paris: Prault, 1786; repr., Chapel Hill: University of North Carolina Press for the Institute of Early American History and Culture, 1963), 2:405. For legislation requiring the erection of signposts at road intersections, see Hening, *Statutes*, 5:31–35.

20. "Dispersed general store" is the term employed by Joseph S. Wood for the rural economy of New England (see Wood, "Elaboration of a Settlement System: The New England Village in the Federal Period," *Journal of Historical Geography* 10 [October 1984]: 331–56; Wood, "Village and Community in Early Colonial New England," *Journal of Historical Geography* 8 [October 1982]: 333–46; and Wood, *The New England Village* [Baltimore and London: Johns Hopkins University Press, 1997]).

21. On relationships among counties, towns, and roads, see Hening, *Statutes*, 5:78–80; and Frederick County Court Orders, 1:97, Frederick County Courthouse, Winchester, Va.

22. Jacques Pierre Brissot de Warville, *New Travels in the United States of America, 1788*, ed. Durand Echeverria, trans. Mara S. Vamos and Durand Echeverria (Paris: Buisson, 1791; repr., Cambridge: Belknap Press of Harvard University Press, 1964), 237; Donald W. Meinig, *Atlantic America, 1492–1800*, vol. 1 of *The Shaping of America: A Geographical Perspective on 500 Years of History* (New Haven and London: Yale University Press, 1986), 160; Mitchell, *Commercialism and Frontier*, 239. On the diffusion of folk culture from Pennsylvania into the southern uplands and middle America, see Glassie, *Pattern in the Material Folk Culture of the Eastern United States*.

23. George Washington to Robert Dinwiddie, April 27, 1756, in W. W. Abbot et al., eds., *The Papers of George Washington*, Colonial Series, 10 vols. (Charlottesville: University Press of Virginia, 1983–1995), 3:59; Washington to John Robinson, April 24, 1756, ibid., 3:50. For a fuller discussion of provisioning the Virginia Regiment, see Raymond Chester Young, "The Effects of the French and Indian War on Civilian Life in the Frontier Counties of Virginia, 1754–1763" (Ph.D. diss., Vanderbilt University, 1969), 211–69.

24. Burnaby, *Travels through the Middle Settlements in North America*, 74. The rapid increase of town lots in Winchester during the Seven Years' War is documented in Hening, *Statutes*, 7:234–36, 314–17; and Frederick County Deed Books 5–6, 8, 9–11, Frederick County Courthouse. Thomas M. Doerflinger discusses the expansion of Philadelphia trade during the 1750s in *A Vigorous Spirit of Enterprise: Merchants and Economic Development in Revolutionary Philadelphia* (Chapel Hill and London: University of North Carolina Press for the Institute of Early American History and Culture, 1986), 70–134.

25. During 1759–60, British forces headquartered in Pittsburgh spent more than eighteen thousand pounds sterling for provisions in Virginia. See Thomas Walker to John Stanwix, October 12, 1759, in S. K. Stevens et al., eds., *The Papers of Henry Bouquet*, 5 vols. (Harrisburg: Pennsylvania Historical and Museum Commission,

1951–84), 4:222; George Mercer to Henry Bouquet, October 9, 1959, ibid., 4:203; Bouquet to Stanwix, December 20, 1759, ibid., 4:372; and Bouquet, account as deputy adjutant general, May 24, 1760, ibid., 4:574.

26. Harry Piper Letterbook, 1767–1775, Albert and Shirley Small Special Collections Library, Alderman Library, University of Virginia, Charlottesville, as quoted in Thomas M. Preisser, "Alexandria and the Evolution of the Northern Virginia Economy, 1749–1776," *VMHB* 89 (July 1981): 289, 287. On the rise in Philadelphia grain prices and its effect on Shenandoah Valley flour production, see Carville V. Earle and Ronald Hoffman, "Staple Crops and Urban Development in the Eighteenth-Century South," in *Perspectives in American History 10*, ed. Donald Fleming and Bernard Bailyn (Cambridge: Harvard University Press, 1976), 77–78; Marc Egnal, *New World Economies: The Growth of the Thirteen Colonies and Early Canada* (New York and London: Oxford University Press, 1998), 46–77; Jacob Price, "Economic Function and the Growth of American Port Towns in the Eighteenth Century," in *Perspectives in American History 8*, ed. Donald Fleming and Bernard Bailyn (Cambridge: Harvard University Press, 1974), 151–56.

27. On sectional patterns of the Shenandoah Valley in Virginia, see Ambler, *Sectionalism in Virginia*; Kenneth E. Koons and Warren R. Hofstra, eds., *After the Backcountry: Rural Life in the Great Valley of Virginia, 1800–1900* (Knoxville: University of Tennessee Press, 2000); and Mitchell, *Commercialism and Frontier*.

28. The value of exports from the United States to Europe more than tripled during the 1790s (see U.S. Bureau of the Census, *Historical Statistics of the United States: Colonial Times to 1970* [Washington, D.C.: U.S. Government Printing Office, 1975], pt. 2, 284–86; and Cathy Matson, "The Revolution, the Constitution, and the New Nation," in Stanley L. Engerman and Robert E. Gallman, eds., *The Colonial Era*, vol. 1 of *The Cambridge Economic History of the United States* [Cambridge: Cambridge University Press, 1996], 388–401). For comparative figures on early nineteenth-century flour production in the Shenandoah Valley, see U.S. Census Office, Third Census, 1810, *A Statement of the Arts and Manufactures of the United States of America for the Year 1810*, ed. Tench Cox (Philadelphia, 1814), 112; and U.S. Census Office, Fourth Census, 1820, *Digest of Accounts of Manufacturing Establishments in the United States and Their Manufactures* (Washington, D.C., 1823), 21.

29. Nicholas Cresswell, *The Journal of Nicholas Cresswell, 1774–1777* (New York: Dial Press, 1924), 47; Hening, *Statutes*, 8:549. On turnpike development across the Blue Ridge, see James Chapin Bradford, "Loudoun County, Virginia, 1790–1800" (Ph.D. diss., University of Virginia, 1976), 64–68; and Fairfax Harrison, *Landmarks of Old Prince William* (Richmond: Old Dominion Press, 1924; Berryville, Va.: Chesapeake Book Company, 1964), 563–65.

30. La Rochefoucauld-Liancourt, *Travels*, 3:204; *Virginia Centinel and Gazette; or, the Winchester Repository*, June 3, 1793; *Virginia Centinel & Gazette: or, the Winchester Political Repository*, January 7, 1791.

31. *Virginia Centinel and Gazette; or, the Winchester Repository*, June 3, 1793; *Virginia Centinel: or, the Winchester Mercury*, October 21, 1789; Thomas Bryan Martin to Philip Martin, June 28, 1790, Wykeham-Martin Papers, 1672–1820, M-1124.2 Microforms Collection, John D. Rockefeller Jr. Library, Colonial Williamsburg

Foundation, Williamsburg, Va. On migration to and population growth in Kentucky and Tennessee, see Bureau of the Census, *Historical Statistics,* pt. 1, pp. 8, 24–37; and La Rochefoucauld-Liancourt, *Travels,* 3:208.

32. Mitchell, *Commercialism and Frontier,* 195–201; Mitchell, "The Settlement Fabric of the Shenandoah Valley, 1790–1860: Pattern, Process, and Structure," in Koons and Hofstra, eds., *After the Backcountry,* 34–47.

33. Fithian, *Journal,* 12.

34. Weld, *Travels,* 1:115.

4 An Early Road to the Old West, 1780–1837

GABRIELLE M. LANIER

In *Notes on the State of Virginia* in 1785, Thomas Jefferson observed that future western trade would develop in the area with the best transportation network. "There will therefore be a competition," he wrote, "between the Hudson and Patowmac rivers for the residue of the commerce of all the country westward of Lake Erié, on the waters of the lakes, of the Ohio, and upper parts of the Missisipi." Jefferson calculated the advantages and disadvantages of both routes to the west, which he assessed in terms of portage length, propensity to freeze, and strategic position in case of war. The link to the Ohio would be considerably shorter through the Potomac to Alexandria than to New York, he concluded. "But," he observed, "the channel to New-York is already known to practice; whereas the upper waters of the Ohio and the Patowmac, and the great falls of the latter, are yet to be cleared of their fixed obstructions."[1]

Jefferson's remarks capture four key aspects of the state of affairs that would affect the Valley Road as well as most other Virginia arteries in the immediate post-Revolutionary period and for several decades to come. First, many observers near the close of the Revolution agreed that improvements were obviously necessary. The existing system of roads and waterways was quickly becoming inadequate, and work clearly needed to be done. Second, binding the eastern part of the state to the western part via improved transportation networks was becoming increasingly critical as the focus shifted westward. But it was the *methods* and *locations* for creating those linkages between the eastern and western regions that caused considerable discussion, especially once the Erie Canal neared completion. Third, Jefferson, like many others of his day, still thought mostly in terms of river rather than overland transport, for even he noted that Virginians had been spoiled by their abundant waterways.[2] Yet it was the very presence and potential navigability of these waterways that drew much of the attention and helped to stymie creation or improvement of other inland overland routes such as the Valley Road, at least initially. And finally, the specter of having to compete with and perhaps lose out to other ports and other parts of the country lent a certain sense of urgency and divisiveness to the push for new transportation routes.

These overarching issues governed the progress of the Valley Road as well as most other Virginia transportation improvements in the late eighteenth and early nineteenth centuries. The post-Revolutionary period eventually saw the genesis of a far more complex transportation system than the state had ever known. By the time that Claudius Crozet completed his 1838 map of statewide transportation improvements, Virginia — which then also encompassed present-day West Virginia — evinced a growing network of developing canals, turnpikes, roads, railroads, and waterways, and the Valley Road was finally being transformed from an "old stage road" into a turnpike.[3] The road had always been an important artery connecting the area west of the Blue Ridge to Philadelphia and points south and west, and would become, in the antebellum years, one of the most well-known turnpikes in the country, linking formerly localized places along the way, and transforming the landscapes through which it passed. Still, this change did not happen overnight. The Valley Turnpike was not officially born until 1838. But between 1780 and 1837, despite the formation of Virginia's Board of Public Works in 1816, advances in road-building technology, and the focus on statewide internal improvements, the Valley Road remained much the same as it had been during the colonial period. Conflicts between local and regional interests, sectional tensions, and worries about Virginia's general agricultural and commercial decline all helped to delay the road's modernization until the end of the 1830s. The road's development during this period was thus caught in the interplay between natural and cultural landscapes: while topographical and geological features had long ago forged the Valley Road's natural lines of communication in a northeast–southwest direction, the prevailing conceptual axis during this period ran in a different direction, from west to east.[4]

After the Revolution, it became increasingly apparent that Virginia's existing transportation routes were no longer adequate. The state's network of roads and waterways had generally served well enough when most of the population was concentrated in the Tidewater and Piedmont, but the population west of the Blue Ridge was growing. The mountains presented engineering problems and clearly complicated any east–west movement. Because of the state's expanding population, the old localized and piecemeal approach that involved petitioning for roads and requiring county courts to administer them through a system of road overseers and their gangs of male tithables would no longer suffice. The economy was also growing more complex. No longer was Virginia comprised primarily of dispersed Tidewater tobacco plantations linked to a lacework of waterways by wagon roads and cartways and oriented eastward toward coastal Virginia and the English ports of London and Bristol. In the early Republic, the prevailing conceptual orientation shifted, and the western part of the state became increasingly important.[5]

In the Valley, too, the economy had diversified away from its earlier emphasis on livestock, tobacco, and hemp and toward wheat cultivation integrated into a general mixed farming system. While the Valley's cattle, swine, and turkeys could be driven to market along the most marginal roads in the colonial period, the midcentury shift toward wheat cultivation introduced a lasting prosperity but also presented different transportation issues.[6] Farmers needed to ship the Valley's surplus wheat to distant markets, and these were largely the major ports of Baltimore and Philadelphia to the north as well as the cities of Alexandria, Richmond, and Fredericksburg across the Blue Ridge.[7] Although the Valley Road remained the region's main thoroughfare, it ran in a southwest to northeast direction, carrying commerce away from the state and toward Baltimore and Philadelphia. Consequently, improvements that might funnel the increasingly important produce of the Valley and points west through the eastern Virginia ports of Richmond and Norfolk, rather than out of the state entirely, tended to receive the attention of legislators and investors in the early Republic.

Population growth also played a part. By the time of the Revolution, the Valley's earlier settlers had already altered the countryside. In 1776, as he traveled northward through the Valley, Philip Fithian wrote that "Every Part of this broad Valley is settleable, & filled with Inhabitants." Fithian remarked that an acquaintance who had lived near Staunton since the 1730s had witnessed profound changes to the Valley landscape, which he remembered as a wilderness penetrated only by Indian or animal paths. "Strange is now the Alteration," Fithian wrote. "A continued Settlement. Broad, well-beaten Roads. And a most rapid Enlargement of the Population."[8] By the 1790s, even though immense tracts of woodland remained throughout the Valley, Isaac Weld remarked that "the whole of this country, to the west of the mountains, is increasing most rapidly in population." Especially near Winchester, Weld observed, the population had burgeoned so much in recent years that wood was becoming scarce, and "the farmers are obliged frequently to send ten or fifteen miles even for their fence rails."[9]

This population growth in the Valley and throughout Virginia had placed new pressures on available land everywhere. Agricultural depression and chronic soil exhaustion in the Tidewater and Piedmont created new demands for less worn-out land. As early as the 1790s, one traveler remarked on the contrast between the "well cultivated fields, green with wheat" that characterized Virginia's Valley and Piedmont landscapes with the "large pieces of land, . . . worn out with the culture of tobacco, . . . lying waste, with scarcely an herb to cover them" east of the Blue Ridge.[10] Yet most of Virginia's best real estate had already been taken, and land values dropped dramatically between 1817 and 1829. An 1816 legislative committee remarked of Virginia that "a very large proportion of her western territory is yet unimproved, while a considerable part of her eastern has receded from its former opulence. How many sad spectacles do her lowlands present of wasted and deserted fields, of dwellings abandoned . . . of churches in ruins?"[11] Between 1810 and 1840, almost half of the counties east of the Blue Ridge actually lost population at the same time as the nation was quickly growing, and many Virginians began to look westward.

At the same time, some observers also saw the state declining agriculturally and politically. Yet Virginians could not agree on the nature of
the decline or the reasons for it. At the Virginia Convention of 1829–30,
Benjamin Watkins Leigh attributed the decline to excessive westward
migration, noting that "none has contributed more to the peopling of the
new States, than Virginia."[12] John Randolph saw the decline differently,
defining it as a loss of political might. Randolph readily acknowledged
the surge in westward emigration to places like Kentucky, where produce
could be grown with just one-fifth of the labor required in Virginia. In a
letter written in 1830, Randolph advised a relative to reconsider his de-
cision to buy property in Virginia, where soil exhaustion was rampant
and where "soil and staples [were] both worn out . . . [and] the country
is in a galloping consumption.[13] While some believed that the problems
related to improper agricultural practices and their attendant evils, others pointed to Virginia's lack of communications, marketing centers, and
effective transportation arteries. In short, these observers thought that
Virginia needed to be more closely connected to the growing West.[14]

Beyond the state of Virginia as well as within its borders, an expanding market economy fueled interest in transportation improvements. Before the second decade of the nineteenth century, because the only way
to transport heavy or bulky goods cheaply was by water, trade and commercial farming were confined to areas within easy reach of coastal and
international markets. Following the War of 1812, however, the American
economy grew more varied. As factories developed in the Northeast and
manufacturing became a more crucial sector of the national economy,
the development of more efficient transportation routes to inland markets
became more essential.

Thus the growing importance of the West, population growth, land
pressures, an increasingly diversified economy, and an expanding national
market revolution constituted the context within which the surge of interest in statewide transportation improvements developed. Early road legislation in the 1780s attempted to lay the groundwork for transportation improvements, but these initial efforts reflected a piecemeal approach rather
than a coordinated statewide plan. But slowly, gradually, this fragmentary
approach evolved into a more systematic vision for statewide internal improvements. A 1785 revision of the general road law constituted one of
the first efforts. This law required county courts to respond to petitions
requesting that new roads be opened or old ones altered; it also provided
construction specifications and outlined procedures for appointing inves-
tigating commissions to report on road conditions. Still, the law did little

to overcome the widespread problems of maintaining roads under the unwieldy county court system.[15] In the 1790s, turnpike companies began to form. These were typically private companies created with the approval of and some financial support from the Virginia legislature to oversee the construction of turnpikes. Turnpike companies usually sold shares in order to raise the money necessary to build the road. Once the turnpike was completed, the company could then charge tolls to earn enough money to repay its investors. Between 1795 and 1812, eighteen such turnpike companies were incorporated, but only about half of them survived, and not surprisingly, all operated in one of the two great market centers of the state—either near Richmond or in the Winchester-Alexandria-Fredericksburg corridor of northern Virginia.[16] Toll roads and lotteries also helped finance road improvements.

Despite slow progress, the drift from local to state control continued. Proponents of statewide improvements lent urgency to their warnings in 1810 and 1811 by contrasting Baltimore to Richmond. The city of Baltimore had multiple banks, its capital was forty times that of the city of Richmond, and its commerce and trade were greater than that of the entire state of Virginia.[17] The prospect of Virginia falling even further behind other parts of the country was, to some, becoming very real. Following the War of 1812, other states turned their attention to internal improvements. Many began to look westward, especially when the first section of the National Road—running from Cumberland, Maryland, to Wheeling, the head of low-water navigation on the Ohio River—was completed in 1818. This established what was viewed as the first part of an essential link to the West, but also siphoned a significant amount of commerce westward. By the 1820s, the next westward link in the road was being planned, for the National Road was already heavily traveled and had fueled the development of towns, taverns, and stagecoach lines along its way. In the midst of this growing national interest in transportation improvements and westward movement, Virginia also began to focus more attention on developing transportation routes within its borders. In 1815, the Virginia Committee on Roads and Internal Navigation reported on the state's transportation needs, and the following year, the Virginia Board of Public Works was established.

The board forged ahead immediately. Charged with responsibility for internal improvements throughout Virginia as well as what is now West Virginia, within the next two years the board established the office of principal engineer and prescribed regulations for incorporating turnpike companies. It also undertook surveys of proposed transportation routes and monitored turnpike construction. Turnpike companies typically up-graded existing routes by improving the road surface and maintaining a consistent width. Accordingly, the board issued specifications for road construction, wheel sizes, maximum load weight, tollgates, toll rates, and methods for bridging watercourses. Turnpike companies were permitted two years to begin construction and ten years to finish. Any company failing to meet these regulations would forfeit its charter. Although the assembly chartered around twenty turnpike companies in the board's first year of operation, most of those early companies failed. Following the economic uncertainty caused by the Panic of 1819, new charters declined, and the board began backing only those turnpike companies that were most likely to succeed.[18]

Road construction usually involved multiple preliminary steps, includ-ing surveying and mapping the proposed route to determine the most du-rable, cost-effective, and labor-efficient construction procedures. Where possible, the board advocated road-building methods that reflected the state of the art, promoting construction "on the most improved modern plan."[19]

The board's discussions in its 1817 *Annual Report* about building a road that would extend nearly one hundred miles between Dunlaps Creek and the falls of the Kanawha in what is now West Virginia typify the kinds of issues they routinely considered. Observing that both France and En-gland had devoted considerable attention to road construction in recent years, the board noted that most roads there were carefully constructed, averaging between twenty-five and thirty-three feet wide and some-times even wider near large towns. For Virginia roads such as the one under consideration, though, the board recommended concave, convex, or sloping road surfaces with paved drains to draw off excess rainwater, but acknowledged that the convexity of the road should be minimized to prevent heavily loaded carriages and wagons from carving deep ruts that could collect water and form dangerous ravines. The most durable roads laid over loamy soil were those made of stone and gravel. The board's pre-ferred construction method, a variant of the Telford and McAdam sys-tem of surfacing roads with layers of crushed stone, involved raising the earth above the surrounding surface, digging a channel the width of the intended road, and filling the channel with several layers of successively smaller crushed stones topped with a layer of coarse gravel rammed into the surface with a roller (see fig. 4.2). But while the board advocated this type of construction, it would have been too expensive for the road under consideration because the necessary materials were too distant from the

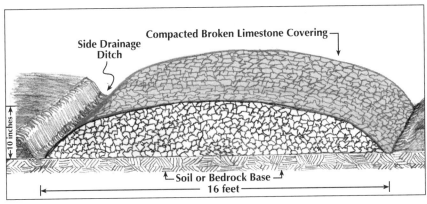

Fig. 4.2. John McAdam's road design in cross-section. No large stones were used, the only foundation being the natural soil or bedrock; a layer of hand-broken stones (about 1½ inches in diameter) was spread to a depth of 8 to 10 inches and compacted. (Gyula Pauer Cartography Lab, University of Kentucky)

road site. Instead, the board recommended an alternative method of raising the roadbed, surfacing it with a coating of gravel, and compacting the surface with heavy iron rollers before using the road.[20]

Topography in Virginia's hilly or mountainous regions could present engineering issues as well as special problems for horse teams and cattle drovers. "Wherever there is a long ascent or descent," the board's report cautioned, "there should be level places found at intervals where cattle may occasionally stop and rest, in going up, so as not to remain in draught, and the carriage stand on a plane surface." For especially long hills, five or six such resting places could be warranted. In the absence of such stopping places, wagoners often blocked their wheels with stones or wood blocks to give their horses a chance to rest. These carefully spaced level spots on hilly mountain roads, the report noted, prevented the horses from having to set off "in full draught," and kept them from losing "their spirits and strength under the inhuman cruelty inflicted with the whip. These resting places give encouragement to the team, and they move off for a few yards on a level, and ascend the next angle with readiness and refreshed strength." Flat spots along the road would also permit water descending the hill to be channeled off in gutters at regularly spaced intervals.[21]

Roads such as the one the board was considering were often proposed along the same routes as existing roads. In theory, this should have lessened the expense and labor necessary to upgrade the route. In fact, however, many existing roads were passable only in places. The board acknowledged that, in the case of the road under consideration, "very little appears ever to have been done in making the old road, except clearing away the wood and timber," and any good sections of road were due only to the qualities of the surrounding soil. No digging to lessen the ascent had been done, few bridges had been built, and little engineering to prevent the encroachment of watercourses had been undertaken. The board recommended that the resident engineer ultimately charged with building a modern road here should therefore plan his approach as if no road construction had yet occurred except clearing timber. The board estimated that the total cost of this one hundred–odd mile road would come to about $372,000, and would consist of new sections as well as upgraded portions of the old road.[22]

The process of surveying was equally involved. Surveyors attempted to straighten crooked ways, find workable routes through mountainous regions, and avoid objectionable soils and excessively rocky or steep grades. Road surveyors were to measure and survey proposed routes "very carefully, along the middle of the roads; to protract them on a large scale in sections, so as to shew all the angles and meanders distinctly; and also on a reduced one to exhibit the whole at one view for general improvement; and also to run a number of lines of experiment on both routes, with a view to improving their location." Locating a proper and suitable roadbed according to the board's recommendations could thus involve passing three times over the ground with instruments, with each survey distinctly marked with a different system of tree blazes and hatchet marks so that the final road alignment would be clear once construction commenced. Surveyors also typically included field observations regarding soil quality, gradients, stream and river crossings, and the availability of stone nearby for turnpike construction.[23]

Recommendations such as these typified the kinds of standards the Virginia Board of Public Works sought to establish for road improvements throughout the state. Despite this flurry of activity between 1810 and 1820, however, improvement projects still concentrated on the same two major market areas: the Richmond to James River and the Winchester-Alexandria–Potomac River region. The focus was on developing transportation linkages within the state in order to develop internal markets. In particular, the James River improvements, of which the road proposed between Dunlaps Creek and the falls of the Kanawha was only one part, received most of the board's attention, money, and energy from the start. Work on the James River and Kanawha Canal had actually begun several decades before the Board of Public Works was formed and continued off and on through the early nineteenth century, eventually extending nearly two hundred miles west of Richmond to Buchanan in 1851. The board's hope had always been to funnel trade from America's hinterland through the ports of Richmond and Norfolk by connecting the James to the Kanawha and the Ohio beyond. This route would involve opening the navigation of the James to Dunlaps Creek, extending the linkage from there to the falls of the Kanawha by road, and opening navigation of the Kanawha from the falls to the Ohio. The Board of Public Works saw this series of linkages as the primary connection between east and west and the centerpiece of the statewide system of internal improvements. In fact, the board suggested that "the consequences of these improvements will be [that] vast quantities of fertile land, now a neglected wilderness, will be brought into cultivation; much already occupied will be better managed, many useful articles, now untouched, will be produced and in increasing quantities" because transporting them would be so much cheaper. Claudius Crozet, who became the principal engineer and surveyor of public works of the board in 1823, underscored this point. "The trade of the west is the common aim of the Atlantic States," he observed; "it is a prize worthy to be contended for."[24]

At the same time, strident warnings about the possibility of Virginia falling behind other states and ports in the competition for western trade continued, lending urgency to the push for statewide improvements. "The western trade appears to be considered an object of immense value: to which the States of New York, Pennsylvania, Maryland, and Virginia, each have their pretensions," the board observed. "It therefore appears, that the benefits of the western trade, exclusive of the shares that will fall to the lot of New York and Louisiana, ought to be enjoyed by that state which can place a ton of merchandise on the bank of the Ohio river, at a suitable point, for the least money, and with the least detention, at any season."[25] In 1819, the board further cautioned that:

If Virginia neglect[s] to use the means of improving her advantages so largely offered to her acceptance, she must consent to hold an inferior rank among her sisters. The State of New York, by her noble enterprises, by her enlightened zeal in developing and applying to internal improvements her own resources, is rising in splendor like a star of the first magnitude in the federal constellation. The cities of Philadelphia and Baltimore are struggling in earnest competition for the western trade. If Richmond do not rise in the scale of cities to a rank second only to that of New York City; and if the Commonwealth do not still maintain a pre-eminent station among the states, it will not be because nature has denied the means.[26]

By 1828, just three years after the opening of the celebrated Erie Canal, the warnings had grown even more clamorous. That year the Board of Public Works described the state of Virginia as "retrograding rapidly," and observed that the state had been declining for the last seven years. "Other States have far outstripped her in public improvements, and are now reaping the rich harvests from those improvements," observed the 1828 *Annual Report*. "Unless the Legislature will interpose, by its energy and wisdom, to arrest this downward march, Virginia, whose resources are ample, and whose natural advantages are incalculable, will be thrown into the back-ground." Still, much of the focus remained on the James-Kanawha improvements. Noting the economic effects of the Erie Canal on New York and the positive impact of a good early turnpike on Baltimore, Claudius Crozet asked, "Why should not a connexion of the eastern and western waters have a similar effect in Virginia?" Virginia had already captured part of the North Carolina trade. "By connecting the Kanawha with the Chesapeake," Crozet reasoned, "she will certainly secure the commerce of the greater part of three other rich states, and reclaim that of her own eastern section, which now flows towards Baltimore or New-Orleans." Making the river navigable for boats all year long seemed of primary importance. Once the canal was completed, the rich counties in the western part of the state "would crowd the canal with their produce," the ironworks lining the James would ship five thousand tons of metal per year, and the New River and Greenbriar valleys "would send hemp, flour, and tobacco in abundance, whereas at present they send nothing to market except in waggons," which was so expensive that "there is nothing to stimulate the husbandman to industry." Improving navigation for the entire distance along this route, the report concluded, "would make the country rich and happy."[27] It was within this context, then, that the east–west connection to Richmond and beyond appeared imperative, and improvements following the Valley's natural corridor to Baltimore and Philadelphia seemed to be of much lower priority.

Concomitant with this initial burst of activity during the board's earliest years was an ongoing debate over which mode of transport would be the best solution for any given area. As the Erie Canal had neared completion in the early 1820s, interest in canals, or "canal fever," dominated, and it became increasingly clear to many that changing the basic mode of transportation and the technology that accompanied it was likely to exert profound changes on the nation's geography. Despite the energy and attention devoted to the National Road in the first few decades of the 1800s, plans for other modes of transportation often eclipsed road-building schemes. In fact, most of the ink in the board's first few annual reports was devoted to discussing prospective canals and their merits. One estimate concluded that overland transport cost twenty times more than transportation by water. "It may well then be stated," the report continued, "that the public would be great gainers, were they to lay out upon the making of every mile of canal, twenty times as much as they expended upon a mile of turnpike road." Observers felt that the greatest advantage of canals would result from the more rapid movement of bulky items that were difficult to transport overland between interior and seaboard regions — items such as fuel, building materials, and certain foodstuffs and domestic items. Furthermore, canals would create altogether new markets and increase demand for products such as plaster of paris, salt, fish products, and foreign imports. Canals could double the value of river fisheries, increase the Chesapeake coastal trade, and promote shipbuilding. Prices of heavy items such as coal, lime, iron ore, and roofing slates could be dramatically reduced by canals. In short, canals during this period promised to revolutionize the economy and profoundly transform existing markets. In the board's view, canals in Virginia would "advance and extend the manufactures, commerce and agriculture, of the most distant ramifications of the Chesapeake."[28]

This focus on canals, waterways, and the obviously favored James–Kanawha route consequently dominated the board's attention in its first few years. In terms of road improvements as well, most turnpike interests generally focused elsewhere in the state rather than in the Valley region. Moreover, turnpike interests were particularly active on east–west routes. In 1806, one observant traveler underscored this point, noting that while a rugged road across the mountains was undergoing modernization by being turnpiked, the Valley Road, which he had just traveled only days before, remained unimproved.[29] New road-building technologies, such as the Telford and McAdam systems of surfacing roads with layers of carefully broken and graded stone, brought sounder engineering principles to road construction by the 1820s, but extensive use of such surfaces was at first concentrated on major arteries such as the National Road.[30]

Turnpike-building efforts in some parts of the region were sometimes redundant and not particularly well planned, resulting in multiple and competing short turnpikes leading in the same direction instead of a single coherent route. In a discussion of the survey of the best route between Middleburg and Strasburg, the board recommended that short turnpikes should not be undertaken before first determining the most favorable direction for a longer main road, or else they might need to be destroyed and

Fig. 4.3. A foot-
bridge spanning
the James River
and James River
Canal bed connects
to the old 1930s
concrete U.S. 11
highway bridge on
Buchanan's north
side. (Scott Jost
2003)

rebuilt or somehow incorporated into the main road. Such solutions were
clearly not cost-effective and were also deemed to be "detrimental to the
best location of the whole line."[31]

When railroads entered the mix in 1827 with the appearance of the Baltimore and Ohio (B&O) Railroad in Virginia, a new era of debate began,
especially regarding transportation developments serving the Valley.
"Well constructed cast iron rail-ways," the board reported, "are next in
importance and value to the best canal and lock communication; and may
frequently be constructed in situations where the latter would be imprac-
ticable." Like canals, railroads also offered lowered transportation costs.
One report estimated the cost of transporting goods via turnpike to be

Fig. 4.4. An old mill
and B&O Railroad
bridge on the north
side of Martins-
burg, West Vir-
ginia, a short dis-
tance from U.S. 11.
The mill building
and related water-
control structures
were built from
local limestone.
(Scott Jost 2004)

about eight or ten times higher than moving the same goods on a railroad.
With the railroad, new connections and routes suddenly became possible,
but new tensions also arose. In addition, because the Valley's natural lines
of communication led not in an east–west direction, but away from the
state, toward Maryland and Pennsylvania, there was growing fear that
out-of-state ports like Baltimore might begin to siphon off Valley trade.[32]
In 1828, the Board of Public Works warned that if the state legislature did
not move more quickly to create east–west linkages to Virginia ports,
farmers in western Virginia might turn to states other than their own in
order to reach markets expeditiously. "Such are the difficulties experienced by our brethren in the western parts of the State, in reaching our
seaports," the board warned, "and such has been the tardiness with which
the Legislature has moved on this subject, that many of them are prepared
to accept this deleterious draught, in order to obtain an outlet and market for their surplus produce, the profits of which will centre in a sister
State."[33] Proponents of the James River developments were particularly
opposed to any linkage between the Valley and the B&O.[34]

Taken together, these obstacles delayed significant improvements to the Valley Road until the mid-1830s. Because Virginia's prevailing approach to transportation in the Valley was predicated on an east–west orientation, and because one of the overarching goals was to forge a link with the Ohio River to open up western trade, the state's initial strategy was to link the Valley's trade to the east by constructing routes across the Blue Ridge.[35] Thus, while other regions of Virginia experienced intermittent bursts of transportation improvements in the first two decades of the nineteenth century, Valley residents were, as one historian has argued, caught between several conflicting agendas. They could wait for Piedmont and Tidewater improvements to extend to the Valley; they could build their own lines eastward; or they could follow their natural line of communication northeastward toward Maryland, along the course of the Valley Road. During the early nineteenth century, the state's approach to the Valley's transportation problems focused mostly on attempts to divert the region's trade and keep it from seeking outlets beyond Virginia's borders.[36]

Still, the Valley Road continued to function as an important regional thoroughfare throughout this period of statewide transition. But what were actual road conditions like? According to most accounts, traffic along the road during this entire period was quickening, but road conditions continually made travel uncomfortable. By the time of the Revolution, the Valley Road was already heavily traveled. In 1775, writing of the traffic near Winchester, Philip Fithian remarked: "We see many every Day travelling out & in to & from Carolina, some on Foot with Packs; some on Horseback, & some in large covered Waggons — The Road here is much frequented, & the Country for an hundred & fifty miles farther West, thick inhabited."[37] The road surface itself usually responded to the season, freezing hard to ice in the winter, kicking up dust and stones in the summer, and dissolving into muddy ruts in rains and thaws. Fithian complained about the hard and icy surface conditions as he traveled northward from Staunton in February 1775. He called the road "the iron Road" and complained, "Rough & hard is the Beginning of our Ride." Only two days later, though, conditions nearby had changed. "There is a Thaw," he wrote. "Instead of our Horses Feet sounding on the Ice-paved Road, as last Monday, we are now in Danger actually of Miring!"[38]

Conditions on the Valley Road probably did not change much over the next few decades. When the peripatetic but usually optimistic Methodist Episcopal bishop Francis Asbury traveled the road in a sulky between Strasburg and Harrisonburg in 1806, he railed about the road surfaces he encountered. "I have travelled fifty miles to-day, over rough, rocky roads," he wrote. "I rested my feeble body on Saturday."[39]

In the early 1800s, stagecoach lines connecting some major cities and towns had just recently begun extending farther south. Writing in 1805, François Michaux noted that, prior to 1802, the public stages from Philadelphia extended no farther southward than Petersburg, Virginia, but that regular stagecoach travel between Petersburg and Charleston, South Carolina, had just been established. The journey of 650 miles took fifteen days. By that time, public stages were also running between Philadelphia, New York, and Boston as well as between Charleston and Savannah.[40]

Another traveler described one of these typical stagecoaches as being "a kind of open coach." The stagecoach itself was a closed carriage that stood about chest-high and was topped with six or eight small perpendicular posts that supported a roof. Leather curtains attached to the roof could be drawn up or let down and buttoned at the bottom to seal out rain or cold. The inside contained four front-facing seats, each of which could hold three passengers. The driver sat in the foremost seat, under the same roof as his passengers. This traveler described stagecoach travel as far more pleasant than being "imprisoned in a close[d] coach, inhaling and exhaling the same air a thousand times over, like a cow chewing the cud."[41]

By the time that Bernhard, Duke of Saxe-Weimar, visited Natural Bridge in 1825 and 1826, stagecoaches were running regularly on the Valley Road. Still, though, despite the added convenience of regular stage travel, road and coach conditions remained bad enough to elicit comment. The duke traveled from Harpers Ferry to Winchester in "an ordinary stage," but remarked "the improvement of stages, appears not yet to have extended beyond the Blue Mountains, because we were obliged to be contented with one, which was in every respect very uncomfortable." The duke's stage passed through difficult terrain and went "for a considerable distance on rocks; on the road, a great many loose stones were lying." Surprised that what he called the "miserable vehicle" did not break into pieces over the rough and rocky road, he changed stages at Winchester for a vehicle he deemed better, "although still very inconvenient" in his opinion. This one was made of hickory wood, so its natural elasticity made it better suited for the rocky roads. Setting out from Woodstock, the duke again suffered in what he called "a very miserable stage, and proceeded to Staunton, seventy-one miles southward," on a thoroughfare he described as being "a still more rugged road than that of yesterday." In Staunton, he described the tavern where he lodged as "unpleasant" and complained, "this long and uncomfortable journey, in an extremely bad stage, and upon a very rough way, made me quite uneasy." Obliged to remain in Staunton for an extra day because the stage to Natural Bridge ran only every other day, the duke again found himself two days later "in a miserable stage . . . upon a very bad road" heading to Natural Bridge. If the road conditions were rough, the company in this public conveyance was also disagreeable compared to the more refined passengers the duke had encountered farther north near Baltimore, Philadelphia, and Bethlehem, Pennsylvania. Upon his return northward, he left the "wretched tavern at the Natural Bridge, and returned to Staunton in a crowded stage," where he took his seat "as usual alongside the coachman where [he] had more room and fresh air."[42]

Henry D. Gilpin, a young Philadelphia lawyer on a business trip, traveled the Valley Road a year later and encountered many of the same road conditions that caused the Duke of Saxe-Weimar to complain. Although Gilpin admired the Valley's beautiful landscape, he found the road itself to be deplorable. Gilpin endured a "terrible journey" along "the worst road in the universe." The route through Winchester, Middletown, and Woodstock was "the most horrible you can conceive; . . . you pass over naked ridges of limestone rock, through ravines which it is astonishing any one ever though[t] of using for a path, up & down hills almost perpendicular."[43]

Although the terrible road conditions usually elicited comment from travelers like Gilpin, many also remarked on the striking appearance of the countryside they passed through, often underscoring how critical the Valley Road was in shaping the surrounding landscape. During this period, the Valley's landscape was one of dispersed farms, hamlets, villages, and market towns woven into earlier open-country neighborhoods. "This happy valley," one observer wrote in 1833, "is divided into farms of two or three hundred acres, cultivated by proprietors of the soil. Towns are interspersed at short distances."[44] This town and country network, the Valley's distinctive topography, and its diversified grain-livestock agriculture created a prospect that was quite different from the tobacco and plantation landscape farther east. Absent were the grand houses and large slave populations that travelers typically encountered in the Tidewater. In the Valley, by contrast, the farm and the household organized production. Farms, mills, shops, and towns punctuated the countryside, and roads connected them.[45]

In 1795, Isaac Weld found the Valley's natural landscape — particularly its mixture of forested hills, meadows, wandering streams, and mountain backdrops — to be particularly beautiful, but he bemoaned the modifications that settlement had wrought. To Weld, the beauty of the American countryside was spoiled by newly cleared fields bristling with tree stumps.

The landscape was also "much impaired by the unpicturesque appearance of the angular fences, and of the stiff wooden houses, which have at a little distance a heavy, dull, and gloomy aspect." Weld encountered heavy traffic as he traveled along the Valley Road. He "met with great numbers of people from Kentucky and the new state of Tennessee going towards Philadelphia and Baltimore, and with many others going in a contrary direction" to seek new land in the West. "The people all travel on horseback," he wrote, "with pistols and swords, and a large blanket folded up under their saddle." They used these blankets for bedding when they passed the night in the woods. Although, by the time Weld penned his account, most travelers rarely needed to use the weapons they carried against Indians, he observed that "formerly it used to be a very serious undertaking to go by this route to Kentucky, and travelers were always obliged to go forty or fifty in a party, and well prepared for defence. It would still be dangerous for any person to venture singly; but if five or six travel together, they are perfectly secure." The expansion of settlement along the roads had also bred increased safety. "There are houses now scattered along nearly the whole way from Fincastle to Lexington in Kentucky," he wrote, "so that it is not necessary to sleep more than two or three nights in the woods in going there." At the time Weld passed through Lexington, Virginia, it consisted of about one hundred houses, a courthouse, and a jail. Staunton contained nearly two hundred dwellings and a church, mostly built of stone. Weld described Winchester as "the largest town in the United States on the western side of the Blue Mountains." With a population of about two thousand, Winchester featured "regular, but very narrow" streets, four churches, and around 350 houses, all of which were "plainly built." To Weld, Winchester and the other Valley towns seemed relatively unremarkable.[46]

Traveling through the Shenandoah Valley more than two decades after Weld, Lieutenant Francis Hall found the entire Valley to be "remarkably fertile, particularly in wheat." The houses Hall encountered were mostly small, built of log, plank, brick, or stone, and clean enough to elicit comment. "There are more farm-houses and fewer negro huts in this valley, than in the Lowlands," he wrote, but slavery was still present, for he saw advertisements for runaway slaves at every tavern along the way. "Betwixt Staunton and Lexington," he continued, "the villages have a mean appearance."[47]

On his trip southward from Harpers Ferry in 1825–26, the Duke of Saxe-Weimar provided an extended commentary on the development of this dispersed town and country landscape. Near Harpers Ferry, the duke and his companions occasionally saw gristmills, but "houses were seldom met with." He found Winchester itself to be a pleasant country town with mostly masonry houses, a long main street, a market house, and several stores. Traveling south of Winchester, however, the duke again commented on the sparseness of the Valley's settlement, remarking that "the places between Winchester and Woodstock were not considerable" except for Strasburg, which was older and more populated. Around Woodstock, the Valley's distinctive topography began to elicit extended praise. As the duke and his companions passed through the wide Shenandoah Valley, bordered on the left and right by mountains, he remarked, "the formation of these parallel ridges is very singular, and no instance occurs of it in the other parts of the world." The countryside also appeared prosperous and well cultivated, and the duke observed, "by the exterior appearance of many country-houses, we were induced to believe their inhabitants enjoyed plenty." Old fences enclosed most fields, but carefully constructed masonry fences stood closer to the dwellings. Horses were a common mode of transport. The duke noted how, "on account of great distances between the plantations, almost all the ladies can ride on horseback; we met several of them elegantly dressed, and also black women." Teams of oxen and horses drew many of the carts he encountered. Like the towns in the northern end of the Valley, the duke also deemed the towns along the way between Woodstock and Staunton to be "mostly insignificant" and not worth mentioning, except for Shryock (now Edinburg), New Market, Big Spring, and Harrisonburg, which at the time boasted between eight and nine hundred inhabitants living in mostly wooden houses. "This part of the state of Virginia," he sniffed, "does not bear comparison with Massachusetts, New York, or even Pennsylvania. The great number of slaves in this state, makes also a very bad impression."[48]

The duke found the land between Woodstock and Staunton to be mostly cleared of forest, very hilly, well cultivated, and laced with multiple streams. By the time it reached Staunton, the Shenandoah River had narrowed to a small brook; the town itself was surrounded by forested hills. Staunton, like several of the other towns along the way, appeared small to the duke, consisting only of two main streets intersecting at right angles. Most of the houses there were built of wood and covered with shingles. Because Staunton was "the chief place of Augusta county" and court was in session during his visit, "a great many lawyers were present." Between Staunton and Natural Bridge, the duke and his party traveled through mountainous country and passed by "many very handsome country-houses." Nonetheless, he considered only Fairfield and

Lexington worthy of mention. At that time, Lexington had abou~
inhabitants, with a court, a high school, and a large arsenal n
visiting Natural Bridge, the duke and his party headed for
traveling through a hilly, forested landscape dense with pa
snipes and punctuated periodically by limestone rocks and caves. .
the way, they encountered "lonely houses and met with many travelers c
horseback."[49]

Travelers such as these were not the only people along the crowded
Valley Road. Wagoners driving loads of farm produce bound for market also frequented the roadway in large numbers. One traveler, passing
through the Shenandoah Valley in 1833, encountered a typical bivouac of
wagoners camped near an inn where he had stopped for the night. Each
wagon carried three tons, had narrow wheels, and was drawn by a team
of four horses. The wagon drivers usually traveled cheaply and in a group,
bringing with them staples like coffee, sugar, meat, bread, and corn for
their horses. The wagoners typically "set out early in the morning," the
traveler wrote, "and proceed until ten o'clock, when they stop in a shady
wood, near a spring of water. The horses are taken out by one of the party,
whilst another makes a fire, and prepares the breakfast." After the meal,
the wagoners extinguished their fire, harnessed their horses back to their
wagons, and proceeded on their way until nighttime, when they stopped
again to eat heartily. "If the weather is fine," the traveler wrote, "they sleep
in the open air; if it rains, the waggon affords them shelter. They generally
travel in company, and as some of the waggons are loaded with whiskey,
a scene of merriment takes place at night. They travel thirty miles a day,
and thousands of waggons visit every year the markets of Philadelphia,
Baltimore, Richmond, and other cities near the Atlantic coast." Still, the
traveler observed perceptively that this mode of transporting goods to
market would soon die out. He noted that the surge in "canal fever" and
the ongoing debate over Virginia's transportation improvements might
soon curtail such well-established wagon traffic and remarked, "the intended canals to the interior will diminish, or put a stop to, this mode of
transportation."[50]

As this observer predicted, big changes to the way people traveled were
already under way, and the debate over the Valley's position within the
state's transportation scheme would only grow louder as general interest
in statewide improvements increased. In the 1820s and early 1830s, groups
began to lobby for better transportation links, internal improvement conventions were held, and newspapers cried out for action. Still, the controversy over what form and route these links should take, which commercial

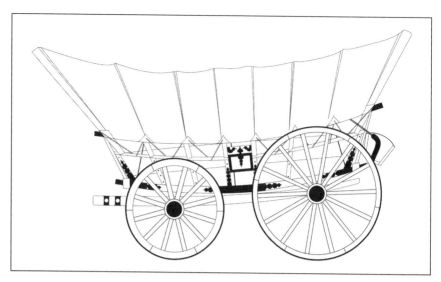

Fig. 4.5. The Newtown wagon. From the 1790s to the 1860s, this type of Virginia freight wagon was made in Newtown/Stephensburg (the present-day Stephens City), where nine different establishments engaged in wagon manufacturing. The wagon shares overall characteristics with Pennsylvania's Conestoga wagons, but it also has distinctive features that separate it into a class of its own. The Newtown wagon was of exceptionally heavy construction and capable of hauling 4,500- to 5,000-pound loads. The harness was very heavy, and all of the metalwork, breast and tongue chains, and tires were made from the highest-quality iron available. (After an original drawing by Linden A. Fravel; Gyula Pauer Cartography Lab, University of Kentucky)

towns would become the primary markets for the state, and which parts of the state would benefit or suffer the most persisted.[51] Newspapers often captured the heated nature of the discussion. In March 1831, the *Richmond Enquirer* outlined a debate in the Virginia legislature about what extending a railroad link to the B&O would mean in terms of routing valuable Valley trade away from Virginia and toward Baltimore. On the one hand, some argued that the proposed improvements would increase sectional tensions, which would be unacceptable to good Virginians. These improvements would divert western trade toward Baltimore, "lessen the profits on the money vested in the state Improvements, injure the Internal Improvement Fund, and thus destroy the hopes which other parts of the state might entertain of assistance from this fund" and would ultimately pull Virginians apart from one another instead of uniting them. The proposed link "would estrange their feelings from each other, and unite their interests with those of the citizens of another state — and that surely gentlemen were too good Virginians to weaken the ties which arise from a community of interest and the connections of commerce." On the other hand, those representing the Valley argued that "it was a violation of the rights of the people of the Valley to cut them off from any market which they might please to seek . . . that it was arbitrary, and tyrannical to deny them this privilege, and would be, in fact, to sacrifice the interests of the Valley to the James River interest."[52] In May of that same year, an article in the *Richmond Whig* echoed the latter sentiment:

> We are not surprized to learn the awakening tendencies of the country at the head of the James River, to connect itself with Baltimore; neither do we regret it, for although unquestionably, it were best for the whole State that Richmond should be the entrepot of Western Commerce, yet if the Legislature and the people interested to make it so, persist in withholding the indisposable facilities, the people of the Valley and beyond it, deserve applause for directing their eyes towards those who woo their intercourse by splendid enterprize and Herculean exertions. If Richmond and the James River people will *not* do any thing, we are glad that there is a portion of the population of Virginia, resolved that they will.[53]

Just as the *Richmond Enquirer* had suggested, the author of this article agreed that the inhabitants of Baltimore and the Valley had every right to promote their own interests by connecting themselves more directly with one another, because "the commerce of the West is a fair and wealthy heiress, to whom the Atlantic Cities are all suitors, and let the prize be worn by that one which deserves it."[54]

The same year, in the midst of this ongoing debate, the state directed a survey of the Shenandoah River and the adjacent countryside to determine the best method of opening up the Valley. This 1831 survey was intended to determine the most suitable mode of transport — whether by means of "locks and dams, or by a canal, or railroad through the said valley," and to compare the estimated costs of each method. Nonetheless, the Valley Road remained largely unimproved, for when James Herron surveyed and mapped the Shenandoah River the following year in anticipation of these improvements, he still rendered the Valley Road as the "Stage Road" extending from Harrisonburg to Winchester.[55]

Finally, in 1834, the Valley Turnpike Company was incorporated. The company was authorized to build a seventy-odd-mile stretch of turnpike from Winchester to Harrisonburg, and the charter empowered the company to use as much of the "old stage road" as was feasible. In 1837, a second stretch of macadamized turnpike to link Harrisonburg and Staunton was begun.[56] Although the turnpike was still under construction when Claudius Crozet completed his map of the state's internal improvements

Fig. 4.6. A fragment of the original Valley Pike at Red Bank Road, five miles south of Edinburg. The contemporary U.S. 11 roadbed lies in the left background. (Scott Jost 2003)

in 1838, the importance of this road to Virginia's overall transportation system was undeniably and clearly indicated on the map, as the future benefits of this improvement were already becoming apparent. Macadamization was still under way in 1840 when an upper Valley resident noted, "they have got the Mcadamized road nearly completed from Staunton to Winchester." Two years later, the same observer wrote: "Our Mcadamised road is beginning to be of some service to the Valley. The large wagons . . . carry from 80 to 85 hundred [pounds of] produce from Staunton to Winchester for 50 cents per hundred."[57] Still, when the head of the Valley Turnpike Company wrote to the Board of Public Works in 1838 to request the appointment of a principal engineer to work on the Valley Pike as soon as possible, he underscored the dramatic change that was taking place in his region, but also emphasized the need to strike while the iron was hot: "The spirit of improvement is awakened in our hitherto sleeping valley," he wrote, "and we fear that delay will lessen the interest which is now manifested."[58]

Thus the Valley Road, about to be revitalized as the Valley Pike, had finally emerged from the conflicted state of affairs and the general neglect of the region that followed Jefferson's observations in 1785. Crozet's 1838 map shows the Valley Turnpike as an integral link in an increasingly sophisticated system of statewide improvements. Although its early modernization was undoubtedly retarded by the inherent conflict between the prevailing east–west conceptual orientation and the Valley's natural topography, and although conflicts between local and regional interests, "canal fever," and the vacillating policies of the early Board of Public Works exacerbated statewide concerns about Baltimore surpassing Richmond and stealing the prize of Valley trade, the "hitherto sleeping valley" was awakening at last.

Notes

1. Thomas Jefferson, *Notes on the State of Virginia,* ed. William Peden (New York and London: Norton, 1982), 16.

2. Jefferson wrote, "Our country being much intersected with navigable waters, and trade brought generally to our doors, instead of our being obliged to go in quest of it, has probably been one of the causes why we have no towns of any consequence" (ibid., 108).

3. Claudius Crozet, "Map of [Virginia] Internal Improvements," 1838, Board of Public Works Collection, Inventory #669, Library of Virginia, Richmond.

4. Robert F. Hunter and Edwin L. Dooley Jr., *Claudius Crozet: French Engineer in America, 1790–1864* (Charlottesville: University Press of Virginia, 1989), 120.

5. David Hackett Fischer and James C. Kelly, *Bound Away: Virginia and the Westward Movement* (Charlottesville: University Press of Virginia, 2000), 136–37; Nathaniel Mason Pawlett, *A Brief History of the Roads of Virginia, 1607–1840* (Charlottesville: Virginia Highway and Transportation Research Council, 1977), 4–5.

6. Kenneth E. Koons and Warren R. Hofstra, "Introduction: The World Wheat Made," in Koons and Hofstra, eds., *After the Backcountry: Rural Life in the Great Valley of Virginia, 1800–1900* (Knoxville: University of Tennessee Press, 2000), xvii–xviii.

7. Ibid., xx. Robert D. Mitchell has argued that because the southern part of the Valley was traditionally tied more closely to fall-line cities east of the Blue Ridge such as Richmond, it tended to develop more slowly, being somewhat isolated from arteries that could connect its produce to eastern Virginia markets (Mitchell, "The Settlement Fabric of the Shenandoah Valley, 1790–1860: Pattern, Process, and Structure," in Koons and Hofstra, eds., *After the Backcountry,* 34–47). On efforts to involve the Shenandoah Valley in extending the navigation of the Potomac and James rivers, see also Robert D. Mitchell, *Commercialism and Frontier: Perspectives on the Early Shenandoah Valley* (Charlottesville: University Press of Virginia, 1977), 194–95.

8. February 8, 1776, and January 21, 1776, in Philip Vickers Fithian, *Philip Vickers Fithian: Journal, 1775–1776,* ed. Robert Greenhalgh Albion and Leonidas Dodson (Princeton: Princeton University Press, 1934), 180, 172.

9. Isaac Weld, *Travels through the States of North America: And the Provinces of Upper and Lower Canada during the Years 1795, 1796, and 1797* (London: John Stockdale, 1807), 1:231.

10. Weld, *Travels,* 1:133.

11. Quoted in Fischer and Kelly, *Bound Away,* 202.

12. William M. S. Rasmussen and Robert S. Tilton, *Old Virginia: The Pursuit of a Pastoral Ideal* (Charlottesville, Va.: Howell Press, 2003), 67–68.

13. Ibid.

14. Fischer and Kelly, *Bound Away,* 202–7.

15. Edward Graham Roberts, "The Roads of Virginia, 1607–1840" (Ph.D. diss., University of Virginia, 1950), 48; Pawlett, *A Brief History of the Roads of Virginia,* 13–15.

16. Roberts, "The Roads of Virginia," 56; Pawlett, *A Brief History of the Roads of Virginia,* 15.

17. Roberts, "The Roads of Virginia," 56–63.

18. Pawlett, *A Brief History of the Roads of Virginia,* 22–25.

19. *Annual Report of the Board of Public Works,* Board of Public Works Collection, Library of Virginia, Richmond (hereafter cited as *ARBPW* by year), 1817: 69.

20. *ARBPW,* 1817: 69–70.

21. *ARBPW,* 1817: 69–72; Howard Newlon Jr. and Nathaniel Mason Pawlett et al., eds., *Backsights* (Charlottesville: Virginia Department of Highways and Transportation, 1985), 68–70.

22. *ARBPW,* 1817: 72–73.

23. *ARBPW,* 1819: 42–49.

24. *ARBPW,* 1816, 1817, 1819; *ARBPW,* 1819: 62; *ARBPW,* 1828: 263; Pawlett, *A Brief History of the Roads of Virginia,* 25.

25. *ARBPW,* 1819: 111.

26. *ARBPW,* 1819: 63.

27. *ARBPW,* 1828: 358, 359, 263, 265.

28. Peirce Lewis, "The Landscapes of Mobility," in Karl Raitz, ed., *The National Road* (Baltimore and London: Johns Hopkins University Press, 1996), 25; *ARBPW,* 1822: 95–96, 99, 103–5.

29. August 22, 1806; Francis Asbury, *The Journal of the Rev. Francis Asbury, Bishop of the Methodist Episcopal Church, from August 7, 1771, to December 7, 1815 . . .* (New York: N. Bangs and T. Mason, 1821), 205.

30. The first macadam surface in the nation was laid on a section of the Boonsborough Turnpike Road between Hagerstown and Boonsboro, Maryland, in 1823. The next year, a Virginia turnpike company experimented with a macadam surface near Alexandria, and two years later, a 73-mile-long section of the National Road between Wheeling, Virginia, and Zanesville, Ohio, was macadamized (Newlon and Pawlett, *Backsights,* 68–70).

31. *ARBPW,* 1829: 505–6.

32. Philip Morrison Rice, "Internal Improvements in Virginia, 1755–1860"

(Ph.D. diss., University of North Carolina at Chapel Hill, 1948), 31–33; *ARBPW,* 1819: 46.

33. *ARBPW,* 1828: 358.

34. Rice, "Internal Improvements in Virginia," 31–33. See also Warren R. Hofstra, *A Separate Place: The Formation of Clarke County, Virginia* (Madison, Wisc.: Madison House, 1999), 56–61.

35. Claudius Crozet's 1827 plan for statewide internal improvements also focused on east–west connections (Pawlett, *A Brief History of the Roads of Virginia,* 26–27).

36. Rice, "Internal Improvements in Virginia," 1, 31–33.

37. June 7, 1775, in Fithian, *Journal,* 25.

38. February 12 and 13, 1775, ibid., 181. In the second reference, Fithian appears to have turned onto a nearby road feeding into the Valley Road.

39. August 8, 1806, Asbury, *Journal,* 203.

40. Of the newly regular stages extending southward, Michaux exclaimed: "There are also stages between Philadelphia, New York, and Boston; as well as between Charlestown and Savannah in Georgia; so that from Boston to Savannah, a distance of twelve hundred miles, there is the accommodation of public vehicles" (François André Michaux, *Travels to the Westward of the Allegany Mountains . . .* [London: W. Flint, Old Bailey, 1805], 30). While John Melish's *A Description of Roads in the United States,* published in 1814, reckoned distances between Fredericktown (Frederick, Maryland) and several towns along the Valley Road extending from Winchester to Natural Bridge, he made no mention of regular stages on that route (John Melish, *A Description of Roads in the United States, Compiled from the Most Authentic Materials* [Philadelphia: G. Palmer, 1814], 24).

41. Francis Baily, F.R.S., *Journal of a Tour in Unsettled Parts of North America in 1796 & 1797,* ed. Jack D. L. Holmes (Carbondale and Edwardsville: Southern Illinois University Press, 1969), 25.

42. Duke of Saxe-Weimar-Eisenach, Bernhard, *Travels through North America, during the Years 1825 and 1826* (Philadelphia: Carey, Lee and Carey, 1828), 188–93.

43. Ralph D. Gray, ed., "A Tour of Virginia in 1827: Letters of Henry D. Gilpin to His Father," *Virginia Magazine of History and Biography* 76, no. 4 (1968): 452, 450.

44. John Finch, Esq., *Travels in the United States of America and Canada* (London: Longman, Rees, Orne, Brown, Green, and Longman, 1833), 259–60.

45. Warren R. Hofstra, *The Planting of New Virginia: Settlement and Landscape in the Shenandoah Valley* (Baltimore and London: Johns Hopkins University Press, 2004), 12, 14, 281, 285.

46. Weld, *Travels,* 1:231–238.

47. Lieutenant Francis Hall, *Travels in Canada, and the United States, in 1816 and 1817* (London: Longman, Hurst, Rees, Orme and Brown, 1818), 353–55, 365.

48. Duke of Saxe-Weimar-Eisenach, *Travels through North America,* 188–90.

49. Ibid., 190–93.

50. Finch, *Travels in the United States of America and Canada,* 260–61.

51. Pawlett, *A Brief History of the Roads of Virginia,* 31.

52. *Richmond Enquirer,* March 22, 1831.

53. *Richmond Whig,* May 3, 1831.

54. Ibid.

55. *ARBPW,* 1832: 414–18, 447–50, 506–7; *ARBPW,* 1833: 9, 99–105; *ARBPW,* 1835: 345; New Shenandoah Company. "Trace Map of the Shenandoah River East and West of the Massanutten Mountain as Surveyed by James Herron in 1832," Board of Public Works Inventory #504:1, Board of Public Works Collection, Library of Virginia.

56. *ARBPW,* 1834: 575; Board of Public Works Collection, Library of Virginia; John W. Wayland, *The Valley Turnpike: Winchester to Staunton and Other Roads* (Winchester, Va.: Winchester-Frederick County Historical Society, 1967), 3.

57. Robert and Sally McCormick, Augusta County, Virginia, to William and Rebecca McCormick, Caledonia, Washington County, Missouri, May 30, 1840; Robert and Sally McCormick to William and Rebecca McCormick, Greenville, Wain County, Missouri, December 25, 1842; both in William Steele McCormick Papers, 1833–79, McCormick Collection, State Historical Society of Wisconsin, Madison. Quoted in Kenneth E. Koons, "'The Staple of Our Country': Wheat in the Regional Farm Economy of the Nineteenth-Century Valley of Virginia," in Koons and Hofstra, eds., *After the Backcountry,* 6, 17.

58. Bushrod Taylor to the Board of Public Works, August 3, 1838, Valley Turnpike Papers, 1838–1865, Board of Public Works Collection, Library of Virginia.

Strategy and Sublimity

A Gallery of Valley Pike Images during the Civil War

5

GERALDINE WOJNO KIEFER
AND JAMES K. BRYANT II

"The pleasant and hospitable town of Winchester, with its polished society, its flower-gardens, and famous market, savored too much of ordinary civilization to detain a party in search of the romantic and wonderful," wrote the nineteenth-century travel writer, tourist, and illustrator Porte Crayon. Riding "up the Valley Turnpike as fast as the horses can trot on a bright frosty morning," Crayon's group of travelers approached the Massanutten Mountains, which rose "to a majestic height in the midst of the valley between the forks of the Shenandoah River."[1] In his journals, illustrations, and maps, Porte Crayon — the literary pseudonym for David Hunter Strother — interpreted the Valley Road for a broad public and during the Civil War transformed the image of that turnpike from a picturesque setting for romantic scenery to a strategic theater in a desperate struggle.

A crucial artery in the Shenandoah Valley for moving troops, maintaining military supply and communications, and fighting battles, the Valley Pike embodied the hopes of the Confederacy early in the war and its despair in the conflict's final year (see fig. 5.1). As in many Civil War campaigns, images not only held strategic significance but also conveyed subtle cultural messages as the war progressed to its conclusion. The aesthetics of visual messages, overlaid by the strategy of military conflict, functioned to bring viewers — military and civilian — ever closer to the theaters of combat. Refigured graphically in postbellum years, strategy, story, and romance commingled with the Valley Pike in their midst. Focusing on the Civil War and its aftermath, this gallery of images lays out the major pictorial paths of the road in the Shenandoah Valley. Views of the Valley serve as guideposts along the way.

The Valley Road Transformed, through 1862

Although there was one Valley Road in the nineteenth century, many "valley roads" appeared in the depictions of artists and photographers. Trade,
travel, and literary culture generated intimate "picture-book" landscapes
featuring the road in the media of cartography, drawing, genre painting,
history painting, and the graphic arts. During the Civil War, the military
culture of heroic, newspaper-style panoramas and campaign maps ampli-
fied these images. Photography now joined the mix of media.

Let us view the Valley Pike, a road with deep cultural meaning and
broad economic significance, in the years immediately preceding 1861. By
the 1830s, maps portrayed it as a tourist's road, a key stage route into the
Valley from the eastern seaboard. Two decades later, an equally bold Valley Road — Augusta Street — carved its way through Staunton in Edward
Beyer's *Album of Virginia,* a collection of town and country panoramas.
Topographical accuracy vied with beauty in Beyer's pictorial promotion
of the town's location, connections, and attractions. Beyer also showed the
accessibility of regional springs, spas, and resorts via the Valley Road. On
the notes of Valley banks in 1860, a wagon road linked fields, farmers, and
produce to railroads and markets (see figs. 5.2 and 5.3). The metaphorical road — a promissory note for the production of wealth — certainly
captured what the real road meant to Valley peoples at the outset of the
Civil War. It was a road to travel, a route to attractions, and an avenue of
economic opportunity.

The Valley of the Shenandoah, Virginia, an 1861 engraving, posed another
context (see fig. 5.4). The artist rendered a scenic road winding among
outcroppings of Three Top Mountain, the northern extremity of the Mas-

Fig. 5.2. (*Top*) Staunton, Va./drawn from nature by Ed. Beyer; Woldemar Rau, lithographer, 1857. (Library of Congress, Washington, D.C., LC-USZ62-15357 DLC)

Fig. 5.3. (*Bottom*) Five-dollar note issued in 1860 by the American Bank Note Company, Staunton, Virginia. (Courtesy of Geraldine Kiefer, Winchester, Va.)

sanutten range in the vicinity of Strasburg, Cedar Creek, and the Shenandoah River. Surmounted by breaking storm clouds and dramatic light, this road emerged from a rocky ledge and revealed a breathtaking view. Represented by the farm in the middle ground, the landscape depicted a traveler's road and a farmer's road, a well-trafficked connector linking produce to markets in the distance. Yet it revealed an anomaly — troops marching in formation and a man in uniform, the artist-chronicler turned correspondent, observing them. The Shenandoah Valley and its roads to markets were being folded into roads to war. The Valley Pike, set in the landscape of the Shenandoah Valley, governed military strategy throughout the region. Macadamized, it accommodated all-weather travel and transport. A Union soldier in General Philip Sheridan's command commented in 1864 that the Valley Pike was "among the best roads in the world." That same year, when Confederate forces under General Jubal

Fig. 5.4. *The Valley of the Shenandoah, Virginia.* (Reprinted from *Harper's Weekly,* November 9, 1861: 709)

Early temporarily controlled the road, a Union prisoner described the "famous turnpike ... [as] the perfection of road-making; so level and straight that we were prone to say that we could see in the morning where we were to camp at night."[2]

One of the great ironies of the Civil War was "the spectacle of Northern — and Southern — generals fighting in their own country and not knowing where they were going or how to get there," according to the historian T. Harry Williams. Neither the federal government nor the infant Confederacy possessed topographical maps essential for military operations except in the West. Most commercial maps were general in nature, useful only for boundary surveys and denoting political districts. Accurate military maps of Virginia were still scarce as late as 1864 and often useless for selecting a line of march, engaging the enemy, determining elevation and fields of artillery fire, or identifying strategically important landscape features. The general terrain of Virginia on the whole proved to be among the most difficult to traverse.[3]

The famed Valley campaign of 1862 established the military legacy of "Stonewall" Jackson and made his name a household word throughout the Confederacy. His role was to protect the Shenandoah Valley — the "breadbasket for the South" — as well as keep a northern invasion route open. The Valley campaign began in earnest on March 23, 1862, with the First Battle of Kernstown. The Battle of Front Royal and the First Battle of Winchester followed in close succession on May 23 and 25; all three were fought on the Valley Turnpike. Three days after Kernstown, Jedediah Hotchkiss, a teacher and self-taught mapmaker, presented his services to Stonewall as a topographical engineer. Near the Valley Pike town of Edinburg, Jackson issued his first order to Hotchkiss: "I want you to make me a map of the Valley, from Harper's Ferry to Lexington, showing all the points of offence and defense in those places. Mr. [Alexander S.] Pendleton will give you orders for whatever outfit you want. Good morning, Sir."[4] It would take Hotchkiss almost two years — not to mention walking, surveying, and documenting hundreds of square miles — to complete this highly detailed topographical map of the Shenandoah Valley, but he continuously supplied smaller maps for Jackson and other commanders as needed. Directly through the center of this map he drew the Valley Turnpike as the major artery of military operations.

David Hunter Strother, the journalist who in peacetime pursued drawing, writing, geology, and botany, joined the Union army in Martinsburg as a volunteer topographer until assigned as a captain on the staff of General Nathaniel P. Banks (Jackson's Valley adversary) in 1862. At the same time that his counterpart, Hotchkiss, was surveying the Valley for Stonewall, Strother — operating in enemy territory with existing and outdated Valley maps — was annotating these documents for Banks. Strother portrayed his illustrated diary entries as "Personal Recollections" and published them in *Harper's Monthly* in 1866 and 1867. In his travels in the Valley of Virginia before the Civil War, this artist had depicted the Valley Turnpike as a means of getting from one town, attraction, or destination to the next, a direct line on a metaphorical tourist's map with no embellishments save views of gorgeous prospects. When he switched roles from convivial diarist to staffer, topographer, and wartime chronicler, Strother portrayed the road as a parade route with dramatic vistas (see fig. 5.5).

With the onset of war, northern news weeklies sent "special artists" to illustrate Valley scenery and towns. Writing for audiences eager for spectacles as well as news and victories, the "specials" limned a road groaning with the means of war, a veritable parade of figures, costumes, and pictorial embellishments (see fig. 5.6). They conceived panoramas whose breadth and scope led the eye from side to side and from adjacent to distant spaces. One of the most dramatic scenes, roiling with storm clouds, tortuous trees, scattered branches, and mounded clods of dislodged earth,

Fig. 5.5. (*Top*) David Hunter Strother, *The Narrow Passage*, 1862. (Reprinted from "Personal Recollections of the War, by a Virginian. Sixth Paper. The Valley of the Shenandoah.—Banks's Retreat," *Harper's New Monthly Magazine* 34, no. 202 [March 1867]: 427)

Fig. 5.6. (*Bottom*) *Second Mississippi Regiment (Wildcats) Passing along Main Street, Winchester, on Their Way to Bunker Hill, Virginia.* (Reprinted from *Harper's Weekly*, August 3, 1861: 493)

not to mention a unit of Virginia cavalry in full gallop over a striated and illuminated pike, is depicted in *Rebel Intrenchments on the Martinsburg Turnpike, near Winchester, Virginia* (see fig. 5.7).

The spring 1862 Valley campaign ended in Confederate victory. As if to make up for Federal stalling and ineptitude, the northern press countered with depictions of a storied, fearsome, and hostile Valley Road landscape. Pursuit, passage, and pathos paved this pike. A figure painter and landscapist, Edwin Forbes, one of *Frank Leslie's Illustrated Newspaper*'s special artists, became the key limner of Valley Road events, troops, and envi-

rons in 1862. For Forbes, the road was never a parade ground. Under his purview, it moved toward a comprehensive chronicle, cued to climax and victory. Particularly memorable was his March 25 panorama from General Banks's fort depicting an occupied Valley Pike and Manassas Gap Railroad clinching the entire Valley, horizon to horizon (see fig. 5.8). By early June, Forbes was on the march with General George D. Bayard, moving to reinforce General John Frémont's Mountain Department engaged near Strasburg. Day by day from June 1 to June 5 in sequence along the road, Forbes detailed Frémont's derailed attempts to catch, capture, and defeat the infamous Stonewall Jackson (see fig. 5.9). That Leslie published these engravings as current news and then again in his *Pictorial History of the War of 1861* (1862) rendered the reputations, if not the actual deeds, of Generals Frémont and Banks heroic and victorious.

Fig. 5.7. Rebel Intrenchments on the Martinsburg Turnpike, near Winchester, Virginia. (Reprinted from Harper's Weekly, September 28, 1861: 614)

The Valley Road in the Civil War: 1864

The 1864 Valley campaign saw the collapse of Confederate General Jubal A. Early and his army in the attempts to relieve pressure on General Robert E. Lee's Confederates, engaged in the siege of Petersburg. Early's

secondary mission, threatening Washington, succeeded only as a threat. This Shenandoah campaign also augmented the fame — or infamy — of Philip Sheridan in postwar art and literature.

By autumn 1864, Early's forces were continually raiding the Baltimore and Ohio (B&O) Railroad. Sheridan seized the opportunity on September 19 to attack the Confederates at the Third Battle of Winchester, turning their left flank and forcing a withdrawal up the Valley Turnpike. Sheridan followed through with an attack upon Early's positions at Fishers Hill on September 21–22, driving his opponent toward Rockfish Gap near Waynesboro. But with reinforcements from Lee, Early made a surprise attack against Union forces camped near Cedar Creek on October 19, pushing Sheridan's men back toward Winchester. Having arrived in Winchester from Washington amid the sounds of his army's rout, Sheridan embarked on his famous ride astride trusty steed "Rienzi" on the Valley Turnpike toward Cedar Creek. Rallying his troops along the way, he launched a counterattack, breaking the back of Early's army. The Confederacy in the Valley was no more. Sheridan's success along with William T. Sherman's capture of Atlanta, Georgia, helped President Lincoln win reelection in November.[5]

Needing accurate topographical information on the Shenandoah Valley and the Valley Pike, Sheridan relied heavily on Lieutenant John R. Meigs, a West Point–trained topographical engineer who had served under other Union generals and also with Strother. It would be Meigs's

death in a skirmish with Confederate scouts while documenting Federal troop positions in Rockingham County that led Sheridan to retaliate against the property of residents in the southern portion of that county on October 4–5, 1864. This action was part of a larger mission ordered by General Ulysses S. Grant to "eat out Virginia clear and clean . . . so that crows flying over it for the balance of this season will have to carry their provender with them." Often referred to as "The Burning" or "Red October," Sheridan's "scorched-earth policy" destroyed mills, barns, and other means of agricultural production. It was akin to Sherman's March from Atlanta to the sea.[6]

Harper's special artist Alfred Waud and *Leslie's* James E. Taylor portrayed General Philip Sheridan's campaign against Early in September and October 1864 as a panorama of pursuit and victory that effectively ended Confederate resistance in the Valley (see figs. 5.10, 5.11, 5.12, and 5.13). They elevated the pike from a Broadway-styled avenue of grand marches to a protocinematic stage for exciting cavalry chases, large-scale infantry movements, burning and smoking barns, and immense wagon-train caravans. Infantry, cavalry, artillery, and wagons appeared in compact formations moving in opposing or single files across Waud's scenes.

Fig. 5.9. (*Top*) Edwin Forbes, *Reconnoissance of the Confederate Position at Strasburg, Previous to Its Occupation by Genral* [sic] *Fremont.—From a Sketch by Edwin Forbes*. (*Bottom*) *Army of General Fremont on Its March up the Shenandoah Valley.—Wounded and Ragged Soldiers.—From a Sketch by Edwin Forbes*. (Reprinted from *Frank Leslie's Pictorial History of the War of 1861*, no. 27 [New York: Frank Leslie (1862)]: 13, 15)

Fig. 5.10. (*Top*) James E. Taylor, *Sheridan's Campaign—Battle of Fisher's Hill, Sept. 22—Charge of Crook's Corps on the Right—Sketched by Our Special Artist, J. E. Taylor.* (*Bottom*) *Sheridan's Campaign—Battle of Fisher's Hill, Sept. 22—From a Sketch by Our Special Artist, J. E. Taylor.* (Reprinted from *Frank Leslie's Illustrated Newspaper* 19, no. 472 [October 15, 1864]: 52, 61)

Armies and matériel literally overran the Valley Pike. Actions followed clinched battles. These images demonstrated the unified command of 1864 and the aggressive leadership under Grant and Sheridan in contrast to the divided authority and ineffective generalship of Banks and Frémont two years earlier. Rather than sketch singular, exciting "moments" on the pike in images of presumptive victory, as Forbes had while following Frémont, Waud and Taylor sketched a continuity of battles and burnings along the pike that confirmed victories already accomplished.

The Postbellum Valley Road

Artists reenvisioned the Valley Road from 1864 to 1880. As campaigns ended, military histories began. The compilation of official records, atlases, multivolume pictorial field books, campaign chronicles, battle synopses, and wartime reminiscences constituted the first phase of preserving the history of the "war of the rebellion." Heroic memorializing also gave birth to a road of Valley heroes and produced the sole history painting of the pike, *Jackson Entering the City of Winchester* (see fig. 5.14).

Fig. 5.11. (*Top*) James E. Taylor, *Sheridan's Campaign—Signal Defeat of the Rebel General Rosser, the "Saviour of the Valley," by Gen. Torbert—Desperate Effort of Rosser at Mount Jackson to Save His Last Gun.—From a Sketch by Our Special Artist, J. E. Taylor.* (*Bottom*) *Sheridan's Campaign—the Army of the Shenandoah at Woodstock, on the Movement from Harrisonburg, after Devastating the Valley.—From a Sketch by Our Special Artist, J. E. Taylor.* (Reprinted from *Frank Leslie's Illustrated Newspaper* 19, no. 474 [October 29, 1864]: 88–89)

In its imagery, the war waxed nostalgic even before it ended. Alfred Waud depicted Martinsburg in late 1864 as an empty slate for memories, evoked by a few lines of occupying troops, small groups of spectators, a Union flag whipping in the wind, and a lowering sky (see fig. 5.15). In Benson J. Lossing's extended sketch tour of southern locales and battlefields, a peaceful country road guided the viewer through the vicinity of Fishers Hill and Cedar Creek (see fig. 5.16). And in Horace Greeley's *American Conflict,* the 1861 Valley of the Shenandoah scene reappeared, redrawn, like the pike in Lossing's text, as an undisturbed rural landscape (see fig. 5.17). These scenes saw warring completed and the land restored. Fully expressed in the 1880s, the "new" Valley Pike was actually a new take on the old — a simple road in the country, bereft of all traffic save solitary and silent observers, a rustic stone bridge, a shepherd with sheep, and a United States flag.

VALLEY OF THE SHENANDOAH—GENERAL SHERIDAN'S WAGON TRAINS AT EARLY MORNING.—[SKETCHED BY A. R. WAUD.]

Fig. 5.12. (*Top*) Alfred R. Waud, *Sheridan's Army on the March up the Shenandoah Valley —Sketched by A. R. Waud.* (Reprinted from *Harper's Weekly* 8, no. 408 [October 22, 1864]: 681)

Fig. 5.13. (*Bottom*) Alfred R. Waud, *Valley of the Shenandoah—General Sheridan's Wagon Trains at Early Morning.—[Sketched by A. R. Waud.],* 1864. (Reprinted from *Harper's Weekly,* November 12, 1864: 724)

Fig. 5.14. (*Top*) William D. Washington, *Jackson Entering the City of Winchester*, ca. 1862–66. Oil on canvas. (Valentine Richmond History Center)

Fig. 5.15. (*Bottom*) Alfred R. Waud, *Views in and around Martinsburg, Virginia.—Sketched by A. R. Waud.* (Reprinted from *Harper's Weekly*, December 3, 1864: 781)

Fig. 5.16. (*Top*) Benson J. Lossing, *Stone Bridge at Fisher's Hill*, 1866. (Reprinted from *The Pictorial Field Book of the Civil War in the United States of America. By Benson J. Lossing, LL.D. Illustrated by Engravings on Wood, by Lossing and Barritt, from Sketches by the Author and Others*, vol. 3 [Hartford: T. Belknap, 1874]: 373; courtesy of the Western Reserve Historical Society, Cleveland, Ohio)

Fig. 5.17. (*Bottom*) Harry Fenn, *View in the Shenandoah Valley*. (Reprinted from Horace Greeley, *The American Conflict: A History of the Great Rebellion in the United States of America, 1860–'64: Its Causes, Incidents, and Results: Intended to Exhibit Especially Its Moral and Political Phases, with the Drift and Progress of American Opinion Respecting Human Slavery, from 1776 to the Close of the War for the Union*, vol. 1 [Hartford: O. D. Case & Co.; Chicago: Geo. & C. W. Sherwood, 1865]: between pp. 294 and 295)

Where did the Valley Road lead in the 1880s and 1890s? Pictured and photographed, it acquired new prominence and visibility — a well-marked trail replete with heroes, the ruins of combat, and the milestones of postwar progress. It marked the route of Jackson's victories and the setting for the intensely poeticized ride of Philip Sheridan. Sheridan's veterans transformed this historic road into a sacred site when they visited and photographed it in the fall of 1883 and 1885. The most dramatic of these images were the imagined ones: limned, engraved, etched, and lithographed to draw out the emotive resonance of cliffhanging tales of heroism, camaraderie, and "saving-the-day" adventure. The most informative, redolent, and malleable, however, were the actual ones — the photographs for and about veteran reunions in the Valley (see fig. 5.18). Haunting, vacant memories shrouded the photographed road and its enfolding battlefields.

Fig. 5.18. Henry F. Warren, *Where Sheridan Met the Retreat*, 1883. Cabinet card, War Views. From Points Selected by "Carleton" (C. C. Coffin, Esq.) and Gen. Neafie. (Massachusetts MOLLUS Photo Collection, U.S. Army Military History Institute, Carlisle Barracks, Pa.)

Our tour ends in 1901 in the country of Sheridan's ride. By the 1890s, the Union commander's dramatic dash from Winchester to Cedar Creek, where he rallied his troops to "pluck glory from calamity," would define his legacy in American Civil War memory.[7] The bathos of Thomas Buchanan Read's 1864 poem "Sheridan's Ride" and the 1870 painting of the same name had been even more inflated by a host of heroic dramatizations in music and art as well as by innumerable recitations, reenactments, and even circus shows (see fig. 5.19). The Valley Pike took center stage in Sheridan aide General George A. Forsyth's 1897 *Harper's Monthly* article, illustrated by R. F. Zogbaum, "Sheridan's Ride" (see fig. 5.20).

Fig. 5.19. (*Left*) W. H. Shelton, *And there, through the flush of the morning light, a steed as black as the steeds of night was seen to pass, as with eagle flight.* (Reprinted from *Sheridan's Ride, by T. Buchanan Read, Illustrated* [Philadelphia: J. B. Lippincott Company, 1891])

Fig. 5.20. (*Right*) R. F. Zogbaum, *To the Front from Winchester.* (Reprinted from George Forsyth, "Sheridan's Ride," *Harper's New Monthly Magazine* 95, no. 566 [July 1897]: 169)

In 1900–1901, the enterprising Washington photographer-illustrator Frances Benjamin Johnston proposed, recorded, and published a *Ladies' Home Journal* center spread "pictorial" on Sheridan's famous 1864 ride (see fig. 5.21). As repackaged by the *Journal's* editors, "The Country of Sheridan's Ride" centered that fabled and poeticized story in the place where it transpired, the Valley Turnpike between Winchester and Middletown. The piece simultaneously fed readers' appetites for picturesque travel, nostalgia, and the burgeoning field of women's photography. Johnston depicted a country road running between towns, with tollgates, mills, historic structures, houses, churches, and taverns. Her photographs showed the Valley Road as Valley residents in 1900 saw and experienced it. What is more, Johnston and the *Journal* effectively packaged the Valley, Sheridan, and Civil War memory into a spectacle staged to evoke an "Old Virginia"

Fig. 5.21.
Frances Benjamin
Johnston, *Where
Sheridan Took to
the Fields a Second
Time*, 1900. (Re-
printed from "The
Country of Sheri-
dan's Ride," *Ladies'
Home Journal* 18,
no. 8 [July 1901]: 17)

setting. Her photographs announced and presaged postcards, coffee-table books, and regional histories. Reimagined and reimaged at the dawn of the automobile age, the pastoral Valley Pike would leave an enduring legacy.

Notes

1. Porte Crayon [David Hunter Strother], *The Adventures of Porte Crayon and His Cousins* in *Virginia Illustrated* (1857; New York: Harper and Brothers, 1871), 72–73.

2. For secondary source background on the Valley Pike, see Roger U. Delauter Jr., *Winchester in the Civil War*, 2nd ed. (Lynchburg, Va.: H. E. Howard, 1992), 2; Gary L. Ecelbarger, *"We Are in for It!": The First Battle of Kernstown* (Shippensburg, Pa.: White Mane Books, 1997), 40; Edward H. Phillips, *The Lower Shenandoah Valley in the Civil War: The Impact of War upon the Civilian Population and upon Civil Institutions* (Lynchburg, Va.: H. E. Howard, 1993), 124–25; Robert G. Tanner, *Stonewall in the Valley: Thomas J. "Stonewall" Jackson's Shenandoah Valley Campaign, Spring 1862* (1976; Mechanicsburg, Pa.: Stackpole Books, 1996), 16–17.

3. T. Harry Williams, *Lincoln and His Generals* (New York: Vintage Books, 1952), 5; *Virginia in Maps: Four Centuries of Settlement, Growth, and Development*, ed. Richard W. Stephenson and Marianne M. McKee (Richmond, Va.: Library of Virginia, 2000), 189; William J. Miller, *Mapping for Stonewall: The Civil War Service of Jed Hotchkiss* (Washington, D.C.: Elliott and Clark, 1993), 53–54.

4. Jedediah Hotchkiss, *Make Me a Map of the Valley: The Civil War Journal of Stonewall Jackson's Topographer*, ed. Archie P. McDonald (Dallas: Southern Methodist University Press, 1973), 10; Miller, *Mapping for Stonewall*, 52.

5. James K. Bryant II and Geraldine W. Kiefer, "Strategy and Sublimity: Mapping and Articulating the Valley Pike in the Civil War, 1861–1865," paper presented

at the "The Valley Road of Virginia: History and Landscape, 1700–2000" conference, June 4–5, 2004, Shenandoah University, Winchester, Va.

6. David Hunter Strother, *A Virginia Yankee in the Civil War: The Diaries of David Hunter Strother,* ed. Cecil D. Eby Jr. (1961; Chapel Hill: University of North Carolina Press, 1989), 232; John L. Heatwole, *The Burning: Sheridan in the Shenandoah Valley* (Charlottesville, Va.: Rockbridge, 1998), 7, 12–14, 89–94.

7. Herbert E. Hill, "Campaign in the Shenandoah Valley, 1864: A Paper Read before the Eighth Vermont Volunteers and First Vermont Cavalry, at their Annual Reunion, in Montpelier, Vermont, November 2, 1886" (Boston: Executive Committee, 1886), 11, as quoted in Jonathan A. Noyalas, "'Regarded As a Species of Apocalypse': Sheridan's Ride in War & Memory," paper presented at the 5th Annual Shenandoah Valley Civil War Conference & Tour, Civil War Education Association, Winchester, Va., May 18, 2007, 7.

The Best Thoroughfare in the South

KENNETH W. KELLER

We do not believe its equal, considering its length, can be found elsewhere in the United States.
—*Staunton Daily News,* September 23, 1914

After American independence, the procession of wagons, travelers, and livestock along the Valley Road not only increased, but also made new demands on the Valley's environment. Virginians converted the path that had been a skein of trails, privately initiated, sporadically maintained, not engineered, and limited in extent into an artery intended to produce profit, expand interregional transport, link distant markets, carry heavier freight, and attract ever greater traffic to the Valley. The evolution of a wagon road into a great artery to distant cities was part of a sweeping change that took place between the American Revolution and the Civil War, a transformation that launched the transition to modern capitalism. This change brought with it not only access to distant customers, new forms of financial organization, technological innovation, new settlements, new uses of land, labor, and capital, and entrepreneurship, but also significant shifts in human behavior, as people paid less heed to traditional moral and religious restraints, family ties, customs, personal relationships and feelings, and more attention to prices and markets.[1] Road building was an integral part of this intensified search for profit. Through the nineteenth century, as road promoters attempted to satisfy new demands of this shift to a freer capitalism, the state's road development enterprise brought the era of building turnpikes, or toll roads, and the most advanced of these highways was the Valley Turnpike.[2] Toll road enthusiasts changed the road's nature and its material surroundings, and the road took on new significance as a political issue, a modifier of human behavior, and a romantic symbol of a lost past. In each of its new roles, the drive for profit transformed the road, its surroundings, and the people who used it. Yet even as it was put into the service of private capitalistic enterprise, its dependence on public support and administration grew, and eventually the drive for profit even undermined the turnpikes.[3]

Before the turnpike and toll road craze swelled in the 1820s, Virginians began early experiments with a more substantial transportation system. Initial experiments centered on the Tidewater, the seat of politically powerful men who controlled state government. It was their desire to build river improvements westward, up the James and the Potomac rivers, and to gain canal access into the Great Dismal Swamp. These efforts began in the late 1780s. When Jeffersonian Democrats came into power in Richmond, and in the national government after 1801, they adhered to a political creed that insisted that such projects should stem from private initiative, and that the letter of the United States Constitution forbade federal assistance to such projects unless these works were directly connected with a federal responsibility, such as delivering the mail. Before the War of 1812, however much they might acknowledge the need for transportation improvements, few Jeffersonians could justify them constitutionally, and people in the Virginia Tidewater saw little value in western internal improvements that would drain capital and population from the east.

The Valley Road as a Toll Road

Immediately after the War of 1812, these supporters of minimal government reappraised their views when the United States began to experience a period of energetic transportation construction that historians call the "transportation revolution." Jeffersonian Democratic governor Wilson Cary Nicholas proposed that the Commonwealth launch a program of funding privately sponsored transportation developments, called "internal improvements," to keep trade from draining to other states and to prevent the stagnation of Virginia's economy. The result of Governor Nicholas's proposal was a bill to create a state Internal Improvements Fund, which he signed into law in 1816. This measure instituted a system of what the scholars Carter Goodrich and John Lauritz Larson called "mixed enterprise" in Virginia, in which the Commonwealth financed a proportion of the construction expenses of a company that had received the legislature's approval for starting some project to build a road, a bridge, or a railroad. Virginia at first financed two-fifths of the expenses of such developments, and later, in the case of most improvements, three-fifths of the cost. In addition, the Commonwealth was to attempt to oversee the affairs of most transportation improvement companies through a state agency created in 1816, the Board of Public Works, to which improvement companies had to report.[4] The Commonwealth appointed a portion of the directors of any such company in proportion to the amount of the company's capital the Commonwealth had supplied. It was the Board of Public Works that would oversee all the major Virginia turnpikes, including the Valley Turnpike.

Within less than a year of board's creation, Virginia also enacted a statute for the general regulation of turnpikes. The new law stipulated how the Valley Turnpike and other toll roads were to take shape. According to its provisions, persons interested in building a toll road could seek incorporation after investors bought a sufficient number of shares in the project. Once investors raised sufficient capital, they were authorized to make dramatic alterations in the land, by clearing and opening a road where none existed, or by improving an existing track. The law further enabled turnpike promoters to take lands along the path, and directed that they could quarry, dig stone and gravel, cut timber, move earth or remove part of any adjacent fence or building. Road builders could even remove dwellings, yards, and gardens, providing that equitable compensation was given landowners. Not a traditional zigzag path or track, the new road was to be sixty feet wide, with a central eighteen-foot strip paved with crushed rock and with parallel earthen "summer roads" on either side, each of eighteen feet. The summer roads were to be cleared of all stumps, roots, rocks, stones, mud holes and ruts, and the travel of wagons of various sizes was limited according to their weight and the season of the year in which the travel took place. The statute set standards for the roads' surfaces, grading, and width, established wagon weight limits, regulated wheel width, and provided a method by which turnpike users who had complaints about its administration could seek redress. Turnpike companies could erect scales along the road to check the wagon weight, because a wagon's load determined the times at which it could use the road, the width of the wheels to be used, and the tolls to be paid. The law set toll rates for various kinds of livestock and vehicles, and allowed turnpike companies to erect tollgates every five miles to collect the tolls. In addition, the law provided penalties for toll evasion and the failure of a turnpike company to maintain the road adequately. Such landscape alterations represented change for the eighteenth-century road.

The passage of a general turnpike law soon led to the first specific proposal for an improved western road from the Potomac to the Tennessee line that would comply with the specifications for construction in the general turnpike law. One of the earliest and most well-built sections of this route became the Valley Turnpike. Previous roads in the Valley linked settlement with settlement, meandering from village to village, without much effort to avoid crooked routes. In 1816, the new interest in transportation improvements led the Virginia House of Delegates to authorize the first effort to build a straightened roadway designed with professional engineering advice and constructed roughly midway between the first ridge of the Appalachians and the Blue Ridge Mountains. A straightened road would ease the transport of bulky freight and more passengers over longer distances from the Potomac to the Roanoke Valley, thus eventually reducing transportation costs and yielding new profits for producers and shippers. This roadway, running through the geographic center of ante-bellum Virginia near Staunton, would be the spine of central Virginia and its economy until the secession of West Virginia.

Since the Virginia approach to building roadways depended upon the initiative of local groups of investors, and not a comprehensive state plan imposed from Richmond, the method by which the roads west of the Blue Ridge were built led to discontinuous efforts to build parts of a road sys-tem, not a continuous road that ran from one end of the state to the other. As booster groups from one town or county envisioned profits for their re-gion, work would begin there. Not until different promoters at some other trade center scores of miles away got similar inspiration, perhaps decades later, would the parts of the road system constructed earlier be joined with other links. Because of this helter-skelter approach to road building, the path of the old Valley Road from the Potomac to the Tennessee line was built in sections at various times. And setbacks in construction and finance led to the frequent project collapse and reorganization. Valley promoters who wanted to build a route from the Potomac to Martinsburg received permission to do so in 1833–34, but had to apply again in 1848–49 for re-incorporation. The road segment from Martinsburg to Winchester got a tardy reactivation of its charter when the reincorporation of the Potomac-Martinsburg route occurred. For the ninety-two miles from Winchester to Staunton along the Valley Turnpike, the legislature gave its permission to build a road at various times beginning in 1816, but not until the 1840s did any completed road appear. It became the best long-distance paved road in Virginia, and, according to some advocates such as Harry F. Byrd, "the best thoroughfare in the South."[5] Toll road promoters south of Staunton were even slower to construct their links to southwestern Virginia. The Junction Valley Turnpike, which ran from Staunton through Lexington to the James and Kanawha Canal at Buchanan, did not secure incorporation until 1849, yet its investors had to amend their charter twice in the 1850s to support construction. The state took it over in 1857. This turnpike was then to connect with the Southwestern Turnpike, incorporated at least four times between 1816 and 1846, which was supposed to run for 175¼ miles from Buchanan to the Tennessee line. Its supporters' plans were

Fig. 6.1. The U.S. 11 bridge across the Potomac River links Williamsport, Maryland, to West Virginia. Williamsport, a key port on the Chesapeake and Ohio Canal, is often regarded as the northern gateway to the Shenandoah Valley. In 1861, Union Army troops, at the direction of General Abner Doubleday, built a cannon breastwork atop Battery Hill, also known as Doubleday Hill, overlooking the river. A flagpole and pedestal-mounted cannon commemorate the site. (Mark Hochstedler 2000)

never realized. Thus, the construction of a long-distance toll road from Maryland to Tennessee was serendipitous at best.[6]

The route from the Potomac to the Tennessee line was not to be the only western route. Intersecting with it were dozens of other ambitious toll roads, some stretching to Parkersburg on the Ohio, Charleston on the Kanawha, and the Big Sandy River on the Kentucky border. From each of these branches, promoters planned other routes to smaller western Virginia communities. Additional roads stretched east from the Valley to the Piedmont and to eastern Virginia's towns. Most of the Commonwealth's turnpikes were western roads because ample navigable rivers drained the Tidewater. By 1856, the state held stock in only five turnpikes in the Tidewater, thirteen in the Piedmont, forty-two in the Valley of Virginia, and fifty-four west of the Alleghenies.[7] Most remained paper roads, for few were ever completed. The most striking exception to this failure was the Valley Turnpike.

Profits and the Turnpikes

Unlike the roads that crossed the Alleghenies heading for the Ohio Valley trade, the Valley Turnpike aimed to connect the Shenandoah Valley's economy with seaports north of the Potomac. Valley Pike developers saw it as a way of creating an economy somewhat independent of Richmond, with Valley towns interconnected with each other on a roadway that would bring merchandise to their stores from Philadelphia or Baltimore, not from Richmond. Indeed, once the pike opened, wagons brought finished goods from Baltimore, New York, and Philadelphia to storekeepers' shelves as far south as its southern point at Staunton. Likewise, the social intercourse the highway was to produce was within the Valley and with Maryland and Pennsylvania. The road was to be the artery of commerce of the Valley towns: it ran through the towns, not around them.

Just as the pike was to bring merchandise from outside the Commonwealth to the Valley, it was also to carry cash crops, especially milled flour, to Baltimore, Philadelphia, or the Potomac towns of Georgetown and, to a lesser extent, to fading Alexandria. From these coastal centers, merchants could sell throughout the Western Hemisphere as well as in northern cities, so the Valley Road would link its communities to an even larger area well beyond the mid-Atlantic region. As one petition from about 1838 for state support for a Valley Turnpike put it, "The Valley seems to be designed as the great thoroughfare between the west and the southwest to the northern cities."[8] When the Valley Turnpike Company initially made its stock available to the public, people in the four Virginia counties through which it ran bought most of the shares, but a substantial number of purchasers were from Baltimore. Stockholder lists that identified Valley Pike investor locations contain no listings for any Virginia city except the towns of the turnpike counties.[9] The connections north with Baltimore did not diminish after the Civil War; instead, Baltimore's grasp on Valley commerce only tightened.

With an accountant's eye for costs and profits, the pike's promoters understood the impact of transportation costs on whether an independent farmer-proprietor made a profit. No farmer could make a profit if the cost of transporting a product equaled its value at the market. The faster a product could get to market, the larger the profits became. As wagon capacity increased, so did transportation costs. The more horses or mules required to pull a wagon, the more costly it became to transport goods. People in the freighting business had to search for an economical way of carrying large cargoes to distant markets. Valley people conjectured about the relative costs and advantages of canals versus turnpikes or river navigation or railroads in driving down the cost of high-volume shipments of a wide range of consumer products. How could transportation be made faster? How could the expense of feeding horses and maintaining a wagon and its driver be minimized? What impact would tolls charged by a turnpike have on a farmer's success? Would the freight rates charged by a railroad or a canal leave the farmer with more or less profit? If a road was blocked by ice or snow, or too muddy for passage, what could be improved to open it up to get the goods to market when the price was right? The calculating Valley entrepreneurs attempted to figure out the costs of transportation to Baltimore by the Chesapeake and Ohio Canal or by the Baltimore and Ohio Railroad, or the expense of sending the same cargo over the Blue Ridge to a destination at Scottsville on the James, where it would be transported to Richmond by canal. They thought of a market network of interconnected merchants, brokers, commission agents, lenders, insurers, and attorneys, stretching throughout a great regional market and then reaching for the world. The shipment of commercial products, not passenger traffic, was so central to early pike developers' concerns that they chose as their emblem a sheaf of wheat surrounded by the words "Valley Turnpike Company."[10]

A financial panic after 1819 slowed down transportation projects, but as prosperity returned in the 1820s, petitions came to the General Assembly from Valley communities for the incorporation of turnpike companies. In the 1820s, as proposals for a national road system floundered in Congress because advocates of states' rights maintained such projects were unconstitutional, Virginians appealed to the General Assembly for aid. In 1828, the legislature incorporated a turnpike company to build a road between Winchester and Stony Creek, south of Woodstock. Claudius Crozet undertook a survey of the potential route in 1831, but capital was insufficient to build the road, so the project died. Shenandoah Valley petitioners appealed for a free road from Winchester to Staunton in 1830, but nothing was done. In 1833, persistent Valley residents held a road convention in Woodstock to demand a road from Staunton to Winchester, and in the same year, the Chesapeake and Ohio Canal was opened from Georgetown to Harpers Ferry. It could provide an easy way for getting flour from the northern part of the Valley to eastern markets. Responding to requests for a better roadway in the Valley, in 1834 the legislature revived the 1828 law by incorporating a turnpike company to build a road from Winchester to Harrisonburg. Because of the financial panic of 1837 and the building of other transportation improvements that drained away capital, road promoters sought and got extensions of the deadline by which the road was to have been completed. Not until 1837 did the law specify that the Valley Turnpike would run to its southern terminus at Staunton. Another statute passed the Virginia General Assembly to authorize the building of a turnpike from Harrisonburg to Staunton, thereby extending the Harrisonburg-Winchester road to Staunton.[11]

The surge of migrants to the new states of Ohio and Indiana in the trans-Appalachian West led Virginians to make sure the new roadway would accommodate a large volume of traffic carrying southern products to the Potomac and eastern seaports. Western Virginians feared that these new western wheat-growing states would outstrip cereal grain production in the Old Dominion, so more petitions went to the General Assembly, this time requesting a road to be paved with crushed stone by the macadamization process. This process, developed by the Scotsman John Loudon McAdam in England in 1816, involved covering newly constructed roads with broken rocks no larger than 2½ inches in diameter. Subsequent wagon traffic would compact the rocks, known as "road metal," to provide a smoother ride for travelers, and the road's surface would resist developing ruts and mud holes. McAdam's ideas caught on in America, and on March 24, 1838, the General Assembly passed a statute that joined the two Valley turnpikes and authorized the creation of a macadamized pike between Staunton and Winchester.[12] The Valley Turnpike was born.

According to Bushrod Taylor, the Valley Turnpike Company's first president, capital was slow to come in, especially from Rockingham and Augusta counties, where potential investors believed that the road might not be completed to the upper Valley, so its construction would have benefited Winchester without helping Staunton and Harrisonburg at all. Consequently, upper Valley shareholders would have been left with an investment that did not help their home counties.[13] Construction slowed because of financial depression, but by 1841 the Valley Turnpike was complete, including the erection of fourteen tollgates, limited to one every five miles, with the number increased to fifteen in 1848, and finally to nineteen in 1912. Nine tollgates belonged to the company, but the remainder were privately owned, occasionally administered by women collectors. Bridges had yet to be constructed over most streams, and much leveling had to be done, but work was under way and would soon be finished.

Modifying the Natural Environment

The construction of the Valley Turnpike and other Valley toll roads led to considerable modification of the natural landscape features. The Valley Turnpike had to be built on a low gradient, following the regional slope with the highest elevations in the southwest to the lowest in the northeast. The Valley's rolling terrain required that the Valley Pike had to be graded to comply with proper engineering standards. Frequent heavy rains washed

out wooden bridges, to the pike's investors' dismay. The macadamization process required rock that had to be quarried from the lands adjacent to the road, so the road builders dug quarries along the route, thus further altering the landscape through which the road passed. The many long ridges of hard, unglaciated limestone that protruded from the Valley surface provided a stout foundation for road construction, thereby allowing the legislature to exempt the turnpike builders from requirements that a summer road be constructed parallel to the main roadway. This limestone did not crumble readily, but repeated traffic produced considerable dust. According to some observers, limestone dust made the road look like a white cord running over the hills into the distance. The road builders also used the Valley's limestone to line ditches and culverts through which water could be drained. Unfortunately for the livestock growers, the hard pike surface was much better suited for iron-rimmed wagon and carriage wheels than for the hooves of driven cattle. To avoid cattle macerating their hooves on the turnpike surface, frequently herdsmen used the unsurfaced Middle Road, sometimes known as the "Ox Road," which often paralleled the pike to the west. Alternatively, they might drove herds along the Back Road, which ran along the eastern slope of the Appalachians along the base of North Mountain.[14]

Fig. 6.2. A spring-fed reproduction horse-watering trough stands beside U.S. 11 at Willow Spout, former site of a turnpike tollgate. (Scott Jost 2000)

Weather was the most destructive force in ruining the surface of nineteenth-century roads, whether they were earthen or paved with macadamized limestone rock. Although the paved surface of a macadamized road provided a firmer base than earthen surfaces, the snow, thick ice, and occasionally heavy rains in the Valley played havoc with the Valley Turnpike surface and caused the company that built it to invest many hours and much money in keeping the road in good repair. Road builders also cut much timber in the Valley to construct the numerous bridges the road required, many of which were covered (see fig. 6.3). Local use of wood for building material, fuel, and fencing meant that long stretches of the pike were unshaded and uncomfortable in the summer heat.

The road builders also molded the environment through requirements for grading, widening, and surfacing. They discovered soon after construction began that a "much larger proportion [of stone] on the whole line has had to be blasted"; broken stones were not abundant enough to allow workers to pick them from the fields and roadsides, as some engineers had predicted could be done.[15] In some places, limestone protruded where the roadbed might go, and in other areas, the stone confined the best alignment to narrow passages. The statute's requirement that the road be forty feet wide simply could not be followed where the path crossed some waterways such as Narrow Passage Creek between Woodstock and Edinburg. There was simply too much rock to be removed by blasting, so in some places the Valley Turnpike narrowed to twenty feet in width, thus making it impossible for two-lane traffic to go in opposite directions at the same point on the road. As a result, travelers reported that, although the pike was "one of the smoothest roads of the kind they ever saw," they objected because of its "want of width."[16]

In addition to the company's construction problems, there were other difficulties, more political in nature, about the way the road builders organized space. Different interests wanted different kinds of roadways. Valley newspapers noted that the original Virginia roads merely went from farm to farm, or along property lines or fences, or followed "pig trails" without any effort to make them straight or to speed travel to distant destinations. State engineer Claudius Crozet wanted roads that could curve around the many hillocks in the Valley or ascend or descend the terrain gradually. Valley farmers wanted straight roads that cut through elevations rather than going around them. Cultivators also wanted straight roads because the straight fencing built along them was less expensive and less likely to harbor weeds. Merchants and farmers wanted straight, shortest-distance roads because they could get their goods to market faster over them, and if

Fig. 6.3. The covered bridge over the North Fork of the Shenandoah River at Meems Bottom, west of U.S. 11 north of Harrisonburg. (Keesha Dickel 2000)

that meant going over obstacles rather than around them, road users would not complain. The lower the road's gradient, the more weight the wagon could carry. The statute that created the turnpike company required it to build a road with a grade of no greater than 3½ degrees. Engineers knew that steep grades hurt horses and led to surface erosion when water poured down the road. Nevertheless, company shareholders wanted steep roads. As a result, a true 3½-degree grade was often not achieved in the building of the pike, in spite of the law. In the stretch between New Market and Middletown, which contained some of the road's straightest stretches, the grade was about 4 degrees; a segment in Rockingham County was 5¾ degrees.[17] Whichever professional engineering standard the engineers applied, they forced a standardized template upon the environment.

It was also essential that the Valley Pike be adequately drained and that strong bridges be constructed, for flowing or standing water and ice were more destructive to the road than wear from traffic and caused more headaches as the workers altered the landscape. Engineers insisted that roads should not be used as drains but that cross drains perpendicular to the direction of travel be constructed in depressed spots. Nevertheless, some farmers insisted on draining standing water onto the roads. On the turnpike itself, water could be diverted to the side to ditches or onto the fields of neighboring farmlands. Farmers, of course, were not happy to see water from the roads cascading into cultivated fields, and at least one sued the company for damages to her wheat, corn, and barley from road runoff. The faster wagons or stagecoaches, and later automobiles, moved on the pike, the greater the jolt when the vehicle wheels hit a cross drain. Since the cross drains could break the automobile springs, after the flivver arrived on the pike, the turnpike company, at considerable expense, had cross drains replaced with underground culverts lined with drain tile. To enhance drainage, pike builders crowned the surface so that the center was slightly elevated above the road's shoulders, allowing water to run off the surface into the side ditches. The pike was a not merely a road, but a "high" way, whose surface was elevated above the surrounding terrain to permit water to flow away from the roadbed. But crowning was dangerous for fast-moving vehicles, which could tip to the side and overturn.[18]

In addition, Virginia roads were famous for lacking bridges and for relying on fords across streams. The Valley Turnpike Company made numerous efforts to build bridges to replace the fords, but the drive to be economical frequently led to trouble. Several bridges on the pike were covered, including one 208-foot-long bridge over the North River at Mount Crawford; the company asserted that the Mount Crawford bridge was longer than any other in the state except those that crossed the James at Richmond. The company at first tried to bridge streams with wooden bridges made of latticework construction with decks that were too wide for the supports beneath, so these bridges tended to sag unsafely under the weight of heavily laden wagons. When spring freshets and floods poured down the streams, the bridges were occasionally moved away from the roadbed or even collapsed entirely when the suspension trusses could not stand the strain. What the floods did not destroy, both Union and Confederate armies did during the Civil War, when both sides burned the turnpike bridges. The company eventually replaced some of its wooden bridges with ones made of stone, with solid foundations based on piers in the streambed, but stone piers proved sometimes too expensive to build because of unstable ground in the river below. During the war, thousands of troops marched and support wagons and artillery further degraded the road surface. Destructive floods in the 1840s and 1870s knocked wooden bridges off their piers or caused them to buckle. Some wooden bridges wobbled ominously when fast-moving carriages or even running pedestrians crossed them. The company attempted to protect the structures with wainscoting in 1866, yet wooden bridges still had to be repaired so often that by 1918 all of them were replaced with steel and concrete structures.[19]

Despite the many costs and challenges involved in building the pike, when it was finished, Valley farmers and merchants saw it as a needed innovation that connected them to distant markets like Baltimore. Few criticized the pike as a solution to the problem of reaching northern market outlets for the Valley's staples. The turnpike company sold its stock to Valley farmers, and the surviving lists of stockholders from the 1840s and 1850s show that farmers as well as townspeople in the Valley bought stock in the popular Valley Turnpike Company albeit in small amounts. Turnpike company leaders asserted that the value of lands adjacent to the pike would be higher than lands distant from it. Hard times in the wheat market could adversely affect the company's profits. The company reported in antebellum times that traffic and revenue on the pike rose and declined in response to rising and falling prices in commercial markets.[20] Wheat farmers of the 1840s and 1850s continued to use the pike to ship flour. In the years before the Civil War, relatively high wheat prices made Valley Pike's tolls affordable, at least until the Valley had a railroad that stretched from Winchester to Staunton in 1874. After 1860 and the burning of the Valley in the Civil War, farmers faced greater difficulties, and criticism of the company grew. The road surface around Winchester sustained considerable damage, as contending armies fought more than a dozen major battles on or near the pike in that town's vicinity, and many other smaller actions took place, all of which tore up the road's surface. Turnpike company leaders argued that the cost of labor and supplies had risen ten to forty times what they had been before the war, so the company needed permission to increase tolls at least eightfold. The company had purchased twenty thousand dollars in Confederate bonds during the war; they were all worthless at war's end. Moreover, the financially strapped Confederate government paid only one-fourth the tolls the company was entitled to collect. The legislature did not agree with company requests to double tolls; instead, counterpressures developed to decrease them.

After the Civil War, although wheat production began to increase dramatically throughout the nation, prices fell, so that the profit margins of wheat farmers shrank. When railroads opened in 1874 leading to the Potomac from Staunton, farmers used them to ship their wheat to market, and the company's pike revenue dropped further. New York and Philadelphia corporations controlled Valley railroads. But because the railways lacked sufficient traffic, they did not receive adequate attention from their absentee owners. The Valley Railroad never had enough rolling stock to serve the Valley producers, and railroad schedules and connections were awkward and inconvenient.[21] By the 1880s, the railroads began to receive criticism from Valley wheat producers as an inefficient, monopolistic way of getting produce to the city. Especially harsh on the railways were the Readjusters, a party of antimonopolistic political insurgents who opposed great corporations and thralldom to northern investors and advocated the repudiation, or "readjustment," of one-third of Virginia's debt, most of which was owed to non-Virginians; these agrarian protestors captured the state general assembly and the governorship between 1879 and 1881. The Valley Pike was not yet the target of criticism, though it was to become so eventually.

Valley Toll Road Critics

In the 1870s, a national protest movement against monopolies, corporations, and deflation swept rural America. Valley agrarian leaders such as Senator H. H. Riddleberger of Woodstock, a Readjuster, began to attack monopolies and urged Virginia to regulate corporations, especially railroads. Inevitably such antimonopolists began to attack the turnpike company monopoly. During the financial depression of the 1870s, pike critics protested its oppressive tolls. One Augusta County critic, "North River," urged readers of the *Staunton Spectator* to boycott paying tolls that he found to be an "unrighteous imposition."[22] Divisions among Virginia's Democrats during the era of the Readjusters heightened political party competition, so the turnpike board became a political issue between the contending factions. One Harrisonburg politician tried in 1882 to get the governor to remove Michael Martz as a director because he was allegedly "a bourbon [conservative Democrat] of the most virulent type."[23] The Democratic Party attempted to purge the turnpike board of directors in 1887, when the new company president, the Harrisonburg attorney B. G. Patterson, tried to remove two directors who had Readjuster sympathies. Patterson was especially hostile to the company superintendent, Joseph Andrews, whom Patterson called "a vile Republican" and accused him of attempting to make the turnpike a political machine by using its supply purchasing power to reward the Democrats' foes.[24] On other occasions, influential politicians sought to have directors removed from the board if their politics were deemed questionable. Rivalries between county of-ficials of one party and state officials of another also interfered with the turnpike's smooth operation. In 1902, the Republican majority on the Board of Supervisors of Rockingham County petitioned the General As-sembly to receive control of the turnpike in Rockingham County so that they might take it out of Democratic hands. Their plea was not success-ful, but it illustrated how the company could become the victim of local political struggles.[25]

The national campaign against economic consolidation continued until the 1920s. In 1892, some of the angry farmers of the lower Valley began to direct their criticism at the once popular pike and call it a monopoly that charged exorbitant tolls. One of them complained that farmers had to haul lumber "by circuitous country roads" that doubled the distance to the local market to avoid Valley Turnpike tolls, which amounted to one-fourth the wood's value. "This state of affairs," wrote C. W. Peery to his state representative, "exists all along the line from Winchester to Staun-ton." He concluded: "This is the day of resistance to monopolies and trusts and this much favored and long endured monopoly should not be slighted. It is the boss extortioner of the state and its high tariff ideas would bring a blush to the 'tin plate' cheek of [tariff] 'Protection' McKinley or even har-row the conscience of a billion-dollar congressman."[26] Pressure built for a law that would force the company to lower the tolls it charged, and in 1898, the General Assembly responded favorably. Of course, people had always attempted to avoid paying tolls. Valley farmers continued to try to evade tolls by using side roads, called "shunpikes," to get their cattle or lumber to market, so the company installed more tollgates to make evasion difficult, as it did in 1869 near Middletown.[27] Businessmen in growing towns such as Harrisonburg and New Market believed that tollgates drove business away from stores in the center of town. Nevertheless, in 1910 the Valley Turnpike Company secured the Commonwealth's permission to build four additional tollgates close to the town limits of Edinburg, Strasburg, New Market, and Woodstock, even though previously the pike company was not allowed to build tollgates closer than every five miles from each other. The building of the new tollgates led to a storm of criticism and a drive to make the pike free of tolls. The legislature did not immediately abolish the tollgates, but a lawsuit in 1912 forced the company to charge tolls proportionate to miles traveled, rather than according to the kind of vehicle used.[28] Undoubtedly making the Valley Turnpike an object of partisan contention distracted its directors and stymied the efficient administration of the road. In the bitter political culture of both the late nineteenth-century state and nation, it was inevitable that the turnpike's political significance intensified.

In addition to complaining about tolls, communities along the pike objected to its general condition and state of repair. Farmers needed to get their crops to market in a timely fashion, but roads in bad shape meant delay. The general turnpike law of 1817 decreed that, if the people who used a turnpike complained to the local county court about the roadbed's condition, the county court could appoint viewers to survey the turnpike. If a toll road was in bad condition, the viewers were to report it to the county court, which could order that tolls be suspended until its owners made the repairs. If a turnpike's owners did not make the necessary repairs in eighteen months, the pike would be forfeited to the state. Generally, the Valley Turnpike Company kept the pike in excellent shape and was able to avoid the suspension of tolls, but the shippers' complaints in Augusta, Shenandoah, and Rockingham counties caused the courts to appoint viewers to examine the pike. In 1912, the Rockingham circuit court concluded that many sections of the pike were unfit for travel. Especially in the pike's early days, the road's surface became rougher the farther one moved away from the Valley's principal market at Winchester, where there was more traffic on the road to wear down the surface. The spread of heavy steam-powered threshing equipment after the Civil War also played havoc with the surface and with unstable wooden bridges, so in 1886 the legislature enacted a law setting tolls for steam-powered vehicles.[29]

Fencing the pike was an aggravation for Valley farmers along it. Using the pike to herd cattle was at times troublesome to these farmers, who had to maintain expensive fences to keep cattle from straying into their fields.[30] A host of blacksmith shops, saddleries, tanneries, as well as the prosperity of the growers of oats and hay, depended on the thriving trade in livestock. Until the advent of the Valley Railroad, cattle drovers had to herd the cattle along the pike, or else use the parallel side roads, especially if they wanted to avoid the tolls. Initially there was ample material in the Valley to build inexpensive fencing: limestone was abundant, and there were forests nearby that could be used for fence posts or rail fences, at least until the extensive cultivation of the Valley removed most of the trees near the pike. Since its earliest days, Virginia had practiced the custom of having an open range, where stock roamed freely and property owners fenced their lots to protect gardens, fields, orchards, and homesteads. By the 1850s, however, pressure began to mount in the Valley for laws requiring the fencing of cattle, not crops.[31] With the coming of expensive barbed wire and woven wire fencing in the 1870s, farmers had to depend on outside suppliers to keep their fences in good repair, thus adding to the cost of operations. In 1874, the Virginia General Assembly passed a fence law to protect fences from being taken down. Photographs of the pike taken in the late nineteenth and early twentieth centuries suggest that most of the pike was fenced, so undoubtedly living adjacent to the pike created additional expenses for farmers.[32] Poorer agriculturalists might not have been able to afford extensive fences. If the turnpike company made repairs, lowered the grade, or straightened the road's course near a farmer's fence, it had to compensate the farmer, but the inconvenience could be costly. For prospering farmers, a tidily fenced farm was a sign of good agricultural practice, but fence maintenance and occasional replacement with woven wire or barbed wire after the 1870s cut into profits in times of falling farm prices. Fencing the pike remained a serious economic concern that also altered the Valley's landscape.

Communication, Capitalism, and Valley Culture

Once the pike opened, it became an essential channel of communication for information from outside the Valley. In 1843, the Valley first received daily mail delivery from the United States Post Office. By 1896, mail leaving Winchester by stage at 4:30 p.m. would reach Staunton by 10:00 a.m. the next morning. In 1896, twenty-five of the pike's towns, villages, and hamlets had post offices. The pike continued to be a mail route long after the railroad had intercepted most of the towns' commercial traffic. Some post offices could be found in small hamlets like Vaucluse, Mauzy, Pughs Run, Melrose, Burketown, and Lacey Springs. With the advent of the telephone and telegraph in the Valley in the 1870s, the new methods of

Fig. 6.4. On the road to Mauertown, a turnpiker sits astride a perch of limestone and swings a round-headed hammer to break stone into road metal. A farmer approaches with a wagon loaded with lumber. Rock and plank fences on both sides help confine traffic to the toll road. (Frances B. Johnston, photographer; "Shendandoah Valley, Road to Winchester"; contact print of a negative, n.d.; Library of Congress, Washington, D.C., Frances Benjamin Johnston Collection, LC-J698-61141)

communication spread from the towns to rural areas, where farmers on the Valley's isolated farmsteads were eager to have contact with town. By the end of the nineteenth century, telephone companies began to string wires along the pike on telephone poles, which brought more diverse cultural stimuli to the Valley's dispersed rural population but soon became a danger to speeding vehicles.[33]

Travelers through the Valley towns brought new fashions and folkways. Since the eighteenth century, there had been a regular procession of ladies and gentlemen from Baltimore, Washington, D.C., Alexandria, and Philadelphia going to the western Virginia springs. At least ten springs in the Valley were operating by the late nineteenth century, and most of them had resort accommodations. The resort springs published accounts of socially elite personages who visited the waters, and the lists suggest the clientele continued to come from Tidewater towns and cities in the days before the railroad. Richmond seems to be less well represented than cities farther north. Adventuresome foreign artists such as William Henry Bartlett and Edward Beyer came to the Valley to draw picturesque scenes. They sketched attractions such as the springs, Natural Bridge near Lexington, Rockfish Gap between Augusta and Nelson counties, and Weyers Cave in Augusta County, but they overlooked mundane landscapes such as the pike itself. Circuses with exotic animals, and girls on their way to the Valley's numerous female seminaries traveled the Valley by carriage before the coming of the railroad. Occasionally a well-known visitor would travel along the pike. In 1899, President William McKinley visited Harrisonburg; he was the first sitting president to do so, and he, like other famous visitors who made the trip — Andrew Jackson, Henry Clay, John Philip Sousa, Thomas Edison, and John L. Sullivan — often received much adulation and newspaper attention.[34] With disdain newspapers also reported the travels of gypsies, horse thieves, and peddlers on the pike.

In the countryside adjacent to the turnpike, the access to distant markets it provided helped create a prosperous and stable rural social order controlled by local families and centered around the milling of wheat, the dominant source of wealth in the Valley in the turnpike era. There were numerous Valley iron furnaces, forges, harness shops, carriage workshops, inns, distilleries, cooperages, cattle yards, and merchants whose livelihood depended upon the pike for customers, but most important to it in the days before the railroad were the hundreds of mills that operated in the turnpike hinterland. Individual families controlled the mills, often over several generations, and these kin groups became some of the most well-to-do-inhabitants of the countryside. Millers were skilled calculators of profit and loss. They kept books, calculated the cost of capital and labor, used sophisticated arithmetic to measure the volume and weight of milled flour, provided credit, accepted country produce or hauling services when cash was scarce, and clearly understood the impact of transportation costs on profits. Although some mill owners were also slave owners, in the Valley many pietistic Protestant miller families did not own or trade in slaves and relied on family and hired labor to do the work of milling and hauling. Not only did the millers serve their rural neighborhoods in making country wheat available for shipment on the turnpike, but they also dealt in cattle, rented pastureland to drovers, sawed lumber, ground plaster, purchased hides, and sold general merchandise. Once miller families accumulated wealth, sons would enter other professions, invest in internal improvement projects like the turnpike, serve on boards of such improvements, or hold local office. Since mills were so essential to the rural communities, local farmers worked cooperatively with local millers and even allowed parts of their lands to be flooded to construct millponds that would power the mills by supplying falling water. Mill raisings attracted many neighborhood hands because neighbors profited from the convenience a nearby mill provided. The mills became major landmarks on the landscape: they were used as reference points in land survey; the roads that led to them from the main arteries were often named for the mill or family that operated it. There is little evidence that the neighbors of the miller entrepreneurs resented the wealth and business acumen of the millers; the neighbors were likely to have viewed the mills as vital to their own economic survival. This cooperative social order, organized around neighborhoods and established local families, remained central to rural people's lives until the advent of the railroad and the large corporation.

One of the best-documented examples of a successful country mill was that of Siram P. Henkel, who operated the Plains Mill in Rockingham County. Henkel, grandson of the pioneer Lutheran minister Paul Henkel, was a member of a prominent Valley family of German descent. His mill, built in 1848 on the North Fork of the Shenandoah River about a mile from the Valley Turnpike, had close ties to the turnpike from the road's earliest days. Henkel was a stockholder in the Valley Turnpike from the time of its first offerings of stock in 1838.[35] Wagons on the pike brought wrought iron, cast-iron fittings, planks, and timber for beams to construct the mill. Although the Henkel family's connection with the German Lutherans was very strong, when the mill was built, fifty-six neighbors from surrounding farms turned out to help Henkel erect his mill, and the workers who came had surnames of English, Irish, and German backgrounds. Religion and ethnicity meant little when an opportunity to improve the marketing of local grain arose. Wagons on the pike hauled his wheat to Winchester, and then to Baltimore and, if prices were not good, to Philadelphia. Other Valley millers brought their flour to him to be shipped with his cargoes, which also included bacon and butter. He operated a variety of moneymaking enterprises including his own sawmill, a cider press, a cooper shop, a smithy, and a general merchandise store as well. The mill even served as a polling place on election day. To attract wagoners to the mill, he operated a free shanty where they could obtain fodder for their horses; he also supplied straw to nearby cattle yards. The mill was constantly busy, and even on religious holidays like Good Friday and Easter Monday, this staunchly Lutheran miller worked at the mill. Labor came before the liturgical calendar at the Plains Mill. Although Henkel opposed slavery and used only hired labor at the mill, sales came before allegiance: he sold flour to the Union and Confederate armies in the Civil War. Henkel created a small rural manufacturing community that survived well beyond the turnpike years. Plains Mill remained in operation for at least 124 years, and was owned by the Henkel family for four generations.[36]

The Challenge of Rail and Auto

Eventually, the drive for profits that created the pike and motivated farmers along it also brought changes that financially undermined the toll road, especially in new forms of transportation. The first of these transportation changes was the railroad. The first railroad to enter the four turnpike counties was the Winchester and Potomac Railroad, which Winchester promoters completed in 1836. Initially, the Winchester and Potomac attracted traffic to the turnpike, for wagoners coming down the pike could deposit their cargoes at the Winchester depot to have them loaded on the railroad. The Winchester and Potomac traveled only from Winchester to Harpers Ferry on the Potomac, where they could be transferred to the Baltimore and Ohio Railroad, which crossed the Potomac there from the Maryland side of the river. The Winchester and Potomac soon experienced financial difficulties and allowed the track to fall into disrepair. Shippers were reluctant to rely upon the railway because it became unreliable, and the road soon began to emphasize passenger service, which was more profitable than shipping freight. The Manassas Gap Railroad was the next to enter the turnpike counties. It crossed the Blue Ridge from Manassas in 1853 and reached Mount Jackson shortly afterward; until 1868, the Manassas Gap stopped at that point. Even before the Manassas Gap opened its route, the turnpike company directors became wary. They appointed a committee to study its route and sent a petition to the legislature protesting the railroad's route, which they correctly believed would take trade away from the pike and make it merely a local road. The railroad would destroy the livestock droving business as well as "ordinary" and "neighborhood" travel, as the directors asserted in 1854. The Manassas Gap Railroad "irreparably damaged" the turnpike, and company directors unsuccessfully sought an injunction to restrain the railroad from building upon a location so close to the pike. Almost immediately, turnpike company revenue began to fall, as freight that might have been carried to Winchester was diverted to the Manassas Gap. Between 1853 and 1856, the pike's toll revenue fell by fourteen thousand dollars in three years' time.[37] As early as 1855, so many Valley Turnpike directors had investments in the Manassas Gap Railroad that the company could not obtain a quorum for a directors' meeting, since the directors were attending the stockholders' meeting of that railroad and the Orange, Alexandria and Manassas line in Alexandria. The Valley Turnpike Company had to change the time of its annual meeting so as not to meet on the same day as the railroad's gathering. In 1854, the Virginia Central Railroad reached Staunton from Charlottesville, and it, too, produced a short-lived upsurge in traffic from Rockingham and Augusta county shippers, who used the line to send goods to Richmond on the eve of the Civil War, after which it became dilapidated until melded into the Chesapeake and Ohio.[38] The Manassas Gap and the Virginia Central were the only two railways that intruded into the Valley Turnpike's trade territory before the Civil War. By 1865, there was still no line that ran the Valley Pike's entire length from Staunton to Winchester.

After the Civil War, though, a boom of railroad building overtook the South, which now sought to refashion itself as a "New South," hospitable to northern capital and investments in its mines and railroads. The Valley's own Jedediah Hotchkiss, a promoter of New South–style industrial development, noted in 1882 that the South had to look to Baltimore "for its progress." As before the war, Baltimore capitalists, determined to continue seeking access to Valley commerce, attempted to exploit the Valley. They organized the Valley Railroad (VRR), which opened a line from Winchester to Harrisonburg. It was, in fact, an arm of the B&O Railroad. By 1874, the Valley Railroad was extended to Staunton, and for the first time the Valley had a railroad stretching along the entire route of the pike from Winchester to Staunton. A year later, the turnpike company reported to the Board of Public Works that "our tolls have reached their lowest point." In 1883, the Valley Railroad extended its line from Staunton to Lexington. Freight that would once have been taken down the pike in wagons was now loaded aboard the VRR and carried to the B&O, which then took the cargo to eager Baltimore merchants. The Valley Railroad was very close to the Valley Pike roadbed. At one point on the road, a VRR station was only thirty-five feet from the pike. Moreover, in 1874 the Valley Railroad crossed the roadbed of the Valley Turnpike at three points between Winchester and Staunton, so that trains stopped on its tracks occasionally blocked passage on the pike. The company sent a memorial protesting the competition to the state general assembly, but by this time turnpike directors realized that railroad expansion was inevitable.[39] Legislative leaders were beholden to railroad interests, who exerted much influence in the capitol. The best the legislature could do was enact a statute in 1884

Fig. 6.5. A new visitors' center under construction at Mount Jackson, between U.S. 11 and the railroad track. The center's architecture is reminiscent of a railroad depot, rather than a hotel, house, tollgate, or other structure that would have acknowledged the pike. (Scott Jost 2003)

that made it illegal for a railroad to block passage on a turnpike. Other railroads provided further competition to the pike, as they extended their lines to other Virginia cities. Thus, the turnpike became a local road for travelers between Valley towns, and its role as a route for shipping flour to market ended, except when strikes, breakdowns, or railroad bridges interfered. Late nineteenth-century photographs of the pike show a lightly traveled road with only a few freight wagons, bicycles, pedestrians, and people riding on horseback or in carriages. The pike looked vacant.

The turnpike sustained the Valley economy before the Civil War, but after 1865, railroads energized the Valley economy and opened its culture to new influences. The railroads surpassed the turnpike as the Valley's commercial artery and, however imperfect their service, brought substantial change to the daily lives of ordinary people in the towns along the route. Railroads organized excursions to the Philadelphia Centennial Exposition of 1876, presidential inaugurations, Mount Vernon, Baltimore, and the Tidewater sights of Point Comfort and Fortress Monroe. Instead of using the pike to travel to Valley events such as picnics, summer resort seasons, county court sessions, meetings of religious organizations, or events to memorialize the Civil War, Valley people took the railroad. Valley town storekeepers advertised in local newspapers the new availability of products shipped in by the railroads and "just received from the Northern Cities": cast-iron stoves, ready-made clothing, medicine, hardware, cutlery, glass, musical instruments, engines, imported porcelain, and many other consumer products previously hard to get in the Valley could be found in local emporia. The *Richmond Times-Dispatch* soon complained that Harrisonburg's merchants would rather do business with the traders in Chicago, Cincinnati, and St. Louis than with those in Richmond. It would appear they did: some newspapers in the Valley regularly gave the market prices for Valley crops offered in Baltimore, Chicago, and Philadelphia, less frequently for Washington and Alexandria, but usually ignored Richmond. By the early twentieth century, the railroads also made possible the commercial shipment of apples and poultry products from Valley farms.[40] The pike did not share in this commerce, and nearly all livestock was sent to market by railroad. The links to new, distant markets seemed to make the pike economically obsolete.

Although the Valley railroads deprived the turnpike of trade essential for revenue, the automobile brought about the pike's demise as a toll road. Automobiles began to appear in the Valley before 1905. The popularity of the new "machine," as the automobile was called, led to the adoption of laws prescribing turnpike tolls for such vehicles in 1904. Automobile drivers paid 6¼ cents for each wheel on each five-mile section traveled at first, but in 1912, the charge was made proportional for the miles they traveled at the rate of five cents per mile.[41] Small-town merchants found their meager inventories were unattractive to customers when motorists could travel to larger towns for consumer goods — albeit at a price. Rural mobility eventually meant the end of many Main Street businesses.

The Valley Turnpike had a reputation as the best paved extensive road in Virginia, and it became a popular place for excursions for out-of-state travelers, some of whom used its long, straight surfaces to "open 'er up" and speed. By 1905, the *Rockingham Register* reported that there was a rapid increase in the number of automobiles "in this section of the country." To cope with congestion, collisions, and speeding, the 1906 Highway Code imposed an automobile speed limit of fifteen miles per hour. The delighted editor of the *Harrisonburg Daily News* noted that on July 8, 1911, at Harrisonburg, thirty-five tourist automobiles passed through the pike

Fig. 6.6. The Winchester Cold Storage Company warehouse on the city's north side has railroad access. The loading dock faces U.S. 11, and a sign on the side of the building confirms that this structure is the "Largest Apple Storage in the World." (Scott Jost 2004)

tollgates in two hours, and there were many more later in the day. But the automobile brought other problems that plagued the pike. Undoubtedly responding to popular opposition to tolls, the 1906 General Assembly banned the construction of any tollgate within five miles of any city limits. This law made it easy for vehicles to elude tollgates by allowing motorists to leave a town surreptitiously, head for a back road, and bypass the pike tolls on their way to their destination. The law deprived the company of substantial income just at the time when increasing traffic could have yielded the income needed to make a profit. Speeding automobiles also tore up the road's macadam surface and stirred up dust, so serious repairs were required to keep the road in acceptable condition. The company appealed for permission to build extra tollgates to increase revenue, and the State Corporation Commission agreed to the request, in spite of growing protests from townspeople and motorists. By 1914, for the first time in years, the Turnpike Company experienced an increase in its revenue as the new tollgates brought in extra income. When Harry F. Byrd was elected Valley Turnpike Company president in 1908, he stirred the company to action and instituted a program of "permanent and enduring reconstruction" that led to the application of tar dressings to the surface, the replacement of wooden bridges with ones of iron and steel, the erection of concrete barriers at dangerous spots, and road widening. Although Byrd was responsible for improving the roadway, he also realized that the pike could no longer finance repairs through tolls, since the repair expenses necessitated by automobiles were too great. So Harry F. Byrd reversed his position on tolls and led a campaign to end them and convert the Valley Turnpike to a free, public, state-maintained road.[42]

A Free Public Highway

Byrd's campaign to transfer the turnpike to the Commonwealth converged with a national movement to provide federal aid to the states to improve their highways. In the 1890s, bicyclists and early automobile owners launched a national campaign for federal aid to the states to build highways. At the turn of the twentieth century, "good roads" promoters organized state and national good roads associations. Good roads advocates soon proposed that the tollgates on the Valley Turnpike be abolished and the state assume control of the road. The good roads campaign became one of the many causes identified with the so-called "progressive" reform movement, a national effort that attempted to prod government into action to adjust the laws to fit the needs of a modern, industrial society. In 1910, when the *Richmond Times-Dispatch* revealed that the turnpike company had appealed to the State Corporation Commission to build five more tollgates on the pike to prevent toll evasion, a controversy broke out in Valley newspapers. One editorial commented that the tollgates ought to be abolished, because in so doing Virginia would be "doing what almost all others of our wide-awake and progressive states are doing today, building state roads free of tollgates." Virginia needed "good, open roads." In a democratic society, roads were public necessities and should be owned by "the people." Valley newspapers, such as the *Harrisonburg Daily News,* that supported the transfer argued that the turnpike was now "out of date" and that toll roads "could not be tolerated in a progressive community." Another writer observed that the abolition of tollgates was "one of the most generous, progressive and patriotic moves." Collecting tolls was a practice unsuited for the twentieth century, and more appropriate for "the medieval days in old England," one correspondent asserted.[43] Harry Byrd's *Winchester Evening Star* noted that since so much out-of-state "foreign traffic" was using the road, the four Valley counties should no longer have to pay for it. Collecting tolls had become difficult, for too many scofflaws from out of state tried to evade them. Moreover, tolls were discouraging business, especially from tourists who would choose to motor elsewhere if the tolls were not abolished, Byrd predicted. The automobile made it necessary to widen the road to three lanes, so that cars could safely pass slow-moving horse-drawn vehicles. He exaggerated the road's unprofitability by maintaining that the turnpike company had never paid a dividend to its shareholders, even though it had paid a few in the 1840s and 1880s.[44] Byrd also frequently pointed out that he owned no stock in the company and that he was voting himself out of a job as company president by supporting the transfer. Byrd's *Winchester Evening Star* gave thorough publicity to his campaign to make the turnpike free.

The national progressive reform crusade gave impetus to federal action that transferred the pike to the state. Good roads advocates secured the passage of the national good roads law during the administration of Staunton's own president, Woodrow Wilson. Popularly known as the Good Roads Act, the Federal Aid Road Act of July 11, 1916, provided a system for encouraging the states to establish state highway systems by taking responsibility for constructing and maintaining the farm-to-market roads from the counties of each state and encouraging the establishment of federally assisted state highway programs. States that began state highway programs could obtain matching federal grants-in-aid to help finance the roadways. While Congress considered the law, the Virginia General Assembly created a State Roads Commission, appointing Harry F. Byrd a member. He was, of course, what his newspaper deferentially referred to as "President Byrd" of the Valley Turnpike. The commission studied the problem for two years, and in 1918, Virginia governor Westmoreland Davis proposed that Virginia create a state highway system, which it did. As the legislature drafted the law, Harry Byrd persuaded the legislature to pass a law authorizing the transfer. The complete text of the law appeared in the *Winchester Evening Star* on a full page with Byrd's personal endorsement and that of the company's directors. In 1918, the legislature passed the statute, which began with a preamble inserted at the request of Governor Davis, pointing out that the state had lent the company large sums of money over the years, and that the money was not being paid back, but that it owed the state, including interest, $115,000. In effect, the transfer was more like a foreclosure on assets upon which the state already had a just claim. Before the pike directors could vote on the company's dissolution, Byrd ordered that pike toll collection cease on August 31, 1918. Thereafter the stockholders approved the transfer, and the state assumed control. In 1919, the state sold the company's real estate, and the toll road

became a free, public road, a part of Virginia's new state highway system. Thereby, in the name of modernization, the Valley Turnpike Company passed into history. Hundreds of automobiles traveled on the free road that first day, despite World War I gasoline-consumption regulations.[45]

Commemorating the Past

The turnpike's history and attributes would acquire cultural meanings other than those related to road construction and use. In the years after the Civil War, the defeated South attempted to keep alive memories of the Lost Cause by literary works, monuments to the Confederate dead, and battle commemorations. Because the Valley Turnpike had been the focus of some of the most important battlegrounds of the war, it became a cultural icon of sorts, a symbol of the valor of the soldiers of both sides in the war. John Esten Cooke and Mary Johnston both produced books of fiction that described the pike and its role in the campaigns of Jackson and other Confederate heroes. The pike played a role in the commemoration

of the war when veterans erected monuments along the pike, such as the one honoring the Fifty-fourth Pennsylvania Regiment above New Market adjacent to the pike, put up in 1905, and the monument marking the spot where Turner Ashby died, also near the pike at Harrisonburg, erected in 1898.[46] Certainly, by 1900 the Valley Turnpike had become part of this culture of commemoration. With the coming of the automobile, the interest in the pike's past heightened, for there was tourist money to be made.

Consequently, the Valley Pike became the obvious route for northerners to Valley tourist attractions. The Civil War sites and monuments played an important part in drawing the tourists, but there were other scenic attractions as well. The railroads played a significant role in promoting the Valley as a tourist destination, but the Valley Pike also became a quaint means of access to the scenery. In 1879, the Commonwealth Department of Immigration and Agriculture began periodically issuing a series of Virginia handbooks designed to attract both investments and tourism to the Valley. The handbooks described the mountains, the tidy farms, the caverns, Stonewall Jackson's exploits in the Valley, and the "famous Valley Pike." With the advent of the automobile in the early twentieth century, picture postcards appeared with pike scenes and events. Advertising from tourist facilities celebrated the pike's role in history. For example, a pamphlet issued in 1915 by Chilton Hall, a Staunton tourist home near the southern end of the pike, boasted that "the macadam road — the Valley Pike — which traverses the Valley, is the joy of tourists, and the pride of those who use it daily." Out-of-state investors sank money into Valley resorts: Edward T. Brown of Baltimore purchased Endless Caverns in 1919 and built a road from the pike to the cave. He and Harry Byrd led a campaign to widen the pike to make it even more inviting. When Virginia commemorated Jamestown's three hundredth anniversary in 1907, the state mounted a Jamestown Exposition near Hampton Roads. The American Automobile Association organized what it called a "National Highway" to and from the exposition; the return route used the Valley Pike. In 1909, the *Atlanta Journal* and the *New York Herald* began a campaign to establish a permanent National Highway from New York to Atlanta. Its promoters included the Valley Pike in the National Automobile Highway. It was part of the first important north–south road in the East, well before U.S. Highway 1 became the main travel route.[47] A 1912 map issued by the American Automobile Association designated the Valley Pike as part of the National Highway and declared it was the path of 95 percent of all travel between the Northeast and the southeastern states. A sign went up by the road in Shenandoah County proclaiming the pike as the National Highway, and so it was called at least until the end of its days as a toll road.[48] The turnpike's cultural significance as a tourist highway was that again outsiders and non-Virginians were welcome in the Valley. Again important sectors of the Valley's economy were oriented toward the North, and Valley business maintained intercourse with the North on a much larger scale than with the mid-Atlantic region.

In its sometimes troubled history as a toll road, the Valley Turnpike reflected several important themes in western Virginia's history and the saga of its roads. It deepened an already commercial society's ties to the northern market and brought about a substantial alteration in the Valley's natural environment, with economic considerations paramount in the decisions people made about building the road. The Valley had an ambivalent relationship to the South, living on its margins and depending for markets, customers, investors, many consumer goods, information, and tourists on the land north of the Potomac. The Valley's people were commercial entrepreneurs, and since the North provided the materials for their commerce, and Richmond gave them little succor, they had few qualms about being what some people called a "colonial economy" for cities outside the old Confederacy, regardless of whether that economy depended on the shipping of raw materials and agricultural products north, the supply of goods from Philadelphia and Baltimore, or upon the gawking of northern tourists. When railroads usurped the road's functions, people converted it into a cultural symbol of Virginia's ties to the Lost Cause, and eventually the "Lee-Jackson Highway." The southern mystique perpetuated in the late nineteenth century attracted more northerners, who came to the Valley to explore the South, and the culture of the Old Dominion moved yet another step closer to the land north of the Potomac.

Notes

The author wishes to acknowledge the generous support of the Mednick Fellowship program of the Virginia Foundation for Independent Colleges, which made this research possible.

1. The scholarly literature on the "market revolution," the name that some historians apply to the shift to a more freewheeling capitalistic economy, is well summarized in John Lauritz Larson, "The Market Revolution in Early America: An Introduction," *Organization of American Historians Magazine of History* 19, no. 3 (2005): 4–7.

2. The local historian John W. Wayland prepared a study of the Valley Turnpike, but he did not live to see the manuscript published. The unfinished manuscript was published by the Winchester-Frederick County Historical Society (see John W. Wayland, *The Valley Turnpike — Winchester to Staunton* [Winchester-Frederick County Historical Society, 1967]). See also Robert F. Hunter, "Transportation Problems," *Proceedings of the Rockbridge Historical Society* 5 [July 1961]: 53–60; and "The Turnpike Movement in Virginia — 1816–1860," *Virginia Magazine of History and Biography* 69 [1961]: 278–89).

3. A useful map of all Virginia turnpikes may be found in S. E. Tompkins, comp., "Map of Virginia Showing Turnpikes," compiled from acts of assembly by the Department of Highways in 1928. There is a copy in the collections of the Virginia Historical Society. The best available published maps of the route of the Valley Turnpike appear in J. M. Lathrop and A. W. Dayton, comps., *An Atlas of Frederick County* (1885; repr., Strasburg, Va.: G. P. Hammond, 1997); J. M. Lathrop and B. N. Griffing, comps., *An Atlas of Shenandoah and Page Counties, Virginia* (1885; repr., Strasburg, Va.: G. P. Hammond, 1991); Lathrop and Griffing, comps., *An Atlas of Rockingham County, Virginia* (1885; repr., Strasburg, Va.: G. P. Hammond, 1995); and Jedediah Hotchkiss, *Historical Atlas of Augusta County* (1885; repr., Verona, Va.: Mid Valley Press, 1991).

4. George Rogers Taylor, *The Transportation Revolution, 1815–1860,* vol. 4 of *The Economic History of the United States* (New York: Holt, Rinehart and Winston, 1951); Carter Goodrich, "The Virginia System of Mixed Enterprise: A Study of State Planning of Internal Improvements," *Political Science Quarterly* 64, no. 3

(1949): 355–87; John Lauritz Larson, *Internal Improvement — National Public Works and the Promise of Popular Government in the Early United States* (Chapel Hill: University of North Carolina Press, 2000), 91–97; "The Virginia Board of Public Works," *Niles's Weekly Register* 10, no. 18 (June 29, 1816): 298; John S. Salmon, comp., *Board of Public Works Inventory* (Richmond: Virginia State Library, 1978), ix–xii.

5. Harry F. Byrd, president of the Valley Turnpike Company (1908–18), as quoted in the *Staunton Daily News,* July 25, 1917.

6. Commonwealth of Virginia, Acts of Assembly (hereafter cited as AA by year), Acts of March 30, 1837; March 24, 1838; January 25, February 14, 1839; January 28, February 28, 1846; January 29; March 17, 20, 1849; January 19, February 25, 1850; March 20, 1851; May 11, 1852; March 31, 1853; February 25, 1856; April 7, 1858; Resolutions No. 3, March 9, 1849; No. 5, March 29, 1851. The legislature authorized the town of Staunton to purchase stock in the Valley Junction Turnpike. It did so.

7. *Annual Report of the Board of Public Works,* Board of Public Works Collection, Library of Virginia, Richmond (hereafter cited as *ARBPW* by year), 1855–56: tables A–E. Twenty-four turnpikes ran between two or more sections of the Commonwealth. Twenty of these followed routes between the Valley and the Piedmont.

8. *Staunton Spectator,* May 8 and 22, 1850; Kenneth W. Keller, "The Wheat Trade on the Upper Potomac, 1800–1860," in Kenneth E. Koons and Warren R. Hofstra, eds., *After the Backcountry* (Knoxville: University of Tennessee Press, 2000), 21–23; Frederick County Petitions; undated petition to the legislature for a Winchester-Staunton Road, File No. 11770, Legislative Petitions Collection–Virginia State Archives (hereafter cited as LPC-VSA), Library of Virginia.

9. Lists of Stockholders for 1838–43, 1846–49, 1852, 1854, 1857, Records of the Board of Public Works, Internal Improvement Companies, Turnpike Companies, Valley Turnpike Company–Virginia State Archives (hereafter cited as VTC-VSA), Library of Virginia. The town of Winchester was the only Valley town to buy stock in the Valley Turnpike Company.

10. *ARBPW,* 1842: 598; *Martinsburg Gazette,* June 9, 1831. A printed version of the seal appears on a note of J. S. Calvert to John S. Rice, April 15, 1853, VTC-VSA.

11. "Survey of Part of the Shenandoah Valley from Staunton to Stony Creek through Harrisonburgh [*sic*] by Crozet 1831," Microfiche 1831, no. 644, Maps, Plans, and Drawings of the Board of Public Works, Map Collection, Library of Virginia; petition from the inhabitants of the Shenandoah Valley for a free road between Winchester and Staunton, December 8, 1830, Shenandoah County Petitions, LPC-VSA. Delegates from Frederick, Shenandoah, and Rockingham counties attended the Woodstock Road Convention of November 11–12, 1833. See petition of December 4, 1833, with printed account of Road Convention in Woodstock, Shenandoah County Petitions, Legislative Petitions Collection, LPC-VSA; Commonwealth of Virginia, An Act to Incorporate the Valley Turnpike Company (March 3, 1834), *ARBPW,* 1835: 575; Act of January 13, 1835, AA, 1835: 131; Act of March 30, 1837, AA, 1837: 147–48.

12. Petitions of the inhabitants of Rockingham County, January 18 and 24, 1838,

Rockingham County Petitions, LPC-VSA. The petition of January 24 noted that between Bangor, Maine, and New Orleans, there were only seventy miles of un-improved road, the road in the Valley; Act of March 24, 1838, AA, 1838: 167.

13. Bushrod Taylor to the Board of Public Works, June 30, 1838, VTC-VSA. The legislature authorized the town of Winchester to purchase shares in the Valley Turnpike Company.

14. By the count of John W. Wayland, local historian of the pike, some thirty-one streams, creeks, and runs crossed the path of the pike; they required that streams be crossed over fords or that bridges be built (see Wayland, *Turnpike,* 162–67; *Art Work of Scenes in the Valley of Virginia,* pt. 4 (Chicago: W. H. Parish, 1897), n.p.; Commonwealth of Virginia, Department of Highways and Transportation, Office of Public Affairs, *History of Roads in Virginia: "the most convenient wayes,"* 14; *Rockingham Daily Record* (Harrisonburg), May 2, 1913.

15. *ARBPW,* 1839: 141.

16. *ARBPW,* 1838 (pamphlet): 2.

17. *Harrisonburg Daily News,* November 22, 1904; "Propertyholder" on "Roads" in the *Shenandoah Valley* (New Market), March 17, 1882. See also the reference to the "natural route" in the petition of the inhabitants of Frederick County for connecting Opequon Creek and Cedar Creek with a road, February 9, 1846, LPC-VSA; *ARBPW,* 1838: 84; *ARBPW,* 1840: 500; *ARBPW,* 1868: 172; AA, 1838: 130.

18. *ARBPW,* 1839: 147; *Shenandoah Valley* (New Market), March 17, 1882; *Rockingham Register* (Harrisonburg), May 18, 1906; Shenandoah County Bicentennial Committee, *Shenandoah County — Dunmore County 1772–1972* (Woodstock, Va.: Shenandoah County, 1972), 83; Wayland, *Turnpike,* 107.

19. See advice to travelers in the American Automobile Association, *Virginia Main-Traveled Routes and Their Connections into Adjoining States,* map (New York: American Automobile Association, 1912), Map 755/R6/1912 in the Library of Virginia Map Collection; Ms. Annual Report of the Valley Turnpike Company to the Board of Public Works, 1879, VTC-VSA. The engineering of the early bridges was poor, leading to many collapses. The worst of many floods in the Valley during the turnpike era was in October 1870 (see *ARBPW,* 1842: 560–61, 596; *ARBPW,* 1843: 54; *ARBPW,* 1851: 115; *ARBPW,* 1859: 451; *ARBPW,* 1862–63: 65; *ARBPW,* 1866: 303–4; *ARBPW,* 1867–70: 173; *ARBPW,* 1871: 159, 224; *ARBPW,* 1872: 134; ms. an-nual report of the Valley Turnpike Company to the Board of Public Works, 1878; *Shenandoah Valley* (New Market), October 6, 1870; November 23, 1872; *Harrison-burg Daily Times,* April 3, 1907). Pedestrians who walked fast over a Shenandoah County bridge on the turnpike could be fined five dollars for causing dangerous vibrations in the structure (see Shenandoah County Bicentennial Committee, 83).

20. Lists of Stockholders for 1838–43, 1846–49, 1852, 1854, 1857, VTC-VSA; *ARBPW,* 1847: 200; *ARBPW,* 1848: 2–3; *ARBPW,* 1851: 113; *ARBPW,* 1854: 372; U.S. Department of Agriculture, Office of Road Inquiry; *Proceedings of the Virginia Good Roads Convention, Held in Richmond, Virginia, October 18, 1894* (Washington, D.C.: U.S. Government Printing Office, 1895), 23.

21. Ms. report of President Samuel Shacklett of the Valley Turnpike Company to the Board of Public Works, March 22, 1864; ms. annual report for 1880, VTC-VSA; *ARBPW,* 1859: 451; *ARBPW,* 1867–70: 121, 157, 159, 173; *ARBPW,* 1874: 200;

ARBPW, 1876: 156; *Shenandoah Valley* (New Market), November 23, 1872; *Harrisonburg Daily News*, April 13, 1904; June 9, July 29, 1905; *Harrisonburg Daily Times*, May 6, 1907; *Bridgewater Herald*, August 18, 1905; *Shenandoah Valley* (New Market), September 1, 1870; May 5, 1876; February 2, 1877; John P. Stover, *History of the Baltimore and Ohio Railroad* (West Lafayette, Ind.: Purdue University Press, 1987), 306. See also Jefferson R. Keen, "The Development of the 'Valley Line' of the Baltimore and Ohio Railroad," *Virginia Magazine of History and Biography* 60 (1952): 537–50.

22. *Staunton Spectator*, September 2, 1873.

23. James Sullivan to Thomas E. Pollard, June 27, 1882, VTC-VSA.

24. B. G. Patterson to the Board of Public Works, September 15, 1887, VTC-VSA.

25. Resolution of the Rockingham County Board of Supervisors, March 3, 1902, and letter with newspaper clipping from A. M. Newman to the Valley Turnpike Company, March 6, 1902, VTC-VSA.

26. C. W. Peery to Delegate Joseph A. Miller, February 15, 1892, Joseph A. Miller Papers, Special Collections Department, Perkins Library, Duke University.

27. Act of February 24, 1898, AA, 1898: 509. In 1872, the company lowered tolls for pleasure carriages. Joseph R. Strayer to Samuel Shacklett, October 2, 1869; Samuel Shacklett to Dr. Joseph R. Strayer, October 4, 1869, VTC-VSA; *ARBPW*, 1843: 669–70.

28. Commonwealth of Virginia, State Corporation Commission, *Annual Report*, 1910: 35; Act of March 16, 1910, AA, 1910: 433. See *Harrisonburg Daily News*, December 22, 1910; January 15, 1912. The Harrisonburg City Council voted to oppose the installation of a planned additional tollgate north of Harrisonburg; the company did not erect the gate (*Harrisonburg Daily News*, October 23, 1912).

29. Act of February 21, 1817, AA, 1817: 41–55; Letter of William McClene, Henry P. Dickerson, and Hugh A. Hamilton, freeholders of Augusta County and road viewers appointed by the county court, to the Board of Public Works, November 23, 1882, VTC-VSA; *Shenandoah Valley* (New Market), November 12, 1880; February 16, May 11, October 12, 1883; *Harrisonburg Daily Times*, October 11, 1912; Act of March 1, 1886, AA, 1886: 382.

30. The counties of Augusta and Rockingham were, in the words of a legislative petition of 1837, the "centers of the grazing interest" of Virginia (see petition of the inhabitants of Augusta County for a bank, December 7, 1837, Augusta County Petitions, LPC-VSA).

31. Petition of the inhabitants of Rockingham County for a law against the pulling down of fences, December 14, 1852, LPC-VSA; *Shenandoah Valley* (New Market), February 20, 1874; August 24, 1876. See *Shenandoah Valley* (New Market), April 26, 1878; March 5, 1880. Some farm journals and Valley newspapers recommended the use of Osage orange hedges as a natural substitute, but extensive planting of Osage orange was costly, and very cold winters could kill the plants. Unfortunately, Osage orange hedges and worm fences of split rails provided hospitable environments for weeds that were obnoxious to farmers, various agricultural journals reported.

32. On barbed wire versus woven wire, see John Fraser Hart, *The Rural Land-*

scape (Baltimore: Johns Hopkins University Press, 1998), 165, 170, 173. See also Northern Virginia Daily, *Standing Ground — The Civil War in the Shenandoah Valley* (Strasburg, Va.: Shenandoah Publishing House, 1996); and Margaretta Barton Colt, *Defend the Valley — A Shenandoah Valley Family in the Civil War* (New York: Oxford University Press, 1994).

33. *Martinsburg Gazette*, June 1, 1843; *Staunton Spectator*, January 8, 1851; U.S. Department of the Interior, *The Post Office Department and the Postal Service*, vol. 2 of *Official Register of the United States, Containing a List of the Officers and Employees in the Civil, Military, and Naval Service on the First of July, 1895; together with a List of Vessels Belonging to the United States* (Washington, D.C.: U.S. Government Printing Office, 1896), 373–91; *Shenandoah Valley* (New Market), March 7, November 23, 1872; *Harrisonburg Daily News*, April 13, 1906; March 29, 1911; *Winchester Evening Star*, May 14, 1918; John W. Wayland, *A History of Rockingham County* (Harrisonburg, Va.: C. J. Carrier Company, 1980), 234–35; John W. Wayland, *A History of Shenandoah County Virginia* (Baltimore: Regional Publishing, 1969), 8; Richard M. Hamrick Jr., "Local Telephone History," *Augusta Historical Bulletin* 26, no. 2 (Fall 1990): 42–45.

34. Commonwealth of Virginia, Commissioner of Agriculture, *Hand-book of Virginia*, 4th ed. (Richmond: Johns and Goolsby, 1885), 92, 99, 108, 110; Maria G. Carr, *My Recollections of Rocktown — Now Known as Harrisonburg* (Harrisonburg, Va.: Frank Stover, 1959), 40–41; *Harrisonburg Daily Record*, November 18, 1912; *Harrisonburg Daily News*, December 31, 1910; *Rockingham Register* (Harrisonburg), May 2, 1906; July 12, 1907; Carr, *My Recollections of Rocktown*, 50.

35. List of Stockholders for 1838, Valley Turnpike Company (see note 9 above). Siram Henkel is listed as a stockholder in the section of the subscribers' list for Rockingham County.

36. Janet and Earl Downs, *Mills of Rockingham County* (Dayton, Va.: Harrisonburg–Rockingham Historical Society, 1998), 2:543–58.

37. The tangled railroad history of the Valley is explained in Richard K. MacMaster, *Augusta County History, 1856–1950* (Staunton, Va.: Augusta County Historical Society, 1987), 63–68, 99–100, 107–8. See also Warren Hofstra, *A Separate Place: The Formation of Clarke County, Virginia* (White Post, Va.: Clarke County Sesquicentennial Committee, 1986), 46, 71; *ARBPW*, 1854: 175. Petition of March 1, 1839, Shenandoah County Petitions; Memorial of the President and Directors of the Valley Turnpike Company, Frederick County Petitions, January 13, 1840; petition of the inhabitants of Frederick County, January 5, 1846; petition of the Directors of the Valley Turnpike Company, December 8, 1855, Shenandoah County Petitions, LPC-VSA; ms. report of the Valley Turnpike Company, October 3, 1854; ms. "A Statement of the Distance from the Centre of the Valley Turnpike to the Centre of the Manassas Gap Railroad," October 3, 1854, VTC-VSA; *ARBPW*, 1854: 174, 372–73; *Harrisonburg Daily News*, April 7, 1905; *Shenandoah Valley* (New Market), January 15, 1869.

38. *The Virginias* 5, no. 3 (May 1884): 69; ms. annual report of the Valley Turnpike Company to the Board of Public Works, September 30, 1880, VTC-VSA.

39. *ARBPW*, 1867–70: 121; ms. "Statement of the Distance from the Centre," VTC-VSA.

40. *Shenandoah Valley* (New Market), October 13, 1876; April 10, May 18 and 25, 1877; January 14, July 26, August 9 and 16, 1878; October 29, 1880; August 3 and 7, September 7, 1883; *Rockingham Register,* May 21, 1885. The most common origination of these products was Baltimore. See advertisements in the *Shenandoah Valley* (New Market) November 16, 1871; July 26, 1878; February 14, August 12, 1879; October 22, 1880; January 7, October 27, 1881. See *Harrisonburg Daily Times,* February 16, 1907; *Harrisonburg Daily News,* April 7, 1905; April 6, 1907; January 12, 1906; October 17, 1906; *Shenandoah Valley* (New Market), January 15, 1874.

41. The act of March 1, 1886, specified tolls for steam-powered vehicles, most likely threshing machines and traction engines (see AA, 1886: 382). The law of February 27, 1904, provided for tolls for vehicles "moved or drawn, in whole or in part, by steam or other motive power," thus acknowledging the growing use of the internal combustion engine (see AA, 1904: 78; see also *Harrisonburg Daily Times,* October 23, 1912).

42. *Rockingham Register,* August 1, 1905; *Harrisonburg Daily News,* December 5, 22, and 23, 1910; July 8, 1911; January 15, 1912; Act of March 19, 1906, AA, 1906: 571; *Rockingham Daily Record* (Harrisonburg), March 8, 1913; Commonwealth of Virginia, State Corporation Commission, *Annual Report,* 1910: 35; Wayland, *Shenandoah County,* 351; *Harrisonburg Daily Times,* October 11, 1912; *Winchester Evening Star,* January 31, February 4 and 11, March 11 and 21, April 13, 1918.

43. U.S. Department of Agriculture, Virginia Good Roads Convention, *Proceedings.* As quoted in the *Harrisonburg Daily News,* November 21, December 5, 16, 21, 23, 27, and 30, 1910.

44. *Winchester Evening Star,* July 12, 1918. In 1922, Harry Byrd corrected himself by noting that the only time the company had paid a dividend after the Civil War was in 1888 (see *Winchester Evening Star,* October 10, 1922). This clipping may be found in the Harry F. Byrd Papers, Valley Turnpike File, Special Collections Department, University of Virginia Library).

45. Karl Raitz, ed., *The National Road* (Baltimore: Johns Hopkins University Press, 1996), 212, 385. On the politics of the creation of the State Highway Commission, see Jack Temple Kirby, *Westmoreland Davis — Virginia Planter-Politician — 1859–1942* (Charlottesville: University Press of Virginia, 1968), 87–89. Kirby does not acknowledge the importance of the Good Roads Act and federal grants-in-aid. See also Ronald L. Heinemann, *Harry Byrd of Virginia* (Charlottesville: University Press of Virginia, 1996), 10–18; and Virginia Department of Highways and Transportation, *History of Roads,* 13; Frederic J. Wood, *The Turnpikes of New England and Evolution of the Same through England, Virginia, and Maryland* (Boston: Marshall Jones, 1919), 411–12; *Harrisonburg Daily News,* February 13, 1909; July 8, 1911; *Winchester Evening Star,* January 11 and 17, February 4, 6, and 11, March 21, July 12 and 15, August 21, September 2, November 8, December 26, 1918. See also An Act to Permit the Transfer of the Valley Turnpike to the Commonwealth of Virginia . . . , March 20, 1918, AA, 1918: 633–35. The original investors received six cents for every dollar of stock they owned (see Wayland, *Turnpike,* 68; and Act to Authorize the State Highway Commissioner to Sell at His Discretion, Houses Formerly Used as Toll Houses on the Valley Turnpike, 5 September 1919, AA, 1919: 71. To celebrate the opening of the free road, the Winchester-Frederick

County Chamber of Commerce organized an automobile caravan to travel from Winchester to Woodstock, complete with a band carried in Stewart Bell's truck, flags, banners, bunting, advertisements for the Winchester Fair, and thirty-three automobiles representing different Winchester businesses. Stewart Bell's truck was the first such vehicle mentioned in the local press to have used the free road. By the 1920s, commercial trucking services appeared in Valley towns.

46. *Harrisonburg Daily News,* April 8, 1904; Wayland, *Turnpike,* 57; James I. Robertson Jr., *Civil War Sites in Virginia — A Tour Guide* (Charlottesville: University Press of Virginia, 1982), 6–12.

47. Ron Steffey, *The Shenandoah Valley — A Pictorial History* (Staunton, Va.: B.O.O.S.T. Publications, 1980). See also the postcard collections of the Virginia Historical Society and the Photo and Pamphlet File of the Special Collections Department of the University of Virginia. See also *Winchester Evening Star,* May 9, 1913; June 1, 1918; Chilton Hall pamphlet, Pamphlet File, Special Collections Department, University of Virginia Library; Wayland, *Turnpike,* 68; *Rockingham Register* (Harrisonburg), September 21, 1906. U.S. 1 was created when the federal government introduced a numbering system for U.S. federal highways in 1925. The now public Valley Pike became U.S. 11 (see Tim Hollis, *Dixie before Disney — 100 Years of Roadside Fun* [Jackson: University of Mississippi Press, 1999], 6). For a reference to the pike as the National Automobile Highway, see the Commonwealth of Virginia, Department of Agriculture and Immigration, *A Handbook of Virginia,* 7th ed. (Richmond: Davis Bottom, 1919), 132.

48. American Automobile Association, *Virginia Main-Traveled Routes,* map. The map stated that Virginia was known for bad roads and that streams frequently had to be forded, since there were few bridges. Virginia was catching up with other states, for in 1910 the Commonwealth adopted legislation that exempted nonresident motorists from registration of their vehicles for two periods of seven days each. In the opinion of the AAA, continuing to insist on such registration would have hindered north–south traffic in Virginia (see also Joseph B. Clower Jr., *Yesterday in Woodstock — According to Fred Painter* (Woodstock, Va.: Woodstock Museum of Shenandoah County, 1981), 52.

7 The Turnpike Towns

ANN E. McCLEARY

In June 1808, as settlers pushed across the Allegheny Mountains of western Virginia, thirty-year-old Lewis Sommer departed from his family's plantation in Alexandria to go west in search of a new tract of land for his father. Ten miles after he crossed the Blue Ridge Mountains at Thornton Gap, he encountered the "handsome little town" of New Market, situated along the wagon road halfway between Winchester and Staunton. Impressed by its "thriving appearance," Sommer described the houses as "well built of brick, stone, and frame." He made note of its orderly plan with "straight streets, crossing at right angles" and its "footways," which were "generally paved" so that residents need not walk in the mucky roadbed. As a regional commercial center only a little more than twenty years old and already home to five to six hundred residents, New Market featured "a good many stores full of goods" to serve both travelers and local residents. Sommer spent the night at Deary's Tavern, "a very good house," before heading south along the wagon road to Harrisonburg the next morning.[1] Almost thirty years later, in 1835, the year after the creation of the Valley Turnpike Company, New Market had grown in population to seven hundred and in size to almost a mile along the road, filled with more stores, taverns, churches, doctors offices, a brick academy, and a wide array of "mechanical pursuits."[2] Like other eighteenth-century towns along the wagon road, New Market found itself ideally situated to grow and prosper with the development of the Valley Turnpike.

Turnpike towns were the engines of the Shenandoah Valley's flourishing economy (see fig. 7.1). They provided lodging and accommodations for the many people traveling through this most important transportation artery, whether heading east to the major coastal trading centers or west to the hinterlands. Families in covered wagons moving west into Kentucky and Tennessee to find new farmland and East Coast urban residents seeking to vacation in the mountain springs resorts passed drovers directing

Fig. 7.1. The Valley Road turnpike towns. (Gyula Pauer Cartography Lab, University of Kentucky)

noisy herds of cattle or swine from the backcountry to Baltimore markets. Teamsters guided wagons carrying surplus supplies of flour, bacon, beef, butter, beeswax, tallow, and other produce from small western towns and villages to larger eastern cities, only to return back west packed full of goods farmers could not produce at home.[3] But the turnpike towns were more than stops along a busy highway: they connected residents to trade, commodities, and ideas far from home. The gristmills and distilleries in these towns and villages collected and processed local farm products to ship to distant markets along the East Coast, such as Baltimore or Alexandria, and from there to ports farther abroad in Brazil, the West Indies, England, or Holland.[4] Town merchants imported luxury goods, glass, sugar, salt, and other necessities from throughout the transatlantic world — from Europe and Asia to New England seaport towns — to stock on the shelves for their curious customers. Craftspeople and artisans produced supplies needed by area families — tables, harnesses, hats, boots, wheels, wagons, barrels, and earthenware pots — but also traded their wares through growing commercial networks in the Valley and farther west. The turnpike towns articulated the economic landscape not only of the Shenandoah Valley but also of its connections to broader national, transatlantic, and transnational markets.[5]

At the same time, the turnpike towns became the culture brokers of the Shenandoah Valley. Travelers along the turnpike brought news and ideas — from evangelical temperance reform to progressive agricultural practices — which they shared with local residents at the stores, craft shops, mills, taverns, and hotels they frequented and which local newspaper editors printed in their English and sometimes German papers distributed in town and throughout the countryside. The large collections of public spaces in these turnpike towns — the courthouses, city squares, public markets, commercial establishments, churches, schools, and meeting halls — helped to transform these communities into the Valley's foremost social and cultural centers. Residents and visitors gathered to conduct business or share gossip along the boardwalks lining the main road and in the muddy side alleys, in the formal central halls and parlors of stylish brick homes sitting directly along the road, in the kitchens and on the work porches where wives, children, and enslaved workers performed daily tasks at the back of the house, and in the stables, blacksmith shops, and yards behind the houses where residents milked the cows or tended their gardens. In these boisterous, lively towns, with the steady movement of people up and down the road and in and out of buildings, with the clatter of wagons and stagecoaches along the turnpike's macadam surface, the private world of family and work intersected the public world of commerce, society, and culture. Within these towns, local leaders and town governments sought to strengthen community life by incorporating improvements that spoke of the democratic and forward-thinking character of their American societies.

Yet at the same time that the turnpike networked the Valley to a global economy and boosted trade and industry, it also helped knit together a distinctive Valley culture. The turnpike towns provided the physical space where national and transnational ideas interfaced with local needs, values, and traditions to create a regional identity that defined the resi-

dents: progressive yet conservative, willing to adopt some
thinking while holding onto deep-seated, often ethnic or
ues. The decoration on an earthenware pot, the distinctive
"Newtown" wagon, or the molded cornice on a brick home
part of an expressive material culture exchanged among loc ... residents
living and traveling along the turnpike. By facilitating communication
within the Valley, the turnpike promoted a common local architectural
and cultural aesthetic still seen today in these towns. The turnpike towns
followed similar patterns of architectural development while still evolving
their own distinctive character.

Some of these towns developed as commercial centers during the eighteenth century, almost eighty or ninety years before the incorporation of
the Valley Turnpike. Others emerged as speculative ventures in the 1820s
and 1830s, when plans for the new turnpike were being developed. The
turnpike towns ranged in size from small hamlets containing a handful
of homes clustered around a mill, store, church, school, or artisan shops to
large cities that served as important markets for the backcountry. While
most of these communities experienced tremendous growth during the
height of turnpike travel in the mid- to late nineteenth century, it was ultimately access to another new form of transportation — the railroad — that
would secure a stronger future for some of these towns over others. By the
early twentieth century, the Valley Turnpike boasted a dense web of cities,
towns, villages, and hamlets stretching from four to ten miles apart along
its length from Winchester to Lexington. Ultimately, the popularity of
the automobile in the early twentieth century would commodify and promote this regional identity while at the same time contribute to its gradual
decline.

Creating the Towns

Beginning in the late 1720s, European immigrants, particularly Germans and Scots-Irish, moved south from Pennsylvania into the fertile
lands of the Shenandoah Valley. Some purchased property in the newly
opened land grants and began to establish farms. Others — including
settlers, peddlers, and cattle drivers — utilized the Valley as a corridor to
push even deeper into the southern backcountry, continuing on into the
New River valley or the North Carolina Piedmont. Frontier skirmishes
and the Seven Years' War increased the movement of people and goods
through the Shenandoah Valley in the eighteenth century and accelerated the growth of towns, especially in the northern Valley. Although initial settlement remained relatively dispersed in open-country neighbor-

hoods, trade needs and opportunities led to the creation of villages and towns along the wagon road by the mid-eighteenth century. In contrast to eastern Virginia, where government efforts to create new towns proved challenging throughout the colonial period, many towns emerged in the Valley during the eighteenth and early nineteenth centuries as "business propositions" to connect the growing hinterlands to broader regional and national trade networks.[6]

Three factors influenced the location of these new towns and villages. First, most towns developed where the wagon road intersected a major travel route heading east through a gap across the Blue Ridge. These crossroads locations increased opportunities for trade and commerce by offering contact not only north to Philadelphia but also east to cities such as Baltimore, Alexandria, Fredericksburg, or Richmond.[7]

Access to waterways proved to be a second factor in urban development. Rivers in the Shenandoah Valley proved impractical for travel, so their value lay in the potential for local industries.[8] Communities sprouted up where the wagon road crossed or ran alongside a river or creek that could generate enough power for agricultural enterprises such as grist and fulling mills or sawmills. Towns with access to both waterpower and trade routes proved most promising for future growth because farmers could bring their goods there to be processed and then shipped to distant markets. According to the "central-place" theory proposed by geographers, a hierarchy of towns evolved, their importance based on the array of services and functions they could perform.[9]

The third factor influencing the development of Valley towns was the opportunity to gain the political status of county seat. While Virginia could grant this rank to only a handful of Valley towns, those that received it would realize increased business in trade and legal affairs as well as enhanced land values. Monthly court days especially brought large crowds of people into the county seat to patronize town stores and shops. Further, Virginia tended to focus its road-building efforts on improving those roads that led to the county seats, thus adding an incentive for merchants or artisans to open businesses there.[10] The first two towns established in the Valley became the county seats of the new trans–Blue Ridge counties Governor Gooch created in 1738: Frederick County to the north and Augusta County to the south. In both cases, enterprising speculators with eastern political ties proved successful at securing these county seats on their land, even when the sites were less than desirable.[11]

Meeting for the first time in 1743, the newly established court of Frederick County appointed James Wood, a well-connected local surveyor, as clerk. By the following spring, Wood had surveyed a plat for a county seat on his own property, creating twenty-six lots with two streets and a public square for civic buildings. To gain support for his site, he worked through Lord Fairfax, the "real power broker in the community," who platted additions to the town from his own land holdings. "Frederick Town" sat along a key eastern route through Chester Gap eastward to Alexandria, but a half mile away from the wagon road. Without Wood's survey, observes the historian Warren Hofstra, it is doubtful that a town would have even appeared at this location. One contemporary noted that it sat in a "low and disagreeable location," while another complained that "only as much water is found as required for the use of houses," but clearly not enough for other industrial and business enterprises. To improve transportation access to Wood's new town, the court rerouted the wagon road to the west so that it now connected to the main street of Frederick Town.[12]

William Beverley, a wealthy Tidewater planter and aristocrat with strong ties in Williamsburg, offered a twenty-acre tract of land near his "mill place" to establish a town and courthouse for Augusta County in 1746. The governor had given Beverley a large land grant totaling 118,491 acres in the upper Valley ten years earlier. To sweeten his offer for the county seat, Beverley constructed a log courthouse, described as quite primitive, on a two-acre "public" tract, a typical size for courthouse lots at that time. Beverley's proposed town sat strategically where the north–south Valley route crossed the Indian road leading through Rockfish Gap to Richmond, one of the few opportunities to cross the Blue Ridge Mountains in the southern half of the Valley. Still, the committee reviewing the offer in 1746 found the site "intirely inconvenient and useless being most part of it on a Barron hill or Mountain." Drawing on his personal connections in the House of Burgesses, Beverley was able to convince the assembly to create the county seat here, and he set about surveying and building the new town (see fig. 7.2). As at Winchester, Staunton was situated west of the wagon road, so the Augusta Court similarly requested that the road be redirected six miles to the west to run through it.[13]

As other counties split off by the end of the eighteenth century, they also established their seats along the wagon road. Harrisonburg, in Rockingham County, and Lexington, in Rockbridge County, were both established at the crossroads of the wagon road, with routes that headed to eastern Virginia through gaps in the Blue Ridge Mountains. Woodstock, in Shenandoah County, was the only county seat without direct access to the east. Begun as a speculative venture in 1752, the small village of Muellerstadt was platted in a gridiron plan by the speculator Jacob Muel-

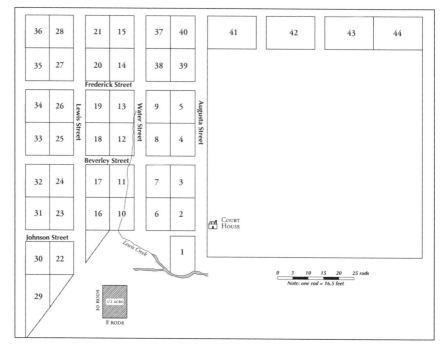

Fig. 7.2. The original survey and plat of Staunton, ca. 1747, showing the courthouse lot and Lewis Creek. (After Augusta County Deed Books, 1749; Gyula Pauer Cartography Lab, University of Kentucky)

ler in 1761 and centered around a log church. In 1772, after establishing Dunmore County, later renamed Shenandoah, the House of Burgesses recognized the town as a county seat, and the founder's son-in-law, Abram Brubaker, deeded two lots on the main street for the courthouse and jail. "A testimony to the contribution of local government to the urban fabric," writes the geographer Robert Mitchell, "is the fact that three of the four largest, and six of the twelve largest, places in the valley were seats of county courthouses."[14]

Official recognition as a town, whether a county seat or otherwise, required action from the colony of Virginia. Landowners such as Wood or Beverley had to petition the General Assembly to establish a town and to demonstrate that it met official requirements. First, the settlement had to contain a minimum population of about 100 to 120 people, or approximately twenty to twenty-five families, living in close geographic proximity and able to carry out the defense of the town and other civic duties. Second, the community needed to agree "to be governed by a group of local trustees and to conduct annual fairs."[15] As towns grew in size, they could request to be incorporated, which offered opportunities for more autonomy: to elect a council or board of alderman and a mayor to govern the town, to impose taxes, and to create their own ordinances without requiring the approval of the state legislature. Virginia granted Winchester this status in 1779, followed by Staunton in 1801.[16]

Besides the county seats — which proved necessary to administer legal control — other towns emerged in the eighteenth century primarily to meet local and regional needs. Villages and towns appeared first in the northern Valley, which had a greater population density and more contact with eastern markets. By 1765, Stephensburg, Strasburg, and Woodstock had emerged, stimulated in part by the economic opportunities brought by the Seven Years' War. While the number of official towns remained low in the eighteenth century, numerous small villages and hamlets grew up around taverns or stores along the wagon road, as entrepreneurial residents sought to take advantage of the potential to service local residents. The number of taverns increased dramatica̱ teenth century; Augusta County approved one hundred tavᴇ.. between 1746, when Staunton was established, and 1776, the year o. ᵗʰᵉ outbreak of the American Revolution.[17]

Many settlements also clustered around rural industries. Lacey Springs, for example, began not only with a tavern but also with a tanyard and sawmill. Stephensburg developed a reputation for producing a distinctive type of wagon, while Staunton, with its Scots-Irish settlers, became a center of the linen and textile industries. But by far, gristmills proved to be the most powerful magnet for town development because they served farmers turning increasingly to wheat as a cash crop. Encouraged by expanding trade opportunities during the Seven Years' War, farmers needed gristmills to process their wheat into flour. By the 1760s, Valley residents were shipping flour to Alexandria and Richmond.[18]

Many of the new communities in Shenandoah County developed around gristmills, where the rivers and creeks running along the wagon road provided excellent opportunities for waterpower. Travelers through the Valley in the 1740s and 1750s described a gristmill operated by Samuel Funk just outside the present-day town of Strasburg, where they could obtain supplies and spend the night. Farther south, Benjamin Allen established a gristmill on a four-hundred-acre tract of land he bought at the confluence of the North Fork of the Shenandoah River and Mill Creek in 1746. Other industries followed, including a hemp mill, carding mill, sawmill, and cabinet shop. First called Mount Pleasant, this industrial community later became known as Mount Jackson. Edinburg, sited along Stony Creek, one of the main tributaries of the Shenandoah River, also began with a gristmill and sawmill, first mentioned in 1805. Some villages took their names from the mill: a hamlet with three mills where the North River crossed the wagon road at the border of Augusta and Rockingham counties is still known today as Burkes Mill. By the early nineteenth century, almost all of the towns and villages along the wagon road boasted at least one merchant mill for processing wheat.[19]

In the last two decades of the eighteenth century, after the American Revolution came to a close, the Valley experienced a town-building boom that accelerated the growth of urban communities along the wagon road. As Americans moved west across the Appalachians into the expanding territories that would become Kentucky and Tennessee, they could now expect to encounter towns spaced about two to twelve miles apart in the northern Valley and twenty-two to thirty miles apart in the less-populated southern Valley. Local residents platted fifteen new towns and villages between 1785 and 1800, and speculators fervently purchased town lots in hope of making a profit. While some purchasers sought to cash in on the increased trade in the region by establishing businesses and shops, others purchased lots for their investment potential. Greenville exemplifies the fast pace of town development during this post-Revolutionary period. Thomas and Jane Steele platted the town on their property halfway between Staunton and Lexington in 1794, and within a few years, it had become a regional trading center and popular stagecoach stop. The population grew to 162 residents by 1810.[20]

While many of the key crossroads locations had been taken by 1800, landowners along the wagon road continued to create new towns into the early nineteenth century, especially as talk intensified about improving the wagon road into a turnpike. Often, residents platted towns at locations that had previously boasted some type of business activity. Mount Sidney illustrates a typical evolution of these early nineteenth-century turnpike towns, which often brought order to open-country settlements. As early as 1780, John McMahon and his family operated an inn about halfway between Harrisonburg and Staunton. This open-country settlement around McMahon's inn, about two miles in length, included a post office, two ordinaries, and four merchants by 1820.[21] When two entrepreneurs platted Mount Sidney in 1826, local business owners purchased lots and moved their operations into the town. When the post office moved from McMahon's tavern to Mount Sidney the following year, it symbolized the rising status of the town and the decline of the less-centralized, open-country neighborhood.

Often the town founders were local businesspeople themselves, hoping to capitalize on their location. Mount Sidney founders Hugh Glenn owned a store and Henry B. Roland operated a tavern along the wagon road by 1824. They platted the town around their businesses, which became the commercial core of the village. Glenn already owned buildings worth eight hundred dollars on the four lots he kept, likely a home that may have contained his store, but he added a new brick store valued at $680 in 1827, the year after he established the town. Roland, who solidified his interests in the town by marrying Glenn's daughter Patsy, kept a two-acre tract across the wagon road from his father-in-law's lots. Anticipating the town's founding, Roland constructed new buildings valued at almost two thousand dollars on these lots between 1826 and 1828, including a stylish brick tavern, the most expensive structure in town, adjacent to a two-story brick store building. Both still dominate the Mount Sidney landscape.[22]

While the towns platted in the central and southern Valley in the early nineteenth century evolved as commercial settlements to provide a convenient stop for travelers, they also functioned as local trading centers, which were still scarce in the area. Some town sites, such as Mount Sidney, lacked industrial potential because they had no waterpower, but they still boasted an array of small craft shops and businesses. In contrast, Mount Crawford, established in 1825 about nine miles north of Mount Sidney, was situated where the wagon road crossed the North River, an ideal location for the gristmill and sawmill that developed by 1835.

Not all of the early nineteenth-century plats proved as successful as Mount Sidney's or Mount Crawford's. Some locations were too close to well-established towns. In 1839, with the construction of the new turnpike, residents of the crossroads community of Hay's Tavern, two miles north of the flourishing town of Lacey Springs, petitioned to have their community declared a town. They selected a new name — Sparta — which they later expanded to Spartopolis, a trendy Greek name reflecting the popular democratic spirit of the United States in the Jacksonian era. Yet even with its pretentious new name, the town failed to attract more residents. By 1912, the sleepy community of Mauzy, as it had come to be called after the name of the family who operated the tavern here, had a population of only twelve residents, the same number as when it was first platted. Even with the economic boom of the antebellum period, there was already an abundance of new towns from which speculators could choose, causing some to remain simply "paper towns." In at least a few cases, local residents may have chosen not to expand the original plats. The sociologist Clay Catlett wrote in 1927 that the town of Burkes Mill in Augusta County "never progressed much because none of the farmers chose to sell off their land."[23]

By the mid-nineteenth century, the string of communities along the Valley Turnpike reflected a hierarchy of settlement. Winchester, the largest city, boasted the strongest ties to markets at Baltimore and Alexandria, and Staunton remained the primary trading center in the southern Valley. The greatest concentration of towns along the turnpike occurred from Shenandoah County north, including the thriving courthouse town of Woodstock. To the south, the county seats of Harrisonburg and Lexington competed as upcoming regional trading centers.[24] Smaller linear towns and crossroads hamlets filled the area between the cities and larger towns, spaced no more than a day's ride along the Valley Turnpike and often much closer. In contrast to eastern Virginia, the Shenandoah Valley was becoming an urban place with a profusion of towns in all sizes.

Laying Out the Towns

The colonists who settled along the wagon road replicated three forms of settlement patterns typical of their homelands: the grid, the linear plan, and the unplatted hamlet. The first towns to appear along the wagon road, those dating from 1740 through 1780, illustrate the grid design that the English brought to the north of Ireland, eastern Virginia, Philadelphia, and rural Pennsylvania in the seventeenth century (see fig. 7.3). The English, German, and Scots-Irish settlers carried these ideas farther west into the southern backcountry, including the Valley of Virginia.[25] Inspired by ancient Romans and promoted by Renaissance planners, the well-ordered grids found in the Shenandoah Valley, as throughout the Virginia back- country, feature square or rectangular blocks with half-acre lots. William Beverley divided Staunton into a square with nine blocks, each containing four half-acre lots; Lexington began with four blocks featuring four half- acre lots; and Strasburg's rectilinear plan featured five blocks with eight lots per block. Most of the town fathers followed an Old World tradition of offering an "out lot" with each town lot for residents to use for pasture, gardening, or woodlots for fuel and building materials and thus to ensure a greater measure of self-sufficiency. Winchester and Woodstock offered three- to five-acre out lots, while William Beverley offered larger fifty-acre woodlots for the first people to purchase city lots in Staunton.[26]

Valley grid plans typically included a central square for public use, again drawing on precedent in Europe and especially Philadelphia, which be- came a model for many towns in Pennsylvania and farther west.[27] Most, like Strasburg (1761) and Stephensburg (1758) incorporated the town mar- ket in the square, though residents in Strasburg considered the square wasted space and soon requested it be divided up and sold. Harrisonburg, platted in 1780, placed the courthouse in this two-acre space, creating the familiar courthouse square that became popular in the upper South and Midwest throughout the nineteenth century. Woodstock created a square

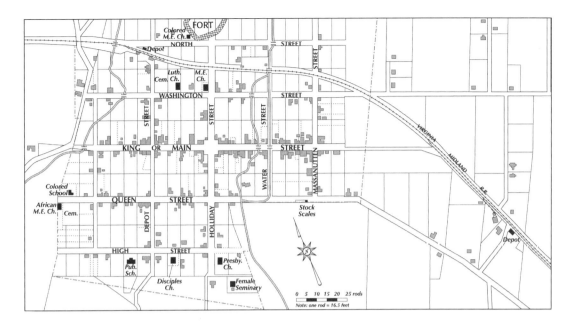

around the church in the middle of town. When it became the county seat in 1772, town leaders designated a two-acre courthouse lot at the main crossroads and set the buildings back accordingly. As in both Old and New World communities, these squares became the commercial and economic centers of the town. Stores, taverns, and other important businesses and later hotels congregated here.[28]

County seats without a central square designated a public lot for government buildings, usually around two acres, to include a courthouse, prison, clerk's office, stocks, pillory, whipping post, and ducking stool. Beverley incorporated a two-acre lot for a courthouse to the side of his grid, while in Winchester, Wood placed the "public lots" in one corner of the primary intersection. The town fathers of Lexington, platted in 1778, simply identified two lots on Washington Street for use as the courthouse and prison and called this block the "court house square" or "public square." Businesses clustered around the courthouse, wherever it was.[29]

The second model of town development that settlers brought from Europe into the Virginia backcountry was the linear plan, characterized by ribbons of deep, narrow half-acre lots lining both sides of the road for a mile or more (see fig. 7.4). Cross streets or alleys divided the strip into blocks, and back streets often extended along the back of the lots to enclose the plan. Residents built their homes and businesses directly on the main road, creating a dense landscape of formal building facades. The geographer Wilbur Zelinsky describes this rhythm of buildings when he writes that the "most measurable peculiarity" of these towns is their "sheer

Fig. 7.3. Strasburg. The grid plan for Strasburg, laid out in 1758, featured a central square that contained the town market. This ca. 1885 map also shows the route taken by the railroad that came through the town in the late nineteenth century. (After Lake's *Atlas of Shenandoah and Page Counties,* 1885; Gyula Pauer Cartography Lab, University of Kentucky)

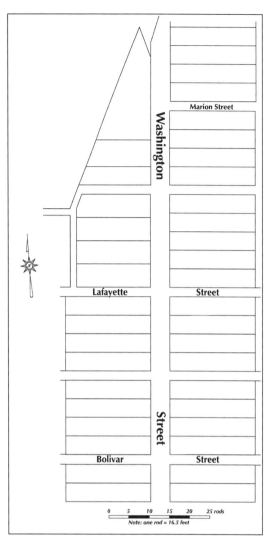

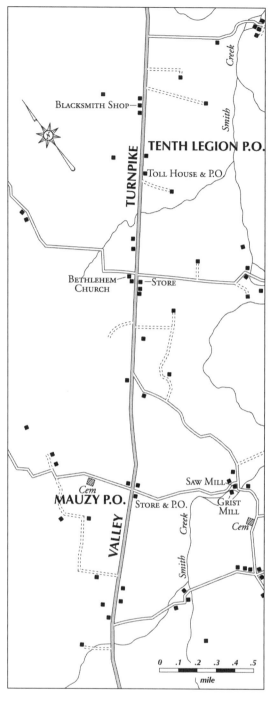

Fig. 7.4. (*Above*) Original survey and plat of Mount Sidney, ca. 1826, showing a linear town plan with deep lots, alleys, and back roads. (Adapted from plat in Augusta County Deed Books, 1826; Gyula Pauer Cartography Lab, University of Kentucky)

Fig. 7.5. (*Right*) Rural hamlets on the Valley Turnpike, ca. 1885. Tenth Legion and Mauzy were representative of the rural hamlets that developed along the Valley Turnpike, often clustering around shops, stores, churches, or industries. (After Lake's *Atlas of Rockingham County*, 1885; Gyula Pauer Cartography Lab, University of Kentucky)

compactness and tightness." Stores, businesses, shops, churches, schools, and homes mixed indiscriminately along the main road, often abutting side walls and stretching across the entire lot width.[30]

The less public work areas occupied the lot behind the street-fronting buildings. Here, town residents and their enslaved workers toiled at their daily and weekly tasks: washing clothes, smoking meat, tending gardens, milking cows, and feeding chickens, all using the wide array of outbuildings and small barns typically found on Valley farms. The historian Lisa Tolbert observes that "the town lots resembled farm yards" because of all of the work and outbuildings they encompassed, including detached kitchens, smokehouses, washhouses, or dairies. The back roads and alleys also serviced the less glamorous needs of travelers along the wagon road, providing corrals, barns, and stables to house the droves of cattle or swine headed to market or the teams of horses pulling the wagons and later stagecoaches. To feed their livestock and those of travelers, local residents used the land just outside the town plat to raise fodder or establish more pasture; if the land were wooded, they might cut fuel here.[31]

The linear plat became the most popular town plan by the end of the eighteenth century and continued to be used well into the nineteenth century, in part because it offered considerable flexibility for future growth. Landowners could plat new roads and strips of lots behind and running parallel to the turnpike to accommodate increasing populations. In New Market, for example, the original plat of 1785 included thirty-two half-acre lots along the wagon road, but Abraham Savage, who bought the entire town site, soon extended the town so that the back roads — Water Street and Lime Street — provided access to a second row of town lots. By the mid-nineteenth century, some residents actually preferred to live in these more quiet neighborhoods. Cross streets heading out of town also became valuable for commercial and residential use, because many towns sat at important regional road intersections with significant traffic. Speculators in Mount Crawford, for example, laid out additional lots along the crossroads.

The third type of settlement was not a planned town but rather a crossroads hamlet that consisted of a cluster of homes, shops, and other buildings often centered on a tavern, mill, church, or store. In many cases, such as Tenth Legion in Rockingham County, these communities served as centers of commerce and culture, but they were never platted by landowners (see fig. 7.5). Originally the site of a mid-eighteenth-century Quaker meeting, Tenth Legion hosted a stone church, tavern, and other commercial establishments in the nineteenth century. By the early twentieth century, Rockingham County built a consolidated school here, reflecting this hamlet's continued significance, though it had grown very little. Although houses, commercial buildings, and some farmsteads may have lined the road, they were arranged in a more irregular and dispersed collection on larger lots — depending on existing property lines — and were not packed as closely or neatly together as platted towns or villages.[32]

Building the Towns

As colonists settled along the wagon road in the eighteenth century, they created a sparsely populated urban landscape sprinkled with impermanent wooden buildings based on plan types and construction techniques from their European homelands. With energies focused on survival, they built structures necessary for this purpose: homes for their families, barns and stables for their animals, and gristmills, sawmills, lumber houses, storehouses, shops, stores, and taverns to facilitate industry, trade, and travel. While few buildings remain from this period — primarily a scattering of more substantial stone structures built toward the end of the century — a few surviving examples and historical documents suggest that most residents constructed homes that integrated family needs and public activities, doubling as taverns, stores, artisan shops, and meeting houses (see fig. 7.6). By opening their homes to board travelers or to trade goods, residents found a convenient way to augment their family incomes, regardless of house size.[33]

The most typical house type — a small, one- or two-story rectangular plan — provided a flexible arrangement of one or two first-floor rooms that could be used for commercial endeavors and family activities and a loft or second floor for sleeping and storage. Often of log construction attributed to the German immigrants and serviced by an end chimney, this "typical southern mountain cabin," defined by the folklorist Henry Glassie, became common throughout the Shenandoah Valley. A few still survive in towns along the wagon road. Most had small wooden barns, sometimes covered with thatch roofs. As their financial resources grew in the late eighteenth century, Valley residents began to improve their homes. They spruced up the exteriors with porticos and weatherboarding. Many enlarged their living space by adding rooms to accommodate their growing businesses and to offer more privacy for family life and by building detached outbuildings such as kitchens or smokehouses to remove domestic tasks from the home. Artisans moved their shops to a room on the end of the house to eliminate some of the dirt and commo-

Fig. 7.6. The house on the right illustrates the rectangular log home that appeared along the turnpike beginning in the eighteenth century and continuing through the late nineteenth century. This particular building, an early-nineteenth-century example later covered with brick, served as Smith's Tavern in the growing turnpike town of Greenville in Augusta County. (Scott Jost 2003)

tion from the family's living space. However, even the weal
to combine work and family under one roof.[34]

Given the array of services provided within homes, Val
communities exhibited few specialized building types in t⟨ ⟩ns or crossroads communities during the colonial period. With their two- or sometimes three-story elevations, gristmills dominated these fledgling urban
landscapes (see fig. 7.7). Originally wood-frame structures with dimensions ranging from twenty to fifty feet, mills were among the first public
buildings to be built of stone by the late eighteenth century, mirroring
the rising economic power of the Valley's wheat trade. Smaller wooden
industrial structures — such as sawmills and lumber houses — clustered
around the gristmills to create industrial neighborhoods along the rivers
and creeks.[35]

With the small number of public buildings, taverns became the focal
point of social life. Tavern keepers distinguished their buildings from domestic architecture and thus advertised their services by adding a wooden
piazza across the front and shed additions to the ends, creating a more

Fig. 7.7. Gristmills, such as the Grandstaff Mill near Edinburg, provided important services to wheat-growing farmers throughout the Valley. Towns and hamlets often developed around the Valley's mills. (Scott Jost 2004)

elongated appearance. The front porch provided a public place for local residents and travelers to exchange news and ideas as they waited for the stagecoach or to enjoy conversation before or after their meals. The local historian Oren Morton describes the role of the porch at Steeles Tavern in Augusta County: "In the summer, they sat on plain benches on the verandah. To the Virginian of his time, the bench in front of his tavern was a necessity." In addition, tavern keepers created an array of adjacent public spaces, including a stable and stable yard, often called a wagon stand, to the rear of the lot to unhitch teams and water, feed, and shelter the animals. Many taverns were sited at, and sometimes known by, a substantial spring, such as Lacey Springs in Rockingham County or Willow

Spout in Augusta County, that served as a popular publi
elers to water their coach and wagon horses or the swine
were driving to market. Blacksmiths, wagon makers, anc
settled around taverns to assist travelers with wagon repairs,
their homes or in separate shops.[36]

The communities along the wagon road assumed an increasingly refined urban appearance as a building boom swept through the Shenandoah Valley and the broader mid-Atlantic region by the turn of the
nineteenth century. The turnpike towns became the hubs for a thriving
regional economy, with roads and additional turnpikes radiating outward
to rural villages, industrial communities, and springs resorts. Town populations increased, new businesses and shops opened, and more permanent and fashionable buildings filled expanding town plats. The greatest
changes in rebuilding the architectural stock began with a burst of stone
construction in the years after the American Revolution but intensified
with an explosion of highly decorated brick buildings in the 1820s and
1830s. Valley communities exhibited a new regional architecture that reflected the region's growing prosperity and prominence. The incorporation and construction of the Valley Turnpike in the 1830s further accelerated the economic growth of and architectural change in these roadside
towns.[37]

Joseph Martin's *A New and Comprehensive Gazetteer of Virginia and the
District of Columbia* provides a window into the expansion of these towns
by 1835, the year after the Valley Turnpike was incorporated. These up-
and-coming urban landscapes now featured a growing number of businesses and public activities housed in specialized buildings, rather than
homes. Almost all towns had at least one church, a school, one or more
mercantile stores, at least two taverns, and a handful of tanyards, blacksmiths, and craft shops. Larger towns contained "handsome" schools,
physicians, lawyers, a greater diversity of businesses and shops, some
small factories, a few hotels, and general as well as specialized stores.[38]

The variety and types of buildings depended on the size, location, and
age of the community. Small and relatively new towns such as Mount Sidney, with 190 residents and thirty houses, had three stores, one school,
one church, two saddlers, one hatter, two boot- and shoemakers, one cabi-
netmaker, a pottery, and a milliner as well as three stores and a "hotel."
The larger, strategically situated commercial center of New Market, with
its seven hundred inhabitants, boasted seventeen trades, including house
joiners, wheelwrights, silversmiths, coppersmiths, gunsmiths, printers,
and locksmiths, leading Martin to write that there was "no town in the

state of the same size where mechanical pursuits are carried on to a greater extent than this." County seats featured a wider array of artisans than did more rural towns. Woodstock, for example, contained four tailors, five carpenters, two hatters, a tinner, two saddletree makers, two saddletree platers, two brick masons, a watchmaker, two plasterers, and a wagon maker. The town also included an earthenware factory, five boot and shoe factories, and a stoneware factory, as well as three lawyers, three physicians, three churches, six schools, and a Masonic hall. As the largest and oldest city in the Valley, Winchester had forty-six trades employing 170 "master workmen" and "several hundred journeymen" in addition to a plethora of more specialized stores and an array of schools, churches, cultural institutions, and benevolent societies.[39]

The greatest changes in the physical landscape appeared around the public square, where it existed, or along the main street, usually the Valley Turnpike. Within the square, county governments replaced rudimentary wooden courthouses with substantial stone or brick edifices, as in Winchester, Staunton, or Woodstock. Counties often rebuilt their other public buildings as well; Martin notes that Augusta County built a stone jail and a brick courthouse for the chancery court and clerk's office on the square by 1835. Strings of one-story brick law offices also clustered around the courthouse, still seen today in Woodstock and Staunton.[40]

Several of the largest towns, including Winchester, Staunton, Harrisonburg, and Stephensburg (now Newtown), erected brick public market buildings on or adjacent to the courthouse square in the early nineteenth century (see fig. 7.8). By creating a public space to house the sale of farm products such as meat, eggs, cheese, and bread, towns could establish and enforce regulations to ensure fair and ethical trade practices. The architecture of the market house spoke of its very public character: the arcaded walls welcomed the public into its midst. Inside, hucksters arranged their goods in rented stalls, while city residents streamed through the open interiors several times a week to purchase goods for their families. Larger cities such as Winchester added an additional floor above the market to provide space for town government meetings and other public functions. Without a courthouse square, Newtown placed its market in a prominent location: in the middle of the wide wagon road and within what had emerged as the commercial core of the town. By the mid-nineteenth century, market use throughout the Valley began to decline. Woodstock converted its building to serve other civic uses in 1850, including a town hall and fire hall, while the Staunton City Council voted to tear down its deteriorating market in 1853.[41]

Surrounding the square and clustered along the Main Street neighborhoods of the larger towns, merchants and shopkeepers erected stylish, two-story commercial buildings (see fig. 7.9). Many still contained both the store or shop and the family's living quarters, but business owners increasingly divided public from private space either horizontally or vertically. Some of the earliest examples feature a store and home side by side, the store or shop identified by large display windows and the home with smaller windows and a private door to the other side. Increasingly, however, merchants in larger cities and towns adopted a new two- or sometimes three-story commercial design, popular throughout the broader mid-Atlantic region, which devoted the entire first floor to commercial activity. Families might still live in the upper floor, but they lacked privacy as businesses filled the downtown blocks. Prospering merchants often preferred to move their families to private homes in the growing residential districts and to devote the upper stories of their buildings to other public uses such as offices, hotels, or meeting halls.[42]

In these larger cities and towns, the downtown business districts emerging along the Valley Turnpike and around the courthouse square became dense settlements of brick commercial buildings, sharing end walls in the narrow town lots. Stores and shops became quite decorative, mimicking popular new styles that illustrated the merchant's status as "economic and culture broker" of the community. The molded brick or delicate wooden cornices and fanlights from the Federal period popular in the early nineteenth century yielded to heavier wooden Italianate brackets above the windows and parapet façades by midcentury. Inside these stylish exteriors, city storekeepers stocked a tantalizing assortment of familiar and

Fig. 7.8. A view of the public market building in Winchester, from James Taylor's *Sketchbook*. Market buildings, such as this Winchester example, stood near the center of many early turnpike towns, but they fell into disuse and were removed by the 1850s. (Courtesy of the Western Reserve Historical Society, Cleveland, Ohio)

Fig. 7.9. Illustration of Loudoun Street in Winchester by A. Howe, 1848. By the mid-nineteenth century, the larger turnpike towns had become high-density assemblages of tightly packed buildings, including taverns, businesses, shops, and homes. Brick had become a popular construction material by the mid-nineteenth century. (Virginia Historical Society, Richmond, Virginia)

novel goods from the region and around the world, proudly displayed in the shelves lining the wall and on the counters wrapping around the interior. These shops offered a more refined shopping experience than the older, boisterous public market buildings. Female shoppers from town or the countryside could stroll along the "improved" plank sidewalks and "well-paved principal streets" in the downtown neighborhoods of larger towns to patronize mercantile establishments selling dry goods and groceries; specialty stores selling confections, fruit, books, and stationery; and artisan shops offering locally made and sometimes custom-produced hats, dresses, tin ware, or watches.[43]

Several other new building types emerged as additional signs of the growing sophistication and thriving economy of these turnpike towns in the early to mid-nineteenth century and of the increasing differentiation between public and private space. As travel intensified with the improved roadbed of the Valley Turnpike, more genteel visitors demanded new services and better lodging facilities. Although taverns still lined the turnpike at regular intervals, hotels began to replace them around the square and in the busy downtown commercial neighborhoods of larger turnpike towns by the 1830s and 1840s (see fig. 7.10). Boasting a more stylish brick construction and often rising three to four stories in elevation, hotels catered to a different clientele that demanded more amenities, including private rooms, while still retaining the familiar porch for socializing stretched

across the street façade. Joseph Martin described several "commodious" and "excellent" hotels in turnpike towns by 1835, with the greatest number clustered around the courthouse square in the larger towns.[44]

New schools and churches further flaunted the growing wealth and refinement of these booming turnpike towns, introducing popular new architectural styles to downtown and Main Street neighborhoods. Although Virginia did not fund free public education until 1870, local residents began to open private schools in homes or churches as early as the late eighteenth century. By the 1830s, larger towns and county seats offered a variety of educational opportunities and more specialized instruction: several schools, like Bernhard Willy's "Latin Academy" in Woodstock, taught a classical curriculum, while other communities offered separate male and female academies that reflected the diverging gender roles popularized during these years. Those schools successful enough to build new structures typically utilized the new Greek Revival style, exemplified by the Augusta Female Academy in Staunton. Still open today as Mary Baldwin College, this fashionable brick building sat several blocks north of the main street but perched proudly on a hill overlooking the town. Joseph Martin described the "brick academies" in towns such as Strasburg, New Market, and Woodstock as "commodious" and "handsome," adding sophistication to these growing urban communities.[45]

Valley residents proudly planted more permanent and increasingly stylish churches in the downtown neighborhoods of the turnpike towns by the first half of the nineteenth century. Denominations expressing the ethnic character of the region — such as the German Reformed, Lu-

Fig. 7.10. The Harrisonburg courthouse square as depicted by James Taylor during the Civil War. A Federal-style brick I-house stands to the left, a tavern or hotel with the distinctive long front porch to the right. The city spring, adjacent to the courthouse, features a pagoda roof. (Courtesy of the Western Reserve Historical Society, Cleveland, Ohio)

theran, Brethren, or Presbyterian — mixed with the Methodist and Baptist churches popularized by the frontier revivals of the Great Awakenings. With limited resources at first, congregations often built a log "union" church where several congregations might share the same building. During the 1820s and 1830s, however, residents began to construct more permanent brick sanctuaries, such as the Union Church, built ca. 1822, which still stands along the turnpike in downtown Mount Jackson. By the mid-nineteenth century, wealthier congregations proudly displayed their success by constructing new churches around the courthouse square or directly on the turnpike. While many of the ethnic congregations erected conservative structures in the local style — brick construction with a hint of Greek Revival detailing — Episcopal churches introduced the trendy Gothic Revival style in Middletown, Staunton, and Winchester, where Joseph Martin describes the 1829 church as "one of the best specimens of Gothic Architecture in the state." Martin mentions only one African American church in any of the turnpike towns in 1835, a Methodist church in Winchester, but some congregations allowed blacks to worship in segregated balconies.[46]

With their attractive public squares and new courthouses, surrounded by stylish brick commercial buildings, hotels, and "handsome" schools and churches, all connected by the new macadam turnpike and plank sidewalks, the downtown neighborhoods of the turnpike towns became a marketplace not only of goods but also of ideas. The turnpike and its travelers integrated Valley residents into a national popular culture. Town residents established Masonic Lodges and temperance societies, sometimes building separate halls but more often using the upper floors of downtown commercial buildings for their meetings. Sunday School Unions and Bible Societies joined an array of benevolent organizations that appealed to urban women who gathered formally in their parlors or churches as well as informally on their porches and in their backyards. Male residents in town congregated with farmers on the public square or in the downtown stores to share local stories, talk politics, and discuss the news coming from outside the region. Printing offices established in these turnpike towns during the early nineteenth century, such as the Henkel Press, in New Market, produced newspapers and publications that spread these new ideas all through the countryside.[47]

The enhancement of civic culture extended into the day-to-day improvements of urban life. Turnpike towns faced the same problems as other cities throughout the country. Increasing populations posed challenges to maintaining health and order and to ensuring productive and attractive communities. One of the most significant issues was ensuring an adequate water supply. Some cities like Winchester and Harrisonburg boasted a "never failing supply of pure, wholesome spring water." Harrisonburg's spring sat right on the courthouse square, but the city covered it with a "grand circular bell-shaped pagoda" for protection, a design that traveler James Taylor claims was "the pride of the townspeople." Woodstock similarly put an "arched and ornamental covering over the pump" to make it "an ornament of the town," noted the local newspaper, and destroyed the old horse trough. Many town governments established pumps serviced by underground water pipes to make water available throughout the town, given the absence of individual wells. One such pump remains along the old turnpike in New Market. Larger cities such as Staunton and Winchester led the way in other urban improvements: passing legislation to require that hogs and other animals running wild through town be confined, purchasing equipment to fight fires and organizing fire companies, installing flagstones to pave the main streets, and requiring residents to whitewash their outbuildings. By the 1850s, some turnpike towns had begun to add gas lighting, which vastly improved opportunities for business and pleasure in the evening hours.[48]

As the towns grew in size and sophistication in the first half of the nineteenth century, so did the homes and residential neighborhoods. Travelers such as Bernhard, Duke of Saxe-Weimar, and Joseph Martin noticed an increasing number of masonry houses in turnpike towns by the 1820s and 1830s. Most of these new dwellings aspired to the classically inspired Georgian ideal, as residents of the turnpike towns participated in the architectural rebuilding sweeping the East Coast after the American Revolution. A Renaissance concept popularized in England during the eighteenth century, the Georgian style diffused to the American colonies as a symbol of wealth and prestige, first to larger colonial cities and then westward as economic conditions allowed. The symmetrical, two-story design featured an ornamented central door, flanked by two windows and end chimneys to each side. Inside, a modern central hall created a formal arrangement of space, often with two rooms to one side of the hall and one larger room to the other side, and incorporated new public rooms such as parlors and dining rooms. Residents built these homes in prominent downtown locations to display their wealth, as exemplified in New Market by the brick and stone houses sited diagonally across the road from each other at the town's major intersection. The brick house, later known

Fig. 7.11. The Hardesty-Higgins House in Harrisonburg. The brick I-house—with a symmetrical façade, a central door, exterior end chimneys, and interior central hall—proved to be one of the most popular house types built in Valley Turnpike towns beginning in the first half of the nineteenth century. This mid-nineteenth-century example includes elements of the Greek Revival style. It was recently remodeled into a visitors' center. (Scott Jost 2004)

as the Lee Jackson Inn, boasts elements of the Federal or Adamesque style popular in the first decades of the 1800s, from its sidelights and transom surrounding the door to its delicately carved wooden cornice.[49]

By the 1820s, the classic Valley "I-house" emerged, a smaller, one-room-deep version of the Georgian design (see fig. 7.11). Built primarily of brick, it became the new status symbol to display one's wealth and social standing not only in the Valley but across the mid-Atlantic region. More economical than its predecessor, it featured an impressive, formal façade that often extended the full width of the narrow town lots, sometimes sharing end walls with neighboring homes. Valley residents interpreted the new style through a regional lens, adding molded or corbelled brick cornices, parapet gable ends, and sometimes decorative brickwork utilizing the glazed ends of the brick. Local builders drew on popular pattern books to provide the most up-to-date details — first Federal details from builder's guides by Owen Biddle and Asher Benjamin and then the Greek Revival, the first "national" style, that became the vogue by the 1830s — but recreated them in a more robust fashion integrated with ethnic symbols and designs and painted the woodwork in brightly colored patterns. City residents pushed the domestic work areas into a rear ell of one or two rooms and one or two stories in elevation. Examples of these antebellum brick I-houses fill town plats up and down the Valley Turnpike and spread out into the countryside, reflecting a new period of affluence as well as the increased stratification of local society. Those wooden buildings that did survive were often enlarged and remodeled into I-houses.[50]

The increasing hustle, bustle, and noise of the turnpike proved too much for some of the more middling- and upper-class town residents, who chose to relocate to quieter but still affluent neighborhoods. As the original town plans filled, entrepreneurial landowners platted new additions, spreading the townscape outward from the turnpike. These residential communities, such as Gospel Hill in Staunton in the 1840s, offered less traffic and more privacy, even if the roads were unimproved. Here, residents built fashionable houses in the popular revival styles on larger, landscaped lots with more generous front yards (see fig. 7.12). Living only a few blocks from the turnpike or the square, residents could easily walk to the downtown to conduct business while securing more privacy and

Fig. 7.12. Dr. A. M. Fauntleroy built this stylish suburban house in the Gospel Hill neighborhood of Staunton in the mid-nineteenth century. The home featured a substantial front yard and manicured landscaping. Increasingly, such trendy homes began to fill the newly established neighborhoods off the turnpike. (Reprinted from Hotchkiss's *Atlas of Augusta County,* 1885)

increased status for their families. According to the historian Lisa Tolbert, these new neighborhoods and homes "defined communal hierarchies" and increased "distinctions among town residents."[51]

At the same time, the expanding industrial communities in the turnpike towns also became increasingly segregated from both the downtown commercial district and the new residential neighborhoods. Most tended to be located at the edge of town, where the gristmills could take advantage of the waterpower along creeks or rivers. As the towns spread geographically, they moved away from the mill sites, leaving this land for new industries, craft shops, and other mechanical pursuits, such as the chopping mill and carding machine that emerged alongside the gristmill at the falls of Lewis Creek in Staunton. Rebuilt and often enlarged, the gristmills remained the centerpiece of these industrial districts.

Some turnpike towns developed new industries to service the region's grain farmers. By 1835, at least six towns — Middletown, Staunton, Newtown, New Market, Strasburg, and Mount Crawford — had manufactories that produced threshing machines or "wheat machinery." Many communities developed specializations that serviced not only the countryside but also provided goods to trade outside the region. Newtown had nine wagon makers who produced a nationally know "Newtown" wagon, sending them to "almost every part of the State" (see fig. 4.5 on p. 128). Strasburg, which had one stone and earthenware pottery factory in 1835, gained another five factories by 1900, leading to its nickname of "Pot Town."[52]

While larger enterprises sat on the outskirts of the community, smaller craft shops and other businesses were located throughout the town. Some artisans still kept work spaces in their homes, but by the mid-nineteenth century, they were beginning to construct shops adjacent to their homes or in the commercial core of town. Some of these buildings still survive, such as the small one-story frame cobblers shop located on Main Street in Mount Jackson. Livery stables, blacksmith shops, wheelwrights, and feed and sale barns were located along the side streets and back roads near the downtown commercial districts to service the horses and wagons for travelers (see fig. 7.13).[53]

The Valley Turnpike Company added a new architectural feature to the landscape: a string of gates, each with a tollhouse, where tolls were collected, located on the edge of cities and towns or within the small hamlets. Historical accounts and surviving structures suggest that the turnpike company utilized existing buildings for tollhouses whenever possible. According to local histories, for example, the brick home adjacent to the

Fig. 7.13. Harry Ritenour's livery stable and blacksmith shop in Mauertown. Small businesses such as this could be found in most turnpike towns along the main roads, back alleys, and side streets. In addition to stabling and shoeing horses and repairing carriages, these shops provided places for residents and visitors to meet socially. (Morrison Photographic Collection, Shenandoah County Historical Society)

Fort Defiance tollgate served as the tollhouse. In some smaller villages, the tollhouses served other functions as well, such as the "toll house and shoe shop" at Mount Tabor and the "toll house and post office" at Tenth Legion, both shown on an 1885 map of Rockingham County.[54]

The Valley Turnpike helped to disseminate new ideas from larger urban centers into smaller towns, villages, and hamlets along the turnpike and throughout the farms filling the countryside in the first half of the nineteenth century. As small towns boomed economically, socially, and culturally in their counties and regions, their townscapes mirrored the transformation. As in the larger towns, a building explosion led to increased physical growth, filling out the town plat with more permanent and stylish buildings of all types that housed a variety of cultural and social institutions and organizations.

Small-town residents mimicked the genteel character of larger communities, but in smaller communities these new ideas came more slowly and in smaller doses. Particularly noticeable in all towns was the appearance of brick construction in homes, businesses, and churches by the 1830s and 1840s. Still, while prospering residents constructed elegant Georgian houses or substantially remodeled older ones in the latest regional fashion and added a full complement of outbuildings and barns, many of their neighbors continued to build conservative, humble dwellings of log and frame in traditional two-room plans. Similarly, some proprietors began to build brick "hotels" to suggest greater sophistication, but the old-fashioned taverns were still commonly found along the turnpike. The "handsome hotel" that Martin describes in Mount Sidney in 1835 is likely Henry Roland's business, which was in a substantial brick I-house that resembles the regional tavern form but that the owner chose to call by a more appealing name.[55]

James Taylor describes the unevenness of this urban development in his diary during the Civil War years. While he notes that Newtown (now Stephens City) "enjoyed unusual prosperity . . . evidenced in its numerous substantial brick and frame dwellings," due to its "wealth derived from wheelwright and farm implement business," he portrays other towns in less glowing imagery. Taylor describes New Market as a "medley of dilapidated houses" and Harrisonburg as "not an impressive spectacle, being stores and dwellings, mostly two-story dingy frames." Similarly, Middletown had only frame and log homes except for the Methodist Church.[56]

Although smaller turnpike communities began to differentiate between public and private spaces, the divisions were less precise than in larger cities or towns. Laid out primarily on the linear plan, these towns lacked a central square or tightly packed downtown commercial neighborhood to provide a focus for civil life or social activities. While clusters of commercial buildings might develop within certain blocks, businesses, churches, shops, and offices were scattered along the turnpike, often adjacent to the homes of the business owners. Some residents built plank sidewalks in front of their businesses, creating places where men congregated (see fig. 7.14). But there were few strings of wooden walkways running throughout the town to allow travelers or residents, especially women, to walk safely along the turnpike to shop, visit, or engage in other business.

Small towns contained fewer buildings for public use. The new public buildings that emerged, especially churches, often served multiple purposes. In Mount Sidney, the town fathers designated a lot for a church when they platted the community, and the small wooden structure doubled as an "academy." Private homes still housed many social and cultural activities, blurring the distinction between public and private space. Some teachers opened schools in their own homes. Popular new fraternal organizations like the Masonic Lodge often met in homes or churches rather than establishing a permanent meeting hall. The Mount Sidney chapter of the Sons of Temperance rented rooms in town for their Saturday-night meetings, and members moved the society's "furniture" to the meeting place each week. Although they had fewer social organizations, women

Fig. 7.14. Several men congregate on the plank sidewalk in front of Harper's Store and post office in Mount Sidney. (Ralph Coffman Collection, Augusta County Historical Society)

found opportunities to meet friends and neighbors in churches and in their homes.[57]

As they moved out of the home, stores emerged as a distinct public space, especially for men, in the early nineteenth century. Here, farmers from the countryside, townspeople, and travelers exchanged news, visited, and perhaps picked up the mail while trading goods, conducting business, and inspecting the newest merchandise. Mount Sidney illustrates three types of store plans that appeared in the antebellum period. Merchant William Bruffey moved his store into a one-room, one-story brick addition to his home, providing it with its own separate entrance. A few lots north, town father Henry Roland built a more common design for small-town commercial buildings: a detached, rectangular, gable-entry building. A prospering merchant, Roland built a two-story store with brick construction and a decorative cornice but little other embellishment. Across the street stands a modest but more typical translation of this plan: a one-story frame store with a gable-end entrance built in the 1840s or 1850s. While its orientation belies its use, it lacks any other decoration and its scale, windows, and doors suggest the region's domestic architecture.[58]

Urban improvements developed more slowly in smaller towns. Like larger cities, towns and villages created a watering trough in town for

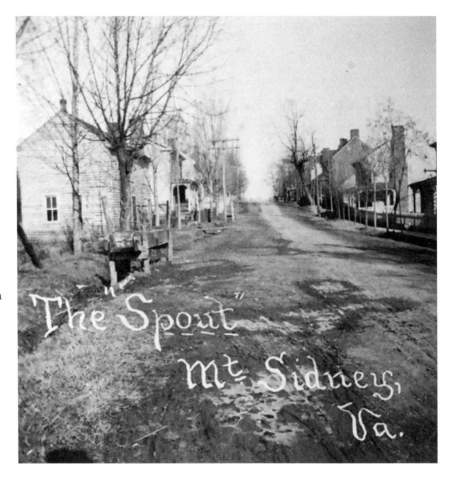

Fig. 7.15. A wooden watering trough at Mount Sidney sat along the turnpike, available for use by both travelers and residents. Rows of wooden houses with brick end chimneys, some I-houses, as well as two-room log houses covered with weatherboarding stand along the tree-lined road. (Ralph Coffman Collection, Augusta County Historical Society)

household and animal use, often fed by springs. Without a natural water supply, Mount Sidney piped water from a spring west of town to a springhouse in town and from there to a wooden watering trough located on the south end of town (see fig. 7.15). While some of these towns took on a more polished look during the antebellum period, with shade trees and fenced front yards lining the turnpike, the back roads and alleys remained muddy and unimproved, and animals roamed more freely than in the larger cities.[59]

The Coming of the Railroad

Ultimately, the railroad, more than the turnpike, would have the greatest impact on the growth of Valley Turnpike towns in the late nineteenth century, strengthening their ties with urban trade centers both to the north and to the east. The Winchester and Potomac Railroad penetrated as far south as Mount Jackson by 1859, linking these towns with trading opportunities along the Potomac River. Other railroads pushed west across gaps

in the Blue Ridge Mountains to link the turnpike towns to trading centers to the east, such as the Virginia Central Railroad, which connected Staunton with Charlottesville in 1854. Although the Civil War wrought devastation to existing tracks, the railroad companies quickly revived their efforts when the war ended, rebuilding existing lines and creating new ones. By the 1880s, a network of railroad lines ran the length of the Valley and crossed east–west through the major mountain gaps, knitting Valley Turnpike towns into a larger national economy and providing better access to a wider array of urban markets than had the turnpike.[60]

The railroads stimulated rapid growth in those turnpike towns and villages through which they ran. Some turnpike communities began to resemble the railroad boomtowns of the late nineteenth century. Businesses and industries abandoned the turnpike and moved to the railroad track, creating new commercial and manufacturing centers. Speculators platted new neighborhoods near the railroad lines, pulling residential development away from the turnpike. At Mauertown, a two-story store building illustrates the increasingly schizophrenic character of many of these turnpike towns. Wedged between the turnpike and the railroad track, the store has a formal façade on both of its gable ends to service both constituencies (see fig. 7.16).[61]

These new railroad communities attracted an array of industries. With

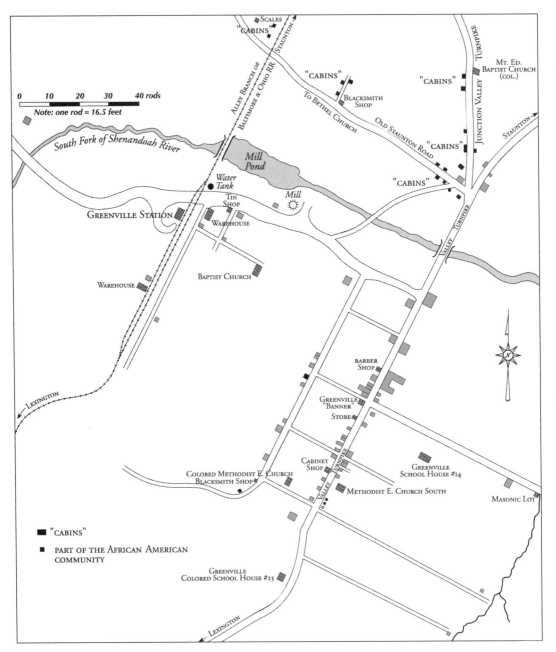

Fig. 7.17. The town of Greenville reached out to embrace the new railroad, developing industries and shops along the track. Soon after this 1885 map was drawn, the land between the railroad and the turnpike was developed and filled with stylish turn-of-the-century homes in a suburban-style neighborhood. An African American community developed on the north end of the town, where the homes on the map are labeled as "cabins." (Adapted from Hotchkiss's *Atlas of Augusta County*, 1885; Gyula Pauer Cartography Lab, University of Kentucky)

more expedient access to major cities, agricultural businesses emerged that could collect, process, store, and ship local farm products. Freed from dependence on waterpower, the "roller" mills processed wheat more efficiently and warehoused the flour until it could be transported by train to its destination. Poultry-processing operations replaced the old country store by purchasing live chickens and shipping them "on ice" to cities. Creameries sent trucks to neighboring farms to collect milk and cream for processing and shipping to market. Many train stations had a cattle yard where farmers could take their cattle to be held before being shipped by train to slaughterhouses. The railroads also serviced the new apple business in towns such as Mount Jackson and Winchester. Larger craft shops, such as sash and window companies, moved their businesses to the railroad to take advantage of improved transportation. Roads along the track, such as Commerce Street in Woodstock, filled with warehouses and other businesses.[62]

Smaller villages and hamlets along the turnpike experienced considerable growth if the railroad came within their reach. Mauertown in Shenandoah County boomed with the addition of two stores, two blacksmith shops, a carpentry shop, a chair factory, a sawmill, a shoe shop, a tin shop, and an icehouse, all clustered around the new railroad depot. Even small villages like Fort Defiance and Mint Spring in Augusta County gained additional commerce. Mint Spring, for example, acquired a railroad station and post office, and it became more of an economic and cultural center, with a church, school, and store, while the railroad helped to improve access to and enrollment at Augusta Military School near Fort Defiance.[63]

The depot stood as the foremost symbol of progress in these turnpike towns (see fig. 7.18). Its eclectic board-and-batten style in the late nineteenth century or brick construction by the early twentieth century set the stage for the "boomtown" character. Fashionable hotels were built near the railroad depot to accommodate train passengers, including tourists headed to the mountain springs resorts. Entrepreneurs opened boardinghouses to lodge traveling salesmen, or drummers, while their livery stables hired out horses and buggies so they could sell their wares in the countryside. Larger stores and banks sprouted up along the tracks to cash in on the new business opportunities provided by the railroad.[64]

Landowners took advantage of rising property values near the railroad to plat neighborhoods with more commodious lots than could be found along the turnpike (see fig. 7.17). In Greenville, where the railroad ran two miles west of town, speculators established a new neighborhood that quickly filled with Victorian homes. Often, these developments became

Fig. 7.18. The clapboard railroad station at Mauertown has wide, projecting eaves, a style typical of the wooden railroad stations found in many turnpike towns during the late nineteenth century. Groups of men and young boys are visiting on the benches in front of the station. (Morrison Photographic Collection, Shenandoah County Historical Society)

the elite residential districts in town, such as Gospel Street in Mount Jackson, Muhlenberg Street in Woodstock, or Capon Street in Strasburg, where wealthier residents, merchants, and industrial leaders built homes in the Queen Anne or other popular styles. Several prominent local architects and builders flourished in Valley towns and cities during this period by catering to this new sensibility for fashion, from the well-known Staunton architect T. J. Collins to the Eutlser Brothers from Grottoes, who built a distinctive type of Victorian house plan with gingerbread decoration that became common in turnpike towns in both Augusta and Rockingham counties (see fig. 7.19).

If the railroad ran more than a mile or two away from the turnpike, towns seldom spread that far to embrace it. In Mount Sidney, where the tracks paralleled the turnpike about one mile to the east, the only commercial building to crop up along the railroad was a store that doubled as the depot. Near Mount Crawford, a separate community called "Mount Crawford Station" emerged along the track and featured a cluster of businesses that competed with those on the turnpike. In other instances, entirely new "railroad" towns emerged, stunting the growth of older turnpike towns. Steeles Tavern, or Midway, a popular stagecoach stop halfway between Staunton and Lexington, found itself flanked by two railroads,

Fig. 7.19. Mount Crawford boasts one of the most stylish collections of Victorian homes along the turnpike. Many were older houses embellished in the late nineteenth century with turrets, jigsawn trim, and fashionable wraparound porches. (Scott Jost 2004)

but neither touched the town limits. The new towns of Raphine, which emerged on the Valley Railroad to the west, and Vesuvius, situated on the Shenandoah Valley Railroad to the east, both drained commerce away from the older turnpike town. In Rockingham County, where the tracks ran miles to the west of the turnpike, new railroad towns such as Linville, Broadway, and Timberville pulled much of the commercial growth from older turnpike communities such as Lacey Springs, Tenth Legion, or Melrose.[65]

Yet with or without the railroad, larger turnpike towns continued to benefit from the economic growth and prosperity that the Valley experienced in the late nineteenth century. Townspeople built new brick stores, from two to sometimes three stories high, and bedecked them with two-story wooden galleries with decorative scrollwork or spindle friezes, a few of which still survive. The upper levels of stores provided spaces for entertainment and cultural events, from fraternal meeting halls to theatrical performances and the opera. Fraternal organizations constructed their own fashionable buildings that resembled other commercial struc-

Fig. 7.20. The Masonic Lodge (*center*) in Greenville, with its decorative and heavily bracketed cornice, still stands in the middle of the commercial district along the old turnpike. In familiar local fashion, the first floor served as a store, with its recessed entry between large plate-glass windows, while the Masons used the second floor for their meeting hall. (Scott Jost 2003)

tures, incorporating commercial space on the first floor and meeting space above, as in the two-story frame Masonic Building in Greenville (see fig. 7.20). The Junior Order of the American Mechanics built what they called a town hall in Mount Sidney around 1900, providing the first floor with a stage to use for school plays, oyster suppers, traveling road shows, and later moving pictures, and using the upper level as their meeting hall (see fig. 7.21). Small wooden shops, usually one story high, filled in the urban

Fig. 7.21. The Junior Order of United American Mechanics Lodge building, Mount Sidney, ca. 1905–10. Two women and a child rest and visit on a bench outside this building, which local residents called Town Hall. The first floor served as a space for school plays, oyster suppers, and traveling road shows. The Mechanics held their meetings in the second-floor rooms. (Ralph Coffman Collection, Augusta County Historical Society)

landscape, producing a variety of wares needed by local residents, from furniture to shoes.[66]

The economic prosperity of the late nineteenth century ushered in a much more flamboyant spirit in the domestic architecture in the turnpike towns. Wealthy professionals and businesspeople who chose to live along the turnpike built larger and trendier homes that sat farther back from the road, often sporting a well-landscaped front yard. The turrets, projecting bays, and half-timbered gables of S. P. Lonas's house on Main Street in Mount Jackson, for example, made a bold statement about his role as a prominent town merchant, bolder still for its location right along the turnpike rather than tucked away in a more reclusive new neighborhood. Prospering residents living in older homes along the turnpike added a gloss of Victorian ornamentation to illustrate their desire to keep up with the new architectural styles and ideas. In Mount Crawford, turrets, wraparound porches with turned and jigsawn trim, shingled front gables, and stylish window treatments created striking new façades along the old turnpike. Doctors and lawyers continued to move their workspaces out of the house, either creating an office at one end of the home or building a new office right on the main road. Examples of both types remain in Mount Sidney (see fig. 7.22).

The architectural rebuilding swept through all building forms and types in the late nineteenth century. Church congregations replaced their smaller sanctuaries with larger and more fashionable frame and

Fig. 7.22. (*Top*) The Millard Johnston house in Mount Sidney, a stylish Victorian home typical of the late nineteenth-century prosperity along the turnpike, features a doctor's office with a separate entrance to the far left of the house. Some professional businessmen with homes along the turnpike added offices in just this manner, while others constructed detached office buildings next to their homes. (Ralph Coffman Collection, Augusta County Historical Society)

Fig. 7.23. (*Bottom*) Interior of the Planter's Bank in Staunton. Banks began to appear in turnpike towns by the late nineteenth century, at first often occupying existing buildings. More lavish bank buildings were built beginning in the early twentieth century. The rich interior of the Planter's Bank remains relatively intact. (Scott Jost 2000)

brick ones, often with Gothic Revival characteristics that featured corner towers. Bankers built some of the most stylish buildings in the turnpike towns, including numerous brick Classical Revival banks in northern Valley towns such as Mount Jackson, Strasburg, Woodstock, and Newtown in the early twentieth century (see fig. 7.23).

With the establishment of free public education in Virginia in 1870, public school buildings appeared on the town landscape. The first ones were simple frame buildings, ranging from one to three rooms, exemplified by the central building still remaining at the Lee-Jackson Hotel in Verona. By the early twentieth century, turnpike towns boasted modern brick consolidated schools built on designs provided by the Virginia Department of Education. Excellent examples survive in Greenville, Tenth Legion, Mount Jackson, and Edinburg. Several Civil War veterans opened military schools along the turnpike, including Augusta Military Academy in Fort Defiance, Staunton Military Academy in Staunton, and Valley Military Academy in Woodstock, displaying the Gothic Revival architecture associated with military schools at the time.

African American neighborhoods began to appear in turnpike towns after the Civil War, as families left the Valley's farms in search of better opportunities. The segregation of the Jim Crow era restricted their residential options, so they created their own communities on the edge of the town. Most clustered around an African American school or church, usually an African Methodist Episcopal (AME) church or Baptist church. An 1885 plat of Strasburg, for example, shows an AME church and a "colored school" that marked the location of the African American community on the western boundary of town, away from the commercial square and the railroad depot (see fig. 7.3). In Mount Sidney, African American families formed their own neighborhood centered on a church and school at the south end of town. Residents lived in small log or wooden houses along the back alley and in dispersed lots immediately outside the town plat. In Greenville, a black community described as "cabins" on an 1885 map extended on a road leading from the turnpike to the railroad (see fig. 7.17). A plat of Mount Crawford from the same year suggests that not all African American neighborhoods were totally segregated. While Mount Crawford's black residents tended to live in the north end of town, near their school or church, a few houses were interspersed with those of white inhabitants.[67]

Fledgling efforts at municipal improvements before the Civil War burgeoned during the late nineteenth century, a trend similar to one occurring in urban areas throughout the country. Cities and towns sought

Fig. 7.24. Automobile stopped at a tollgate. The arrival of the automobile brought dramatic change to the Valley Turnpike towns in the early twentieth century. Advertising signs for soft drinks had already appeared at roadside. The trees and front yards along the turnpike in Woodstock soon disappeared with the construction of a wider road in the 1930s. (Morrison Photographic Collection, Shenandoah County Historical Society)

to clean up streets filled, as one Woodstock resident wrote in 1886, with "the stench from some hog pen, rotten swill barrel, closet or cow yard that makes you sorry you are not deaf in your nose!" Woodstock passed ordinances requiring pens for animals and banning stables and privies that drained into the road. To improve pedestrian access, local governments paved the sidewalks and installed gas lamps, hiring a lamplighter to illuminate them at dusk. Shade trees still lined the turnpike in many of the towns, providing a measure of shade and a pleasant appearance for visitors and townspeople walking along the main road in increasingly active communities. By the turn of the twentieth century, many cities began building municipal buildings or town halls. The Edinburg Town Hall, built in 1903, included a fire engine room on the first floor, with a belfry to ring the bell, and a community center, opera house, and meeting room for the Masonic Lodge on the second floor. In civic and cultural life, the turnpike towns increasingly resembled urban communities and small towns across the country.[68]

By the early twentieth century, the cultural landscape of the Valley Turnpike had changed dramatically. Travelers could encounter booming cities, from county seats to railroad towns, that had grown far beyond their original grid plans. Hefty, stylish brick stores and hotels filled the extensive commercial districts, both on the turnpike and by the railroad, and stylish Queen Anne homes punctuated suburban-style neighborhoods. Even the smaller strip towns had become larger and more fashionable, with development radiating behind the original plats. As centers of regional commerce, they featured a wide assortment of building types interspersed throughout the town and decorated with a glaze of new Victorian styles reflecting the region's economic boom. Smaller crossroads settlements filled the remaining gaps along the turnpike, offering a variety of services such as stores, churches, schools, artisan shops, and lodging, as well as a cluster of homes.

In the midst of the growing homogenization of American culture, the Valley Turnpike towns still exhibited a distinctive regional culture rooted in its history and expressed in its ethnic and religious ideas, its thriving agricultural economy, and its architectural and other folk traditions. While travelers might experience some variations between communities, they could expect to encounter residents who shared similar values and traditions, both in town and in the country. The turnpike towns still remained the cultural centers of the Valley, where travelers exchanged new ideas with local people at the stores, in the hotels, or, later, at the depot, and where local residents found frequent opportunities for socializing and entertainment at the churches, meeting halls, and schools as well as on their porches, in their homes, or along the streets and alleys of these growing towns. Though connected to the outside world by both the turnpike and the railroads, residents still remained insular, focused on their own communities. They knew each other through daily interactions, helped each other through churches and community organizations, and faced the outside world with a relatively unified perspective. The turnpike had bound these communities together.[69]

The arrival of the automobile in the early twentieth century would transform this landscape once again (see fig. 7.24). It helped initiate a decline in small-town economy and culture, as residents motored to the larger cities to seek employment and business opportunities, to find greater choices for entertainment, and to attend consolidated schools or larger churches. While some local institutions survived, others disappeared. Small towns may have gained new businesses such as filling stations, restaurants and diners, tourist courts and tourist homes, but they lost much of their industrial and commercial base. Even the tourist trade began to disappear when Interstate 81 replaced the turnpike as the major thoroughfare through the Valley in the 1960s. Ironically, in recent years, the automobile has brought a renaissance of sorts to these neglected turnpike towns. Seeking to avoid the impersonal character of the interstates, tourists have rediscovered the Valley Turnpike to appreciate and enjoy its rich history and architectural legacy. Through these well-preserved turnpike towns, visitors gain insight into the forces that shaped the Shenandoah Valley and its culture.

Notes

1. "Lewis Summer's Journal of a Tour from Alexandria, Virginia, to Gallipolis, Ohio, in 1808," *Southern Historical Magazine* 1, no. 2 (February 1892): 52–53.

2. John Wayland, *A History of Shenandoah County, Virginia* (1892; repr., Baltimore: Regional Publishing, 1989), 139; Joseph Martin, *A New and Comprehensive Gazetteer of Virginia and the District of Columbia* (Charlottesville, Va., 1835), 451.

3. Martin, *Gazetteer*, 427, 445.

4. Kenneth Keller, "The Wheat Trade on the Upper Potomac," in Kenneth E. Koons and Warren R. Hofstra, eds., *After the Backcountry: Rural Life in the Great Valley of Virginia, 1800–1900* (Knoxville: University of Tennessee Press, 2000), 26.

5. Christopher E. Hendricks, *The Backcountry Towns of Colonial Virginia* (Knoxville: University of Tennessee Press, 2006), 94–95.

6. For more on this development from open-country neighborhoods to "a closer integration of town and country in the backcountry," see Warren R. Hofstra, *The Planting of New Virginia: Settlement and Landscape in the Shenandoah Valley* (Baltimore: Johns Hopkins University Press, 2004), 10. John W. Reps describes the slow process of town development in Virginia and the colonial incentives to create towns in *Tidewater Towns: City Planning in Colonial Virginia and Maryland* (Williamsburg, Va.: Colonial Williamsburg Foundation, 1972), 66, 195. The concept of towns as "business propositions" appears in John A. Jakle, *The American Small Town: Twentieth-Century Place Images* (Hamden, Conn.: Archon, 1982), 13.

7. "In the absence of any easily navigable streams," writes the geographer Robert Mitchell, "the development of valley communications during the pioneer period had focused on a rudimentary road network." His maps on pages 191 and 192 reveal the key role that crossroads played in town development (see Mitchell, *Commercialism and Frontier: Perspectives on the Early Shenandoah Valley* [Charlottesville: University Press of Virginia, 1977], 189–92).

8. There were several efforts to make the Shenandoah River navigable for trade, with access to the Potomac and James rivers, and to create links with the Ohio River, but they were unsuccessful. As the geographer Robert Mitchell writes, "Except for settlers at the extreme ends of the Valley, the region was without cheap water transport throughout the eighteenth century, and the functioning of its towns was entirely dependent upon the maintenance of its highway network." The only improvements completed by 1807 included "eight miles of the South Branch above Harpers's Ferry" and the James River to Buchanan, in present-day Botetourt County (Mitchell, *Commercialism and Frontier,* 195).

9. For more on the application of "central-place" theory to the Shenandoah Valley, see Robert Mitchell, "The Settlement Fabric of the Shenandoah Valley, 1790–1860," in Koons and Hofstra, eds., *After the Backcountry,* 35–36. Mitchell argues that classic central-place theory is ineffective in describing the more distinctive pattern of small towns that evolved in the southern United States.

10. Being a county seat did not necessarily guarantee a community more trade and commerce, as several scholars have noted. However, Mitchell observes that the early county seats in the Shenandoah Valley tended to become more urban than those east of the Blue Ridge, in large part because the county seats tended to be at a crossroads of major travel and trade arteries. He notes that one of the reasons why the population of Winchester became so much larger than that of Stephensburg (later Stephens City) in the eighteenth century was because it was the county seat (Mitchell, *Commercialism and Frontier,* 14, 155, 199).

11. Ibid., 11.

12. Hofstra, *The Planting of New Virginia,* 8, 181; Hendricks, *The Backcountry Towns of Colonial Virginia,* 150.

13. Hendricks, *The Backcountry Towns of Colonial Virginia,* 95–96; Historic Staunton Foundation, *Staunton, Virginia: A Pictorial History* (Staunton: Historic Staunton Foundation, 1985), 12.

14. Hendricks, *The Backcountry Towns of Colonial Virginia,* 109–10; Mitchell, "The Settlement Fabric of the Shenandoah Valley," 38.

15. Mitchell, *Commercialism and Frontier,* 196. According to Reps, new towns were expected to provide men between the ages of sixteen and sixty prepared to fight (Reps, *Tidewater Towns,* 195).

16. Mitchell, *Commercialism and Frontier,* 198.

17. Hofstra, *The Planting of New Virginia,* 263; Mitchell, "The Settlement Fabric of the Shenandoah Valley." Lisa Tolbert notes that the development of towns occurred slowly throughout the eighteenth-century backcountry. Robert Mitchell confirms this statement about the Shenandoah Valley, writing that "Urban settlement during the pioneer period had developed at a very elementary level. It was only during the 1760s that moves were made to establish towns in addition to the county seats of Winchester and Staunton (see Tolbert, *Constructing Townscapes: Space and Society in Antebellum Tennessee* [Chapel Hill: University of North Carolina Press, 1999], 20; Mitchell, *Commercialism and Frontier,* 195).

18. John W. Wayland, *A History of Rockingham County, Virginia* (Harrisonburg: C. J. Carrier, 1972), 202; John Wayland, *Twenty-five Chapters on the History of the*

Shenandoah Valley (Strasburg: Shenandoah Publishing House, 1957), 351; Mitchell, *Commercialism and Frontier*, 172, 201.

19. Hendricks, *The Backcountry Towns of Colonial Virginia*, 106; John W. Wayland, *A History of Shenandoah County, Virginia* (Baltimore: Regional Publishing, 1989), 124, 148.

20. Mitchell, *Commercialism and Frontier*, 90, 197–98; Hofstra, *The Planting of New Virginia*, 285; Ann McCleary, "Historic Resources of Augusta County, Virginia" (Richmond: Virginia Historic Landmarks Commission, 1983), 924. According to Mitchell, "speculation in town lots developed an entirely new phase after 1780."

21. Katherine Bushman, "Mt. Sidney — A Brief History from 1826," *Augusta Historical Bulletin* 19, no. 2 (Fall 1983): 47.

22. Ann McCleary, "Survey of the Village of Mt. Sidney," unpublished report for Virginia Department of Historic Resources, May 1999, 17–18.

23. Wayland, *A History of Rockingham County, Virginia*, 201; Wayland, *Twenty-five Chapters*, 249; Clay Catlett and Elliott G. Fishburne, *An Economic and Social Survey of Augusta County*, University of Virginia Record Extension Series 13 (Charlottesville: University of Virginia, 1928), 21.

24. See fig. 3.4 in Mitchell, "The Settlement Fabric of the Shenandoah Valley," 42.

25. Reps, *Tidewater Towns*, 22, 195, 213.

26. Hofstra writes that Stephensburg, platted in 1758, offered out lots for the "self-sufficiency of residents in time of war" (Hofstra, *The Planting of New Virginia*, 261). Mitchell, *Commercialism and Frontier*, 197; Wayland, *A History of Shenandoah County, Virginia*, 131; Hendricks, *The Backcountry Towns of Colonial Virginia*, 122. For a more extensive discussion of town planning, see Hendricks, *The Backcountry Towns of Colonial Virginia*.

27. See Reps, *Tidewater Towns*, 12, for more on market squares in France and Ireland, including Londonderry in Ulster, now Northern Ireland. Philadelphia was the first large city to be built on a grid pattern, with "the houses . . . built in a line." According to Reps, William Penn "requested a rectangular street pattern and uniform spacing of buildings," adding, "let the houses be built in a line." Philadelphia was the first large American city built on the grid plan (see John W. Reps, *Town Planning in Frontier America* [Columbia: University of Missouri Press, 1980], 143). The Pennsylvania model proved popular along the National Road as well (see Karl Raitz, ed., *The National Road* [Baltimore: Johns Hopkins University Press, 1996], 269).

28. Bernard Herman, Thomas Ryan, David Schuyler, "Townhouse: From Borough to City, Lancaster's Changing Streetscape," in Nancy Van Dolson, ed., *Architecture and Landscape of the Pennsylvania Germans, 1720–1920* (Harrisburg, Pa.: Vernacular Architecture Forum, 2004), 78; *Staunton, Virginia: A Pictorial History*, 16; Pamela Simpson and Royster Lyle, *The Architecture of Historic Lexington* (Charlottesville: University Press of Virginia, 1977), 7–9; Hofstra, *The Planting of New Virginia*, 183; Hendricks, *The Backcountry Towns of Colonial Virginia*, 110, 146; Edward T. Price, "The Central Courthouse Square in the American County Seat," in Dell Upton and John Michael Vlach, eds., *Common Places: Readings in*

American Architecture (Athens: University of Georgia Press, 1986), 138–42. In his study of the National Road, Karl Raitz has observed that while the square is found, not many road towns have it because the "strip development" was "all-controlling" and because the square appealed more to towns that aspired to the county seat (Raitz, ed., *The National Road*, 270).

29. Tolbert, *Constructing Townscapes*, 24; Mutual Assurance Records, Lexington, 1816.

30. Raitz, ed., *The National Road*, 262, 269. The geographer Richard Pillsbury calls this the "Linear-r" plan. According to John Reps, these plans were popular in Ireland, where a "single street provided access to dwellings, church, and other structures" (Reps, *Turnpike Towns*, 16).

31. Tolbert, *Constructing Townscapes*, 57; Raitz, ed., *The National Road*, 198, 261–62; Reps, *Town Planning*, 147.

32. Wayland, *Valley Turnpike* (Winchester: Winchester-Frederick County Historical Society, 1967), 37. Robert Mitchell describes a hamlet as "more clustered settlement forms that might include an occasional agricultural unit but were distinguished by supporting three or four non-farm functions, such as those expressed in a store, artisan's shop, mill, or residence of a local justice, minister, or school keeper" (Mitchell, "The Settlement Fabric of the Shenandoah Valley," 34). Other examples of hamlets along the turnpike include Lacey Springs in Rockingham County or Toms Brook in Shenandoah County. John Reps documents these types of crossroads plans in Ireland as well (see Reps, *Tidewater Towns*, 16).

33. These types of buildings are listed in the eighteenth-century policies included in the Mutual Assurance Records for Shenandoah Valley towns. For more on the flexible use of early housing for other purposes, see Tolbert, *Constructing Townscapes*, 50; Herman, Ryan, and Schuyler, "Townhouse," 89; and Raitz, ed., *The National Road*, 270.

34. Judith Ridner's study of Carlisle, Pennsylvania, north of Winchester, reveals that some tavern keepers operated their businesses in homes as small as 720 square feet, while other families provided larger quarters in more stylish dwellings. Ridner notes that even wealthy merchants operated businesses out of their homes at the turn of the nineteenth century (Ridner, "Status, Culture, and the Structural World in the Valley of Pennsylvania," in Koons and Hofstra, eds., *After the Backcountry*, 86). For other descriptions of this pattern, see Raitz, ed., *The National Road*, 220; and Hofstra, *The Planting of New Virginia*, 300. Raitz notes that this arrangement was common in the Pennsylvania town model found on the National Road. National Register nominations for towns along the Valley Turnpike reference many examples of this pattern.

35. Lisa Tolbert argues that in this first period of town development, there were few specialized building forms and that people and businesses were mixed together with little class distinction (Tolbert, *Constructing Townscapes*, 50). Information on mill and other industrial building types and dimensions is taken from the Mutual Assurance Records.

36. Oren Morton, *A History of Rockbridge County, Virginia* (Staunton: McClure, 1920), 157; Wayland, *Twenty-five Chapters*, 237, 252; Raitz, ed., *The National Road*, 198, 262; Herman, Ryan, and Schuyler, "Townhouse," 91. For descriptions of these

taverns, see the Mutual Assurance Records, which often note the piazzas or additions to older homes as they became transformed into taverns.

37. For more on the rebuilding of Shenandoah Valley architecture and the development of a regional style, see Ann McCleary, "Forging a Regional Identity: Development of Rural Vernacular Architecture in the Central Shenandoah Valley, 1790–1850," in Koons and Hofstra, eds., *After the Backcountry*, 92–110. For additional discussion on the general rebuilding of architectural stock across the broader East Coast region, see Bernard Herman, *Architecture and Rural Life in Central Delaware, 1700–1900* (Knoxville: University of Tennessee Press, 1986); Henry Glassie, "Eighteenth-Century Cultural Process in Delaware Valley Folk Building," in Dell Upton and John Michael Vlach, eds., *Common Places: Readings in American Vernacular Architecture* (Athens: University of Georgia Press, 1986); Richard L. Bushman, *The Refinement of America: Persons, Houses, Cities* (New York: Knopf, 1992); Cary Carson, "The Consumer Revolution in Colonial British America: Why Demand?" in Cary Carson, Ronald Hoffman, and Peter J. Albert, eds., *Of Consuming Interest: The Style of Life in the Eighteenth Century* (Charlottesville: University Press of Virginia, 1994), 483–97; Edward Chappell, "Housing a Nation: The Transformation of Living Standards in Early America," in Carson, Hoffman, and Albert, eds., *Of Consuming Interest*, 167–232.

38. Martin, *Gazetteer*, 209–19, 227–46, 424–34, 445–52.

39. Ibid., 318, 344, 451–52.

40. Ibid., 319.

41. Hofstra, *The Planting of New Virginia*, 315, 297; Staunton City Council Minutes, July 13, 1949 and December 16, 1853; Clower, *Early Woodstock*, 11, 35. Harrisonburg had a "neat brick markethouse, lately erected" in 1835, according to Martin, *Gazetteer*, 433. Even smaller towns like Mount Sidney considered created a market building. In 1829, inhabitants asked for permission to hold a lottery to raise five thousand dollars to build a market, town hall, and other buildings, but these efforts do not appear to have been successful (Nelson H. Fogle, "A History of Mt. Sidney, Virginia," manuscript in possession of Ralph S. Coffman, Mount Sidney, Virginia, dated 1967, 28).

42. Richard Longstreth, *The Buildings of Main Street* (Walnut Creek, Calif.: Alta Mira Press, 2000), 24; Raitz, ed., *The National Road*, 270; Tolbert, *Constructing Townscapes*, 96.

43. Martin, *Gazetteer*, 318–19, 343–46; Jakle, *American Small Town*, 18–19; Herman, Ryan, and Schuyler, "Townhouse," 90.

44. Richard L. Bushman, *The Refinement of America: Persons, Houses, Cities* (New York: Knopf, 1992), 357, 367; Martin, *Gazetteer*, 318–19, 344.

45. Martin, *Gazetteer*, 451–52, 318–19.

46. Ibid. All of the turnpike towns described in Martin's account mention at least one church. Many survive and are included in the National Register nominations for towns such as Mount Jackson, Stephens City, Strasburg, and Woodstock.

47. Martin, *Gazetteer*, 344–45; Tolbert, *Constructing Townscapes*, 78; Wayland, *A History of Rockingham County, Virginia*, 281; Wayland, *Valley Turnpike*, 36–37.

48. Clower, *Early Woodstock*, 32, 38; McCleary, "Mt. Sidney," 28; James E. Taylor, *With Sheridan Up the Valley in 1864: Leaves from an Artist's Sketchbook and*

Diary (Cleveland: Western Reserve Historical Society, 1989), 421; Staunton City Council Minutes, 1849–1859, Staunton City Hall, Staunton, Va.; Martin, *Gazetteer,* 344–46.

49. For more development of this idea in the Shenandoah Valley, see McCleary, "Forging a Regional Identity," in Koons and Hofstra, eds., *After the Backcountry,* 92–110, or the additional sources listed in footnote 35 of that article for the process of architectural development and refinement throughout the mid-Atlantic region.

50. Ibid. The term "I-house" was coined by the geographer Fred B. Kniffen in his classic article "Folk Housing: Key to Diffusion," *Annals of the Association of American Geographers* 55 (December 1965): 549–77.

51. Tolbert, *Constructing Townscapes,* 88, 94; McCleary, "The Gospel Hill Community in the 1850s," unpublished report prepared for the Woodrow Wilson Foundation, Staunton, Va., February 1996. Richard Bushman notes that when businesses moved out of homes in the nineteenth century, women gained control of the homes. "Men needed grand houses," he writes, and "they valued the culture of their wives" (Bushman, *Refinement of America,* 442).

52. Martin, *Gazetteer,* 339–40, 433, 450–52.

53. Jakle, *American Small Town,* 29; Herman, Ryan, and Schuyler, "Townhouse," 94–95.

54. Lake, *Atlas of Rockingham County,* 1885.

55. McCleary, "Mt. Sidney," 25.

56. Taylor, *With Sheridan Up the Valley,* 421, 124, 129, 138.

57. McCleary, "Mt. Sidney," 25–26. In his study of the National Road, Karl Raitz notes that the "Pennsylvania town was for trade and the town center was a commercial not a social or religious place." He observed that churches were often built off the main road. In the Valley Turnpike towns with a linear plan, the churches were typically built along the road, because there was usually only one row of lots on each side. By the late nineteenth century, however, as additional lots were laid out behind the main street in towns like Woodstock or New Market, congregations began to build churches on the back roads (Raitz, ed., *The National Road,* 261).

58. McCleary, "Mt. Sidney," 31–32.

59. Fogle, "History of Mt. Sidney," 6–7; Taylor, *With Sheridan Up the Valley,* 139.

60. Mount Jackson Historic District Nomination, 28; Historic Staunton Foundation, *Staunton: An Illustrated History,* 26.

61. As Jakle argues, the railroads "created distinctive landscapes." In these turnpike towns, the railroad landscape was imposed upon the existing turnpike landscape (Jakle, *American Small Town,* 32).

62. Raitz, ed., *The National Road,* 208. These businesses and warehouses are evident on the maps of these turnpike towns in Hotchkiss, *Atlas of Augusta County,* 1885; Lake, *Atlas of Rockingham County,* 1885; and Lake, *Atlas of Shenandoah and Page Counties,* 1885.

63. Wayland, *A History of Shenandoah County, Virginia,* 156; Hotchkiss, *Atlas of Augusta County,* 64, 76.

64. For a general discussion of these railroad developments, see Jackle, *American Small Town,* 16; Raitz, ed., *The National Road,* 206–8. There are many exam-

ples from the turnpike towns listed in the National Register nominations of these communities and illustrated on the 1880s historical atlases of each county.

65. See the maps of these towns in the 1880s atlases, including Hotchkiss, *Atlas of Augusta County,* 1885; Lake, *Atlas of Rockingham County,* 1885; and Lake, *Atlas of Shenandoah and Page Counties,* 1885.

66. Clower, *Early Woodstock,* 36–37, describes several three-story brick buildings built in Woodstock in the late nineteenth century, including the Burner Building (1881); the Irwin Building, which had an opera house on the third floor; and the Kneisley Building, which obtained a third floor in 1914 to house the Masonic Lodge (see Fogle, "History of Mt. Sidney," 25, for the Mount Sidney meeting hall). Jakle argues that the lodge halls and opera houses were often among the most "architecturally refined buildings in town," but in the Valley, the major differences were that they might be three stories rather than two in the larger towns and that the façade might be slightly more stylish (Jackle, *American Small Towns,* 25).

67. These African American communities are visible in the maps found in the historical atlases of the Valley's counties published in 1885, including Hotchkiss, *Atlas of Augusta County;* Lake's *Atlas of Rockingham County;* and Lake's *Atlas of Shenandoah County.*

68. Clower, *Early Woodstock,* 49–61; Jackle, *American Small Town,* 31.

69. Jakle, *American Small Town,* 49.

U.S. 11 and a Modern Geography of Culture and Connection

KARL RAITZ

The Road in Context

J. B. Jackson's observation that the modern, long-distance American road has a complex, multivalent character is apperceptive. Road travel by motor vehicle opened a radically new mode of movement for Americans, a form of transport so compelling that it would soon command vast sums of federal and state monies for road construction, while fostering a host of unforeseen changes in American culture. Motor vehicles changed the way people related to places, especially though travel, be it local and social or long-distance and vocational. As Americans invented new institutions to produce, market, service, and repair vehicles, and to serve travelers' needs, old institutions that had served the overland wagon and coach industry stagnated and began to fade in importance. Motorized travel opened a new social world for isolated rural people while reinforcing the centrality of well-located towns, be they oriented to old roads, canals, or railroads. The nature of motorized movement itself was so different from travel by train or harnessed-horse team that it promoted new personal values and attitudes — geographic mobility over the tyranny of isolation; aspirations to self-improvement over resignation to one's station in life; mechanical aptitude over animal husbandry. In short, motorized movement introduced an era of ascending individualism. The key to the success of this revolution in the culture of mobility, of course, was the road and its successful adaptation to automobiles and trucks.

While roads permit movement, in the largest sense, they also represent a unique form of linear place where the formal, disciplined behaviors of road-building civil engineers splice into the undisciplined, seemingly chaotic, political and social behaviors exhibited by road users and those who take up entrepreneurial residence at roadside. To begin to appreciate the manner in which the interdigitated interests of road builders and users

[B]ut what a complex thing the modern highway has become; how varied its functions and how varied the public which makes use of it! To the factory or warehouse on its margin, it is essentially the equivalent of the railroad; to the garage or service station, it means direct accessibility to the passing public. The local businessman thinks of it as a way to reach and exploit the outlying suburban and rural areas, the farmer thinks of it as a way to reach town; the tourist thinks of it as an amenity, and the transcontinental bus or trucking company thinks of it as the shortest distance between two widely separated points. Each of these interests not only has its own idea of how the highway is to be designed and traced, it brings its own special highway service establishment into being.
—John Brinkerhoff Jackson

came together along the Valley Road, how the routeway was made over into U.S. 11, and how the new motor highway and its attendant roadside evolved together, we must reconstruct, at least partially, the road's technical, political, and social contexts.

Precursor Road

By the early 1900s, in the very early years of the automobile revolution, the Valley Road had been in active use for more than a century as a migration route, as a long- and short-distance commercial thoroughfare for wagon-borne farm and manufactured goods, and as a local linkage between Valley farmers and the market towns that people were building along the road. From the Potomac River in the north to Natural Bridge and Buchanan in the south, about two-dozen road-oriented towns and hamlets grew up at select sites: regional crossroads, stream fords, mills, and taverns. Town dwellers built their homes and places of business as close to the road surface as they could. Farmers and rural property owners recognized the value of property with direct access to the road and bid up the price of frontage land and oriented their homes and farmstead buildings to the road's alignment.[1]

The old wagon road was an organic road in the sense that it tended to follow the most agreeable topography directly, with little effort invested in modifying grades, calculating and building curves to constant radii, or moving rock and earth to produce a straight and level way. Before turnpike companies applied protective macadam road surfacing, the roadbed tracked across bare earth that the passing parade of draft animals and iron-rimmed wagon wheels pulverized into fine dust. Winter frost heaves and summer rains, acting in concert with steep-slope pitches and gravity, rapidly eroded the loose roadway surface, incising it to bedrock so that the road maneuvered rolling terrain by following a sunken trench.[2] The depth of Valley soils from surface to bedrock varied with topographic conditions. With the exception of short sections on shale near Fishers Hill, south of Strasburg, and a few other places, the road tracked across rather stout limestones for much of the Valley's length. Radically different conditions prevailed on low-lying road sections in stream valleys where the track lay atop alluvial soils that became muddy mires after heavy rains. Nineteenth-century road builders converted the old dirt road into a stone-surfaced toll road following John McAdam's technique and thereby transformed the way into an outstanding road — an Appian Way through a wilderness of mud tracks.[3]

Embracing the Automobile

Hard by U.S. 11 at the Buchanan city limits, a blue, black, and gold sign announces to passersby that the town is "Gateway to the Shenandoah Valley." A secondary message admonishes the visitor to "Enjoy It's [*sic*] Beauty Keep It Clean" (see fig. 8.1). In addition to functioning as the Valley's southern gateway for auto-borne travelers, Buchanan has been a transportation hub for two centuries or more. The Valley Pike crossed the James River here. The James River and Kanawha Canal terminated here. And the Norfolk and Western Railroad passes through on the east side of town.

By 1910, the macadam-surfaced Valley Pike was one of Virginia's best roads, but as long as people were dependent upon canal boats, railroads, or stagecoaches to move themselves or their goods, they traveled at the whim of company schedules. The affordable automobile, personified by Henry Ford's assembly-line Model T in 1908, revolutionized personal

Fig. 8.1. On Buchanan's south side, a "Gateway to the Shenandoah Valley" sign along U.S. 11 beckons the traveler. (Scott Jost 2003)

travel in America and offer unfettered mobility to the middle class. The mass-produced auto was democratic both in the sense that its low price allowed middle-class people to buy one new or used, and because it allowed anyone with access to a car and the know-how to operate one to drive anywhere — according to any schedule they chose — that roads might lead them.[4] Farm people living in the countryside employed the car, and its industrial-strength cousins, the truck and the pickup, to deparochialize their communities. With a motorized vehicle, rural folk could readily reach their choice of market towns in a fraction of the time required to travel with team and wagon. Farm women were no longer isolated in deep country byways but now had access to town churches, social clubs, Main Street businesses, and other city amenities.[5] Businesspeople found great comfort and profit in the flexibility that a private automobile gave them — town-to-town sales calls were now a matter of personal convenience, not straight-jacketed by inflexible train schedules.[6] But family physicians pioneered the use of the automobile as a professional conveyance. Though early autos were fraught with mechanical problems and rode on vulnerable tires, doctors found that the upkeep expenses of the automobile compared favorably with those required to maintain a horse and buggy and that the automobile allowed them, in a given day's travel, to go faster, to range farther, and to have contact with many more patients than was possible in traversing the same route by horse.[7]

At the eve of the automobile era in 1910, Virginians owned 2,705 automobiles, but for Shenandoah Valley motorists, only the Valley Pike had a surface sufficiently resilient to entertain long-distance travel.[8] Before Valley residents could deploy the new internal-combustion freedom machines and experience the transformative effects of self-propelled movement, however, the Valley Pike and its ancillary feeder roads had to be linked into a reliable network of all-weather, hard-surface highways. By adopting the automobile, Virginians and their counterparts across the nation initiated large-scale revolutionary changes in social and economic life. And new modes of living, based in individualized mobility, begat new landscapes adapted to travel by car and truck.

On the face of it, the primary problem experienced by everyone who bought an automobile was the lack of quality, all-season roads. Yet placing the automobile into the existing fine-grained landscape outfitted to accommodate the horse and the railroad would require a host of more subtle adjustments as well. Along the Shenandoah Valley floor, business functions were intensely centralized in towns that grew up along the Valley Pike, and town business sites were focused, in turn, at a major crossroads

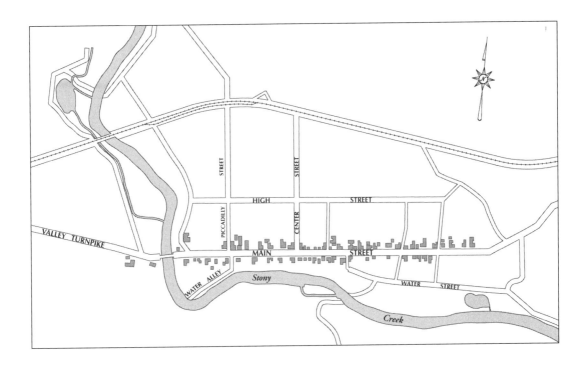

Fig. 8.2. Edinburg town plat. (After Lake's *Atlas of Shenandoah and Page Counties,* 1885; Gyula Pauer Cartography Lab, University of Kentucky)

or a town square or diamond. Small Federal-style homes crowded gable to gable on narrow lots, often built so close to the road that they encroached into the right-of-way. Some north Valley towns such as Edinburg, Strasburg, and New Market were replicas of Pennsylvania linear towns whose road-straddling form was likely platted by Pennsylvania migrants (see fig. 8.2).[9] Strasburg's plat included a central town square or diamond, a signature feature of many eastern Pennsylvania towns, including Philadelphia. Most town residents lived within a few minutes' walking distance of Main Street stores or their places of employment. Industries clustered at long-established waterpower sites or along railroad sidings. Travelers who chose to stay in Valley towns could patronize updated Main Street taverns and hotels. In the open country, five miles or more from the nearest town, isolated roadside taverns offered economical meals and overnight accommodations to coach-borne travelers.

In the pre-automobile countryside beyond the city limits, few buildings other than farmsteads stood beside the Valley Pike. Those buildings that did have direct access to the road often had a symmetrical relationship with road traffic. That is, roadside businesses were usually directly dependent upon road traffic to sustain them. Roadway travelers, in turn, depended upon the roadside businesses that enabled their travel. Adopting the automobile and truck called all such relationships into question. While auto travelers continued to seek food and lodging beside the road, their vehicles also required accommodation in parking space.[10] Commodities delivered by train arrived in town in a boxcar left on a rail siding. The train departed and moved on to the next town. Workmen off-loaded the cargo into a freight depot at the edge of the business district. Merchants could arrange for pickup and customer delivery via horse-drawn wagon. As trucks began to supplement and then replace trains for short- and intermediate-distance delivery, freight companies established storage and transfer terminals in larger cities. Local deliveries to retailers brought invading trucks into business-district streets and alleys, the most compact and congested part of town, where they sought space to park while they off-loaded cargo.

Local businesspeople who could afford to drive a horse and buggy to their Main Street office placed the horse in a livery stable rather than permit the animal to stand all day in the sun unattended. Farmers brought wagons to town to purchase dry goods, lumber, or other necessities, or to deliver eggs, milk and butter, or other commodities for sale. But they left town as soon as their transactions were completed and so did not require long-term parking space for their wagons and teams. On the other hand, auto-mobility carried with it the inconvenience of a rather substantial storage requirement when a vehicle was not in use. Main Street merchants soon found that as their stores filled with customers, the street outside filled with their cars. Idle cars had to be parked whether at home, work, shopping, church, or any other destination. In residential neighborhoods, homeowners either parked their new cars on the street in front of their homes or tried to make room for a small garage in the backyard, provided their lots were of sufficient size to permit inserting driveways between houses. Adapting the automobile and the truck to towns and roads built to accommodate horse-drawn vehicles required major adjustments to streets and roads as well as buildings and social infrastructure.

Perhaps the most important initial adjustment to motorized conveyance was also the most abstract — to build and maintain reliable roads required a transcendence of the traditional local scale of responsibility and an acceptance of the Progressive Era notion that the social, economic, and political ills brought on by a rapidly evolving industrial culture could be best dealt with by honest and efficient government that based its policy and decisions on research and applied science.[11] On the one hand, the expense of road building exceeded the ability of local political jurisdictions to pay, even if they had created a political mechanism to tax themselves to support road construction, which few towns or counties did. Further, the

Fig. 8.3. Old U.S. 11 and Loudoun Street in Winchester. Parked cars line limestone-block curbing and old brick sidewalks that front narrow-lot houses built long before the automobile required builders to provide lots large enough to permit off-street parking. (Scott Jost 2004)

process of creating a system of well-built roads that linked together over long distances implied that the responsibility for road design and construction had to be removed from the realm of turnpike companies and local political units — villages, towns, or counties — and centralized at the state and national levels where the power of taxation and the science of road engineering could be institutionalized. Only when state and federal legislation directed that road construction and maintenance be entrusted to trained planners and engineers whose disciplined and standardized designs could perforce be carried across county boundaries would the full advantage of road access and motor vehicle travel be realized.[12] Once this critical juncture had been reached, and mud ruts had been replaced by macadam, auto travel — local and long-distance — increased rapidly. Auto and truck traffic, moving at speed along the Valley Road in increasing volume, radically altered the long-standing relationship between road and roadside.

Political Adjustment

After a decade of public debate about the quality of Virginia's roads, the state General Assembly in 1906 passed enabling legislation that created the Virginia State Highway Commission, which oversaw and coordinated road construction across the state, and a Convict Labor Force that provided a legal structure for utilizing convicts as an economical source of construction labor.[13] But the highway commission amounted to little more than a commissioner, an engineer, an office, and a few office staff. Not until 1908 did the legislature act to provide funding for road construction, and that required a county monetary match and was intended primarily for those counties that did not have a sufficient number of convicts to provide the county's road-building labor force.[14]

National legislation directed at increasing the federal government's role in fostering road construction and maintenance programs at the state and county levels began fitfully with an aborted attempt by the House of Representatives to pass a bill that provided federal financial backing for the construction of rural mail-delivery roads in 1912. Debate over the merits of federal support for road-construction programs — influenced by the rapidly emerging motor vehicle industry, as well as the American Association of State Highway Officials, the secretary of agriculture, the postmaster general, and the Office of Public Roads — culminated in the passage of the Federal Aid Road Act of 1916.[15] The act provided for federal review and approval of state road-construction requirements and included support for two types of roads; light-duty rural farm-to-market roads of graded dirt or sand and gravel, and more substantial asphalt and concrete city-to-city highways, or what were for a time called "touring roads." The legislation compelled state highway departments to apply for federal support for road-construction projects. If approved, federal funds would underwrite one-half of the construction costs, including bridges and culverts, not to exceed ten thousand dollars per mile.[16] Although the 1916 road act stimulated state interest in quality road construction and planning, the legislation did not require that the road segments built with federal funds connect to other federally funded roads. The result, unless closely planned by state highway departments, was a continuation of county-level construction of short road segments that did not necessarily connect into a cross-state highway system. The oversight was addressed by the Federal Highway Act of 1921, which required federal funds to be allocated primarily to interconnecting highway systems.[17]

Although some federal standards regulating road construction were part of the 1921 legislation — standardizing road width at eighteen feet, for example — federal and state highway engineers and administrative officials remained concerned that a system of interlinked interstate highways did not yet exist. The federal Bureau of Public Roads devised a method for identifying a state's largest and most productive counties as measured by total population and value of forest, mineral, and agricultural products. When plotted on a master map, these centers suggested routes that the most important highways should take to link the largest and most productive places, thereby directing federal highway funds toward the construction of primary roads through those corridors.

Despite the dearth of planned, well-constructed and -maintained interstate roads, the decade from 1910 to 1920 saw a widespread effort to promote automobile travel by an odd amalgam of local city boosters, bicycle enthusiasts, oil companies, and auto manufacturers and parts suppliers, among others. Many such self-interested groups organized at the state or regional level to identify existing road segments, link them together on promotional maps, and then advertise them as a route that invited exploration by the motoring public. The Lincoln Highway Association was one of the first such groups to organize, and in 1912 promoted a route that would link New York City with San Francisco by way of Pittsburgh, Indianapolis, and Omaha.[18] By the mid-1920s, promoters and independent highway associations across the nation had created a chaotic cat's cradle of more than three hundred named highways. Many were little more than roads on paper. Some overlapped with other named roads or had alternate sections or dead-end spurs. Generally these promotional roads lacked continuous road sections over significant distances. Navigating these roads was haphazard at best, in part because they were not formally marked. As navigational aids, some promotional groups advocated a system of painted strips on telephone poles and fence posts unique to each road to guide travelers.[19] Lincoln Highway promoters marked their route with three bands, red, white, and blue. As part of this spate of promotional endeavor, the Valley Road became one segment in the Lee Highway, a coast-to-coast route that supposedly linked Washington, D.C., to San Diego. In 1922, the Virginia General Assembly and the Virginia State Highway Commission designated several named roads across the state including renaming the Lee Highway between Winchester and New Market in the lower Valley, the Lee-Jackson Memorial Highway.[20]

In 1924, the American Association of State Highway Officials (AASHO) requested that the secretary of agriculture appoint a board of engineers representing the federal Bureau of Public Roads and state highway depart-

Fig. 8.4. The Lee Way Restaurant and cabin camp on U.S. 11 north of Lexington. The cabins fronted a horseshoe drive that arced behind the concrete-block restaurant building. (Scott Jost 2000)

ments to identify a national network of principal highways and a numbering and marking system to delineate each road accurately and uniquely. After extended deliberations, the board approved a national highway network of 96,626 miles and a systematic method for numbering and signing each roadway. The AASHO approved the plan in November 1926. East–west federal highways were to be even-numbered, beginning in the North with the lowest-numbered roads. North–south roads were odd-numbered, beginning in the East. In Virginia, the old fall line road from Washington, D.C., to Richmond and Raleigh became U.S. 1; the Valley Road became U.S. 11.[21] Several east–west, trans–Blue Ridge, cross-valley roads also became part of the new federal system. At Winchester, the Berrys Ferry Turnpike to the east and the Northwestern Turnpike to the west became U.S. 50; the Staunton-to-Parkersburg Turnpike, also called the Midland Trail, became U.S. 250; and at Lexington, the road to Richmond became U.S. 60.

Engineering the Road

As federal programs to facilitate quality road construction came into being during the first two decades of the twentieth century, Virginia was also in the throes of creating political structures that promised to foster programmatic road building and maintenance. The Valley Road, though hard surfaced with macadam stone for much of its length and of better quality than most other state roads, retained much of its historic organic character. That is, the route still followed closely the land's surface profile in most places. Low hills and shallow valleys had not been leveled with cuts and fills. In some places, the road climbed abrupt hills; in others it made tight corners in awkward places such as bridge entrances, or the bottom of a steep hill. And although the road had many straight stretches of a mile or more, for much of its length it was narrow with limited or no shoulder space and closely lined with trees and farm fences and buildings. In towns, the road was little different from other streets. The road served as the main street in each Valley town, but only in those towns purposely platted with exceptionally broad main streets did the road have sufficient width to allow a straightforward adaptation to streetside parking for wagons and later, motor vehicles. Woodstock is one example. There the surveyor and landowner Jacob Miller laid out a seventy-foot-wide main street.[22] For automobile drivers traveling the road at upward of thirty miles per hour, the old road was fraught with hazard and in need of rigorous engineering.

The state initiated a highway building and reconstruction plan in 1918 when the General Assembly approved the state's first modern highway program and designated a state system of twenty-eight primary highway routes about four thousand miles in total length.[23] To finance road construction and tap funds available from the federal aid road program, the state needed to raise money. Neighboring North Carolina, and other states, adopted a policy of financing road construction through state bond issues that allowed their highway programs to borrow significant amounts of money to underwrite large-scale highway construction. Virginia, after vigorous debate in the legislature and the press, adopted in a 1923 referendum a "pay-as-you-go" policy based upon taxes and license and registration fees. The state imposed a two-cents-per-gallon tax on gasoline and, by 1928, increased the tax to five cents, then the highest state gasoline tax in the nation. Between 1920 and 1930, the number of registered motor vehicles in Virginia increased from 145,340 to more than 386,000. Together, license and gasoline taxes produced more than $13 million in revenues in 1930 that could be allocated to road-construction projects.[24]

In 1923, the Virginia State Highway Commission established nine divisions, or departments, organized to bring engineering expertise, materials and dimensional standards, and business acumen to the road-construction enterprise.[25] Three of these divisions — testing, engineering, and construction — played a direct role in the physical reconstruction of the old turnpike and consequently in forming the modern motor vehicle road and roadside landscape. Because primary road-construction projects were funded, in part, by federal aid, federal officials in the Bureau of Public Roads served as gatekeepers in controlling state highway design standards, materials quality, and construction engineering. Virginia's road-construction plans, as with federal-aid roads in other states, were subject to review and approval by the bureau and were often modified and upgraded.[26]

The state highway department began a systematic reconstruction program for U.S. 11 in 1928 — a full decade after the state established its modern highway program and designated the Valley Road as one of its primary highway routes. Although highway department officials touted the road as one of the best in Virginia before reconstruction began, engineering the surface, grades, and alignments would transform the route into a high-speed motor vehicle road that attracted a rapidly growing number of vehicles. State highway engineers chose to initiate reconstruction in 1928 on the four-mile, straight section south of New Market, the longest straight section of the entire routeway.

Several other aspects of road configuration required reengineering before the road would be suitable for trucks and automobiles. The old toll road's macadam surface had a high center crown to promote water drainage off either side. On asphalt or concrete roads built for motor vehicles, negotiating a high crown road was akin to steering up a side hill, a hazardous ploy at high speed because overcompensation pulled one into the opposite lane and oncoming traffic, while inattention quickly brought one's vehicle onto the shoulder and into the yawning verge. The high crown was especially risky on corners, where it offered the additional treachery of reverse camber — instead of sloping into the curve, the road surface sloped away from the curve, greatly increasing the likelihood of a skid into the opposite ditch — should one venture across the centerline. Consequently, the crown allowable for Virginia federal aid roads was sharply reduced to a maximum of two and one-half inches for an eighteen-foot road.[27]

To assure that the road surface did not exacerbate the loss of tire adhesion at speed, new construction techniques maintained a nearly level surface on straight road segments that smoothly blended into "superelevated," or banked, surfaces on curves. Engineers also widened highway shoulders — four feet became a minimum standard — eliminated railroad grade crossings where possible, and installed wooden-post guard rails along steep embankments.[28] Steam-powered shovels and other heavy equipment, some of it surplus from World War I, allowed engineers to move large volumes of earth and rock to build up the roadbed above the level of the surrounding land, thereby reducing road flooding during heavy rain. Reconstruction also filled in small ravines, cut through low side-hill spurs, and cut down hills to reduce maximum grades to 5 percent or less. When completed, the reengineered road surface was substantially reconfigured from the original organic track that had closely followed the land's original contour. In addition to radically altering the topographic relationship between highways and adjoining property, reconstructed roads prompted an increase in the value of road-abutting land. During the decade from 1935 to the mid-1940s, rural roadside real estate in Virginia more than doubled in value.[29]

The Valley historian and diarist John Wayland traveled sections of U.S. 11 almost daily during the 1928–36 reconstruction period, and his notes lend a rare insight into the road-building process.[30] Road engineers sequenced and spaced reconstruction in order to undertake several projects simultaneously, with bridge construction taking priority. The 1930s concrete bridges represented the third generation of bridge-building technology, replacing iron bridges erected in the early 1900s, which, in turn, had replaced the original wooden bridges built in the nineteenth century. South of Mount Jackson, straightening the old route necessitated spanning the Dry Fork in three places — three new bridges replaced one on the old toll road that had skirted the stream. One of the route's most dramatic bridging points is on Lexington's north side, where the road crosses the sharply incised Maury River valley near the Virginia Military Institute campus. The original road crossed the river here on a double-track wooden bridge that stood upstream from the new steel-and-concrete structure completed in November 1935. From the new crossing site, engineers realigned the new roadway directly across by way of a deep excavation into the north bank, straightening this section but creating a steeper grade than the old road had required. When I-64 was routed to Lexington in the 1960s, it crossed U.S. 11 at a large interchange about one mile north of this crossing, increasing local traffic significantly. In 2002, the 1935 bridge was substantially modified and widened.

Long stretches of U.S. 11 did not require major realignments; instead, federal and state engineering guidelines could be met by heavily modifying the existing roadbed. This was accomplished by raising, leveling, and widening the bed, followed by application of a new surface. The surface material of choice in the late 1920s and 1930s was bituminous macadam, a crushed-stone surface of two- to three-inch thickness, covered with stiff asphalt that bound the stone together.[31] This combination of asphaltic tar on a macadam stone surface became known as "tarmac."

Fig. 8.5. U.S. 11 in Mount Crawford. Widening the road in the 1930s removed front yards and porches, and forced some property owners to reposition their front doors to the side of the building. (Scott Jost 2003)

Widening the road was the most problematic part of the road-building process for it entailed reclaiming right-of-way from adjoining properties where owners had erected structures that encroached into the road during the early wagon road era. In some towns, the entire main street had been built atop a narrowed right-of-way. About 1930, Middletown was the first urban place to have its main street rebuilt according to the new standards, largely because it, like Woodstock, was platted with a seventy-foot-wide street.[32] But in towns such as Mount Sidney, Mount Crawford, Tenth Legion, Kernstown, Stephens City, Edinburg, and Strasburg, the U.S. 11–Main Street was so narrow that extensive modifications were required before the road could be widened. In some cases, entire buildings, including a gas station at Tenth Legion, were moved back from the road. Some homeowners were permitted to maintain their houses in situ but lost their front yards. In Mount Crawford, the problem was of sufficient gravity that highway engineers gave serious consideration to building a bypass around the town, although this proposal was opposed by Main Street businesspeople, who were convinced that relocating the road

Fig. 8.6. The Staunton business district developed near the point where U.S. 11 and U.S. 250 intersected. U.S. 11 was relegated to one-way streets when road expansion took place in the 1930s. (Scott Jost 2003)

would cause them a significant loss of business.[33] In the largest towns — Lexington, Staunton, Harrisonburg, and Winchester — the business districts were already fully developed, and street widening was not feasible. The solution was to redirect U.S. 11 traffic onto one-way streets to alleviate congestion (see fig. 8.6).

The impact of Depression-era road reconstruction is still evident in the towns that required radical street widening. In some towns, front yards were cut back, leaving only a foot or two of lawn between the front door and the sidewalk. On some properties, cutting the yards back meant reducing the lot level by two to three feet, necessitating the construction of a retaining wall between the sidewalk and yard. Where old Federal-style houses fronted the road, only narrow sidewalks now separate buildings from the right-of-way. Many post–Civil War Victorian homes had their porches cut back so severely that the remaining structures are only two feet deep and function more as stoops than as sitting porches.

For local residents and habitual road travelers, no doubt the most significant alterations to the old road came at those sections where the old bed was abandoned in favor of a new alignment. This often happened in short sections, but it could have the effect of leaving behind orphaned roadside businesses that had oriented themselves to the original track. In other cases, the new road alignment caused the removal of old roadside buildings or was built atop important local historic sites or natural features such as springs.[34] A few miles north of Lexington, near the Mount Carmel Presbyterian Church, at a small roadside community called Timber Ridge, the old road had passed a large formal monument to Sam Houston that sat tight against the road near his birthplace home. Engineers redirected the road several dozen yards to the west by way of a new hillside road cut. The highway department surfaced and maintained the old route as an access road and created a wayside to accommodate tourist parking. At Mauertown, south of Toms Brook, engineers relocated the new road to the opposite side of a small stream, yet the town's houses still stand along the old road, which has since functioned as a private drive for these properties.

Building a New Roadside

Engineers had largely rebuilt U.S. 11 by the eve of World War II, following the exacting science of the transit, level, and Chesterman tape. The road was further disciplined by state and federal regulations concerning informational signage, right-of-way distances, speed limits, and a cadre of law-enforcement officers who ticketed scofflaws and summoned emergency vehicles to wreck sites. While some of the informalities of traveling the old road had vanished with the arrival of the new apollonian order, the availability of cheap vehicles and fuel on the one hand, and the pure pleasure drivers derived from moving along a safe road at speed on the other, was so compelling that people now took to the road in steadily increasing numbers. Those living at roadside took notice of the movable marketplace passing their property, looking very much like a continuous stream of potential customers to those with a merchant's sensibilities. Many started new roadside businesses or sold frontage land to others keen to take the plunge. Few roadsiders knew anything about business, but few formal obstacles such as zoning regulations blocked their way. The result was a raw new roadside that erupted in fits of entrepreneurial abandon as change and dynamism came to characterize the automobile roadside. From the 1920s forward, the roadside never achieved stability but was reinvented again and again as motor vehicle technologies changed, as national and international petroleum companies vied with one another for market share, as business pioneers developed the franchise, and as advertising companies found new ways to represent business at roadside.

The new, high-speed road begat a demand for roadside property, and with rising prices, larger investments were required to buy frontage and build business buildings. By the early 1930s, road-oriented business strips began to form at the gateways to the larger towns. But long-term investors in road frontage land found that the relationship between location, demand, and land value was not stable but changed through time. With the arrival of Interstate 81 in the 1960s, the highest roadside land values moved to the U.S. 11–I-81 interchanges. Roadside buildings created to serve old technologies are often standing on property whose comparative value has declined as demand shifted to new locations. Because it is not economical to remove an old building from devalued land to replace it with a new structure, aging roadside buildings are often either retrofitted to other uses or simply abandoned. This process yields a complex roadside landscape, a palimpsest of material artifacts and social relationships. As roadside buildings age, they settle and sag. Their painted exteriors weather and peel, metal fixtures rust and discolor, neon-lit signs crack and fade. The oldest auto-oriented road sections thus gain a distinctive patina not found at the polished and shiny interchange business buildings.

At a regional — or meso — scale, the purchase and use of automobiles and trucks by rural residents and townspeople alike helped to cement the centrality of the Valley's larger urban centers as foci for mercantile exchange and expansion. Farmers whose weekly trading trip to market by wagon had been geographically limited to those towns within a few miles of the farmstead found that an automobile or pickup truck permitted them to travel many times farther in search of a larger selection of retail goods, cheaper prices, or both. The larger towns, especially the county seats that enjoyed the benefits of serving as a county's node for legal services, attracted more merchants and other service professionals — insurance, banking, accounting, medical — and a larger diversity of retail consumer goods. Generally the larger the population of a place, the larger the selection of low-demand goods that merchants could afford to carry in stock. High-demand goods, food staples for example, were commodities that people consumed frequently or every day so most villages had a grocery store. Expensive, low-demand goods — furniture, jewelry, or fine crystal, for example — were purchased infrequently, perhaps once in a lifetime, so only a few of these stores would be required to serve a large population. With the near ubiquitous access that the automobile afforded, the central-

Fig. 8.7. Ritenour's Grocery and post office near the old Valley Road alignment at Fishers Hill in Shenandoah County. (Scott Jost 2003)

ized mercantile and service functions found in the larger towns were now reinforced as Valley residents traveled longer distances by way of U.S. 11 to shop and conduct business in the larger urban places. Many country stores lost business to town merchants and had to close.[35] Rural church membership began to decline. Rural schools consolidated, and gradually educational functions, too, were ceded to the towns.[36]

As the Valley Road's transformation by steam shovel and dump truck proceeded, the new road, U.S. 11, was increasingly used by two different groups. Valley residents, be they rural or urban, local or from the next county comprised one group. Nonresident travelers heading for destinations within or beyond the Valley were another. The Virginia Department of Transportation began regular traffic counts on state roads in the 1930s, with one of the first comprehensive counts made in 1938. The counts differentiated Virginia cars from "foreign," or out-of-state, vehicles and also counted light- and medium-duty and heavy-duty trucks. By 1938, though the Depression continued to dampen national and regional economies, motor vehicle traffic along U.S. 11 in the Valley's four northern counties

was at or near two thousand vehicles per day. More vehicles of all types used the highway in the vicinity of the larger mid-Valley county seats at Staunton and Harrisonburg. The number of out-of-state vehicles was substantial, outnumbering local cars near Winchester, close to the West Virginia border. Overall traffic volumes were sufficient to encourage the construction of numerous gas stations along the route, and the number of out-of-state tourists and business travelers created a demand for roadside restaurants, overnight accommodations, and attractions. And the road's reputation among critical auto travelers was already established as a "chain of filling stations, sandwich stands, signboards and Sears Roebuck houses."[37]

Fig. 8.8. John Handley High School in Winchester. Built in 1923 with funds donated by Pennsylvania resident John Handley, this Greek Revival structure has served city residents for more than eighty years. (Scott Jost 2004)

U.S. 11 and a Modern Geography of Culture and Connection   257

TABLE 8.1 U.S. 11 Shenandoah Valley motor vehicle traffic, 1938

	Average daily count					
	Total Virginia autos	Total out-of-state autos	Percent out-of-state autos	Total lt. & med. trucks	Total heavy trucks	Total all vehicles
Botetourt	914	449	49	179	55	1,517
Rockbridge	936	545	58	202	76	1,759
Augusta	1,069	707	66	246	107	2,129
Rockingham	965	636	66	328	115	2,044
Shenandoah	901	561	62	285	94	1,841
Frederick	688	863	125	267	58	1,876

Note: For comparison, counties are listed from south to north. Data tabulated for selected road segments (see fig. 8.18) by Johnny Bloomquist, Virginia Department of Transportation, May 2003.

Gas Stations

The earliest gasoline dispensing stations were often simply extensions of existing stores that stored gasoline in barrels and provided fuel to drive-up customers. These curbside operations were soon replaced by dedicated stations with permanent buildings or sheds that dispensed gasoline and petroleum products, although many continued to operate in the smaller towns or at country stores.[38] In Fairfield, in Rockbridge County, Borthwick's Garage still carries a sign that says "Since 1921." Covered with pressed tin sheets that resemble rusticated stone, the building was likely a livery barn before it was converted to service automobiles.

The shed-type station was little more than a small wood, brick, or stucco building at or near the center of town or at a road access point with a gas pump in front. Examples appeared in towns along the Valley Road by the early 1920s. Old stations of this type are rare, although one can sometimes find the residual elements in small settlements that were bypassed when the road was rerouted. An exceptional example still stands along the road north of Middletown. Now sagging with age and covered in faux-brick tarpaper, the station features a canopy on the front that is perched on high metal legs (see fig. 8.9).

In the 1920s, gasoline companies began to build stations at major street intersections in residential areas near the edge of the business district. Land values were lower in neighborhoods than in the business district, and corner lots had greater visibility and accessibility, allowing customers to enter from two streets.[39] Company architects designed the new station

buildings to resemble neighborhood houses to better adapt the business to its new geography. Some house-type gas stations were freestanding; others had canopies attached that offered all-weather protection for pump attendants, and later versions incorporated inside service bays with grease pits.[40] Several canopy-type stations still stand along U.S. 11. In Staunton, north of the business district, three house-type stations stand within two blocks of one another near Churchville and Oakenwold streets. One is now a used-car lot, another is a beauty salon, and a third houses an insurance agency. At Mount Crawford, a canopied house station still functions as a private residence, the gas pumps replaced by oversized soft drink machines. The crown jewel in this collection of house-type stations is a Pure Oil Company station with white brick walls and a steeply pitched blue terra-cotta tile roof that still stands along the old road on the north side of Lexington's business district. It now houses a barbeque restaurant (see fig. 8.10).

The banking crisis and stock market crash of October 1929 marked the beginning of the Depression. Given the nearly ubiquitous demand for fuel,

Fig. 8.10. A 1930s Pure Oil gas station on old U.S. 11 north of the Lexington business district. The house-form station still has its original tile roof and copper door and window hoods. It has recycled through different uses and is now Firehouse Jim's (formerly Pete's) Bar-B-Que. (Scott Jost 2003)

however, the oil industry was one of the first industries to recover. The economic boom of the 1920s and the amazing sales success of the Model T Ford and other automobiles led to a rapid expansion of gasoline retail filling stations, although many more were built than could be supported by the customer base.[41] At least five major gasoline companies — American Oil, Sinclair, Shell, Standard Oil of New Jersey, and Texaco — and many smaller independent fuel suppliers operated in Virginia. By 1932, Virginia had 375,889 registered motor vehicles and 2,430 gas filling stations, or 154 vehicles per station. Industry analysts calculated that a threshold of at least four hundred vehicles was required to support one filling station.[42] Overbuilding meant that poorly located gas stations off the main highway struggled to operate at a profit.

Given the intense competition for customers, gas companies changed their stations' form and function radically during the 1930s. Companies made a concerted effort to sell more fuel through advertising, and added parts and accessory sales, including tires, batteries, windshield wiper blades, and the like. Many new stations conformed to a widely adopted

Fig. 8.11. The Friendly Motor Company on U.S. 11 on the south side of Winchester now sells used cars from an old box-style gas station with Art Deco flourishes. The auto-repair bays are now offices and a display area for a large collection of stock car–racing memorabilia. (Scott Jost 2004)

design: a basic oblong box that was larger, to allow more interior space for accessories display and repair bays, with a simple and austere flat-roofed exterior. Building materials ranged from concrete block to prefabricated steel frames covered in porcelain-veneered steel panels, a material that made the stations resemble oversized kitchen appliances.[43] Gas companies pursued the box station design for the next forty years, into the 1980s, with few alterations other than cosmetic façade augmentation. Gas pumps stood in pairs — regular and ethyl — on raised concrete islands on the apron in front of the station. While the pump island perch seemed awkward at first, its intent was to function as a curb to ward off vehicles whose drivers misjudged the distance between pump base and car bumper or wheel. Gooseneck lampposts fastened to the concrete island between the pumps provided overhead lighting for night service.

Box-type gas stations abound along U.S. 11; many continue to function, some have been converted to other uses, and some stand abandoned. In Greenville, an early porcelain-sided gas station stands at the town's south gateway near the point where the new bypass splits from the old road.

Though the station has been out of operation for some time, its resilient siding still sparkles in the sun, in contrast to the surrounding lot, which is fouled with junked auto parts and wrecked trucks. The gas pumps are gone, and the underground gas storage tanks have been removed in compliance with 1998 federal Environmental Protection Agency regulations, leaving a large hole in the middle of the concrete parking apron, now temporarily filled with crushed stone.

Gasoline companies also built truck stops according to standardized designs, but many independent fuel dealers built their own facilities from the 1930s through the mid-1960s.[44] These locally owned stations were idiosyncratic in form and plan compared to those built according to a franchising company's standards. A 1950s truck stop that once purveyed Texaco products still stands north of Edinburg. The main building was a two-story, concrete-block structure some sixty feet long and eighteen feet deep. The first floor included an office and restaurant, and the second floor offered sleeping rooms to long-distance truckers. The heavily weathered asphalt lot is nearly an acre in size, sufficient to maneuver or park several semitrailer trucks. The fuel pumps are gone, and the building's Texaco green paint has nearly weathered away, but a vivid decal sign in the window still communicates the fuel pump color codes — red for Sky Chief regular, silver for high-test, gold for lead-free, and green for diesel.

In the 1970s, in part as a response to the OPEC oil embargos and an interest by major oil companies to consolidate excess retail capacity in low-profit areas, gas station function and form began to change. In addition, federally mandated pollution-control laws required that automobile manufacturers curtail engine emissions, which they accomplished by installing vacuum, spark, and gas control devices, catalytic converters, and emissions sensors on new cars. In 1981, manufacturers began using integrated circuit computer chips in automobiles, and within a few years, engine management systems were largely computer controlled. While engine emissions were reduced, automobiles became more complex, and mechanics required extensive training, specialized tools, and computer analysis equipment to maintain cars effectively. Straightforward auto maintenance — tune-ups and minor parts replacement — could no longer be performed by a mechanic working in a gas station service bay but were increasingly done at the dealer or specialty mechanic shops. Gas stations either narrowed their focus to the basic remove-and-replace business of auto peripherals such as tires, brakes, and batteries, or began closing their service departments and converting the unused space to convenience stores. The station attendant no longer pumped gas for customers but operated the cash register and managed store functions amidst racks of snack foods, banks of canned drink coolers, and franchise donuts.

Gasoline companies developed a new station form, the canopy-and-booth, in part in response to the sales-only trend. This station form is widely used, especially at interstate interchange locations. It includes a small central booth for the attendant flanked by four or more pump islands. A large overhead canopy covers the booth and the entire pump island area.[45] The canopy edge is wide enough to carry brand-name signs, and it offers all-weather shelter. The canopy's underside is covered in white sheet metal and functions as a large reflector for the dozen or more downward-projecting lights mounted there. At night, the station becomes a brilliantly lit oasis on an otherwise dark and foreboding roadside, at once an advertisement that the station is open for business and that it is safe. This station form is also undergoing modification as the petroleum industry adds convenience stores and co-branded fast-food outlets — nationally franchised sandwich shops such as Subway and Blimpies, for example — to stations in high-traffic locations.[46] The modified convenience store/box-design station can be found in the county seat towns along U.S. 11, and the canopy-and-booth station with the convenience store and co-branded variations now stands at several I-81–U.S. 11 interchanges.

Tourist Camps and Motels

The automobile was a democratic machine that allowed members of the middle class to travel as far as reliable roads and pocketbooks would carry them. Some auto travelers patronized central-city railroad-era hotels or converted stagecoach-era taverns. The Wayside Inn at Middletown, for example, had served coach travelers since 1797, when it was known as Wilkerson's Tavern. In the 1930s, its owner updated the inn and advertised it as "the first American hostelry to cater to automobile tourists only."[47] Many middle-class auto travelers preferred not to overnight in the established central-city hotels, in part because of the expense. At two to ten dollars per night or more by the early 1930s, hotel rooms were comparatively expensive. And parking and meals cost extra. Nationally, wage-earner incomes at this time averaged about twelve hundred dollars annually, while salaried workers received just over two thousand dollars, so that a one-week vacation spent at hotels could expend one-sixth of the annual family income and cost more than the car they were driving was worth.[48] And, the prospect of parading travel-worn and weary through a fancy hotel lobby in front of the local gentry was sufficiently off-putting to encourage auto-borne travelers to seek an alternative mode of accommodation — camping.[49] If travelers packed camping gear into their cars, they could often find campgrounds provided by towns or local land-owners, free or, if basic services such as running water, tables, and benches were provided, for a small nightly fee.[50]

As travelers' demands for overnight camping sites increased, camps proliferated along major highways — one stood along U.S. 11 between Mount Sidney and Burkeville, for example.[51] Many entrepreneurial camp-ground operators began building modest cabins to accommodate those who preferred to leave the tent at home. By the mid-1930s, the cabins were larger, more substantially built, and often included a bathroom and adja-cent parking place.[52] Clustering the houselike cabins in U-shaped rows or in a crescent around the owner's home, a restaurant, or an open parking lot led to the designation "cabin courts," a term that implied a significant upgrade in quality, further separating these operations from the now passé tourist tent camps. By the 1940s, cabin court operators began roofing over the space between cabins, linking the units together under a continuous roofline to create a dedicated carport beside each cabin. When outfitted with doors, these roofed parking places became garages and were very popular with travelers. Increasingly, entrepreneurs built cabin courts at town gateways, adding to the auto-oriented business strip developing beside the road. Some individuals built courts on a farmstead or near a road-front home several miles from the nearest urban place. Whether lo-cated at town's edge or in open country, most early camps, courts, and motels were managed as small businesses, often family-owned operations. As land values on the highway strip escalated, court operators began to build integrated room units, each room sharing a wall with adjacent units, and all under a continuous roof, with a separate attached home for the owner-operator. Termed a "motor court," this configuration used less space and often included a restaurant or coffee shop. By the late 1940s, the term "motel" had replaced "motor court," and owners sought to create a distinctive roadside identity by building linearly along the road to maxi-mize visibility and by augmenting their buildings' façades with colonial, Art Deco–Moderne, or western ranch stylistic details and signs.

By 1950, the Valley's central-city hotels still functioned, although the threat posed by the new suburban motel franchises loomed. In Staunton, for example, travelers could still choose between six different downtown hotels that offered some 395 rooms. Winchester had four hotels and 271 rooms.[53] Holiday Inn was one of the first new chain motels to be repre-sented by franchisees along U.S. 11 in the larger county seat towns. A large, two-story ranch-style inn stood on Harrisonburg's south side, for example, though it has since been converted into a Ramada Inn. Although independent motel operators sought to represent themselves to road travelers through unique names and distinctive signage, large franchise motels employed a different strategy. National advertising transformed the franchise motel into a branded product whose name represented a guarantee that the same predictable qualities could be found in each motel in the chain. A large, distinctive roadside sign was all that a franchise owner needed to remind travelers that a spacious, clean, well-appointed room awaited at their motel.[54] Small-town and country motels were, largely, independently built and owned, although they might join a regional or national referral chain in which owners complied with standards for room appointments and services and participated in a referral and reservation system. A larger form of roadside motel appeared in the 1950s. Termed "motor inns," these motels were often two-story buildings arranged around an enclosed courtyard that usually included a swimming pool, a restaurant, banquet facilities, and meeting rooms.

Examples of motor courts and motels from each era stand along U.S. 11. Whatever considerations entrepreneurs weighed before investing in a cabin camp or court along the highway beginning in the 1920s are lost to us now but can be inferred in a general sense. First, the natural attractions near the road such as Natural Bridge near Buchanan, Endless Caverns south of New Market, and Shenandoah Caverns near Mount Jackson attracted automobile tourists whose presence suggested an obvious demand for accommodations. Natural Bridge and most of the Valley caverns are privately owned rather than being state or federal park property and so have been subject to full-throttle private development. Writing in *Fortune* in 1934, James Agee saw caves as special moneymaking machines, creations of roadside entrepreneurship. Wherever naturally occurring caves could be found at roadside — and a number lie within easy access of U.S. 11 — they were subject to expansive development and exuberant promotion. Limestone caves were "very special to roadside life," Agee opined, because they combined "the art of nature and the art of the entrepreneur. Yet [they were] pure roadside, for [they were] an institution built by and for the roadside."[55]

Cultural and historical places and monuments comprise a second type of place or attraction that stimulated cabin and motel construction nearby. The Valley is richly endowed in such places, including those hagiographic sites that commemorate the birthplace or residence of famous men and Civil War battlefields. Closely related are the "manufactured" attractions such as zoos, snake farms, craft outlets, and a host of museums that commemorate everything from parade floats to major holidays. South of New Market and near the New Market Civil War battlefield, a 1930s cabin court stands on the west side of the road. Two groups of five single and attached cabins, sided in faux Bedford limestone, flank a central office and restaurant building. A metal "gateway" sign at the front door mounts atop two twelve-foot metal supporting posts, and the entire sign assembly straddles the driveway in front of the office. The sign is now covered in weather-resistant, red lead paint. The asphalt drive has crumbled into knuckle-sized cobbles that have deeply oxidized to a light gray. Interstate 81 opened just to the west in the 1960s, and the court closed a few years later. The buildings are now used as storage, and the complex serves as a "sight fence" blocking from the motorists' view a large auto junkyard behind (see fig. 8.12). North of New Market, two 1950s motels, originally independently owned and intended to serve U.S. 11 travelers, continue to operate as motels. One is part of the regional Budget Inn chain that owns recycled motels of this era all along the road, but now offers low-priced rooms to interstate highway travelers who are willing to drive a few miles from the interchanges and their newer, higher-priced franchise accommodations. Near Woodstock, a few miles from the Toms Brook and Fishers Hill battlefields, a 1950s motel continues to operate as a member of the discount Budget Host chain, seeking the same clientele as the Budget Inn units.

Fig. 8.12. An old cabin motel south of New Market. A relict sign suspended by two posts remains in place across the motel driveway. The cabins and office building are now used for storage, and the driveway serves as a kind of podium for used-car sales. A finned 1960 Chevrolet sports "For Sale" signs in its windows. (Scott Jost 2000)

Third, cabin camps, courts, and motels clustered along strips at town's edge, and along strip extensions in the open country. On Harrisonburg's south side, for example, the 1937 Village Inn stands in what once was open farm country but now is near an I-81 interchange. The inn has been completely refurbished with modern appointments, a popular local restaurant, and a swimming pool. On the town's north side stands an abandoned motor court of similar age. Covered garage roofs connected the clapboard-sided, Cape Cod–style double cabins. The relict ensemble stands in double-crescent ranks on a hillside, served by a deteriorating asphalt driveway. Unlike other U.S. highways where many old motels have been recycled into residential use as weekly apartments or retirement homes, many U.S. 11 units stand vacant and in poor condition.[56]

Fig. 8.13. Along U.S. 11, near the Rockingham County Fairgrounds south of Harrisonburg, a 1930s cabin court now serves as by-the-week apartments. Children's toys, charcoal grills, and a phalanx of mailboxes suggest permanency, not diurnal mobility. (Scott Jost 2003)

Strips and Roadside Business

The triumvirate of roadside services that sustain highway truck and auto travelers — lodging, food, and fuel — has evolved distinctive forms, with particular attention given to creating a representational image through signage, color, and logo that is immediately recognized by passersby. But the roadside also attracted other businesses traditionally sited on Main Street. Before 1920, small strip shopping centers begin to appear along the road at edge-of-town gateways. After World War II, new strip centers appeared, followed by suburban shopping centers and malls. At Staunton, for example, highway engineers constructed a U.S. 11 bypass around the old central business in the mid-1950s. A similar bypass rerouted the highway east of central Lexington in 1956. Small businesses quickly collected along the Lexington bypass, creating a new strip business district.

The new roadside accretions were not necessarily destined to be successful business locations simply because they enjoyed direct road access. Roadside business shoppers' psychology became increasingly important

Fig. 8.14. The old Oak Grove Restaurant stands along U.S. 11 north of Winchester. Once a favorite stopover for the country music singer and Winchester native Patsy Cline, the forlorn building and neon sign are being reclaimed by vines and tree sprouts. (Scott Jost 2004)

in determining successful business locations. Clever businesspeople soon realized, and market research would eventually confirm, that some businesses were compatible at roadside and others were not. Similar businesses — retail clothing and shoe stores, for example — were compatible in the sense that people found shopping at similar businesses located side by side or in close proximity a convenience that increased sales at both stores. In most retail locations — be it a small-town service center, a larger city business district, a roadside strip, or a suburban shopping center — grocery stores, meat markets, bakeries, drugstores, and hardware stores were highly compatible with one another, as were stores that offered family apparel, shoes, and variety items. Ironically, auto-oriented businesses were compatible only with others of their kind. Drive-in restaurants, auto parts stores, auto repair shops, gas stations, and used-car lots were so distracting as to be deleterious to other retail businesses. Only mortuaries offered more negative locational associations for retail stores than did auto-related, drive-in businesses.[57] As businesspeople became more aware of consumer preferences, they began to self-segregate their roadside businesses. Auto-related businesses tended to string along the road frontage on individual piano-key lots, whereas retail clothing and grocery establishments clustered into strip centers with common parking lots and eventually into larger L- or U-shaped shopping centers.

Roadside restaurants fit in with other auto-oriented roadside businesses. Early versions were little more than hastily built wood-frame buildings dispensing hot dogs, ice cream, and cold drinks. By the 1930s, some road-oriented restaurants had begun to copy the Main Street café in structure and service techniques, offering sandwiches and hot meals served on plates and eaten with flatware. Howard Johnson's blended the ice cream–serving soda fountain with the traditional café dining room to create the new roadside coffee shop franchise, a restaurant form that persists in chains such as Denny's, T.G.I. Friday's, and Perkins, and in thousands of independent restaurants.[58] The Southern Kitchen Restaurant in New Market is an extant example of a 1950s coffee shop that continues to serve both local patrons and U.S. 11 travelers.

On Lexington's south side, the carcass of an old 1950s Howard Johnson's restaurant stood in the center of a large parking lot on the old U.S. 11 strip. The colonial façade and roof cupola provided clues to the building's heritage. For several years after the HoJo's franchise vacated the site, it was the Virginia House Restaurant. Closed for several years, the building was rehabilitated in 2004 as commercial office space and now stands in the center of a new asphalt parking lot. A second relict Howard Johnson's restaurant stood on Harrisonburg's south side near Mosby Street. The rooftop cupola complete with wind vane, rooster, and clock are all intact, although the clock always reads 8:15. The sun-bleached awning over the front door read "Lloyd's Steak House" in faded letters; a business that, in hermit crab–like fashion, occupied the shell of the old building after the franchisee abandoned the site. The building stood vacant for several years, used only for "indoor yard sales." Outside, untended golden tip junipers and dwarf blue spruce foundation plantings grew tall enough to cover the bottom quarter of the restaurant's windows. The slow-growing spruces, upward of fifty years old, were the size of tobacco hogsheads, five feet across and six feet tall, and would have been highly prized if they grew in someone's residential front yard. In 2004, the building was refurbished, and it now houses an upscale Mexican restaurant. Independently owned drive-in restaurants were also popular along U.S. 11, and in the larger county seat towns — Lexington, Staunton, Harrisonburg, and Winchester — a careful tracing of the 1950s road will locate several such buildings, most now empty or being reused for other purposes.

Though motion-picture theaters had been a fixture on America's Main Street since about 1915, Richard Hollingshead brought movies to the roadside in 1933, when he built the first drive-in theater in Camden, New Jersey. Within fifteen years, more than four hundred roadside theaters were in business nationwide.[59] Along U.S. 11, Hull's Drive-In Theatre stands on a hillside along the road about four miles north of Lexington, adjacent to the relict concrete-block Lee Way Restaurant and cabin camp. Established in 1950, Hull's is still operated on weekends by a nonprofit organization of drive-in theater aficionados. Films project onto a fifty-foot screen, and sound is transmitted through 315 speaker posts and broadcast on FM radio. People who come to the theater in an old car enter the grounds via their own special express lane (see fig. 8.15). A second theater, the twin-screen Family Drive-In, still operates at roadside between Stephens City and Middletown.

Auto dealers once lined U.S. 11 in the larger towns, although most of their garages and lots have been recycled into other land uses. Used-car dealers do take advantage of the lower land prices and rents along the old federal highway, especially at old gas station sites, where small station buildings function as offices and the pump-island aprons offer enough space to park several cars under streamers of fluttering plastic pennants. The new 1960s interstate highway destabilized post–World War II roadside car dealerships, and falling profits forced many to seek new sites near interchanges with more traffic and visibility.

A few manufactured attractions still operate along U.S. 11, usually in close proximity with one of the Valley's caves or other natural features that had long ago been transformed by local investment into "sites" for tourists. Through advertising and promotion, investors hoped to induce travelers to visit the Valley so that they might be entertained by the magnificence and oddity of nature's work. Cave owners provided gravel paths and stairways into the caves for ease of access and ran electric lights to illuminate underground spaces and enhance viewing. Perhaps in recognition that a trudge through a dim, damp, and cold cave would be less intriguing if represented as an exercise in applied science — with detailed explanations of local geology and the geochemistry of cave formation — cave developers instead employed romantic metaphors of art, architecture, and landscape gardening to promote interest in natural calcite formations and implied that the natural processes that created it all were mysterious if not miraculous.

Natural Bridge is the archetype of such sites. Once deeded by King George III to Thomas Jefferson, who found the place an intellectual puzzle, Natural Bridge has been in private hands since and has long been strongly promoted as a tourist destination. Perhaps because few visitors are as enthralled by the natural processes by which Cedar Creek carved the 215-foot-tall span as Jefferson was, Natural Bridge owners through the

Fig. 8.15. Hull's Drive-In Theatre stands beside U.S. 11 north of Lexington. Speaker posts stand in semicircular rows along tiered parking ramps cut into the hillside. A supplementary sign facing the highway announces that a community fund to support theater operations has passed the halfway point, heading for $75,000. (Scott Jost 2000)

years have sought to augment the site's appeal by adding manufactured attractions of their own. Beginning in the 1820s, Natural Bridge has been developed as a privately owned tourist destination. Owners erected the first tourist cabin at the site in 1828. Natural Bridge enjoyed an international reputation as a destination attraction, and attendant tourist facilities underwent cycles of expansion and upgrading. In 1935, Duncan Hines began compiling a list of the nation's best restaurants in his *Adventures in Good Eating*. By 1955, the Herring Hall Inn restaurant at Natural Bridge was one of only thirty-nine restaurants nationwide recommended each of the twenty years Hines published the list.[60] Natural Bridge developers replaced Herring Hall with a large colonial-style motel in 1963, replicating in appearance the Homestead Resort hotel at Hot Springs, Virginia.

Natural Bridge has become a secondary element in a complex that includes a large resort-style hotel, rental cottages, a conference center, wax museum, gift shop, tavern, tennis courts, mini-golf, hiking trails, and a nightly light show called the "Drama of Creation." At the nape of Natural Bridge, the point where U.S. 11 crosses the Cedar Creek gorge, its owners have erected tall wooden fences at road's edge to prevent passersby from stopping for a free view of the scene below.

On U.S. 11 north of Natural Bridge at Buffalo Creek, four 1920s travelers' cabins stand adjacent to a private home. Though the cabins have been relict for a decade or more, the entrepreneurial spirit continues with used pickup truck sales in the front yard. Roadside cabin camps and courts can still be found in proximity to the Valley's other "natural" attractions. The Safari Gift Shop and the Enchanted Castle Studios stand at a strategic gateway position just north of Natural Bridge on U.S. 11. The castle is a walled-in workshop and display area built by an artist who creates large, often whimsical fiberglass sculptures for sale to commercial businesses. The owner opened the complex for tours in the early 1990s and continued until local miscreants set the place on fire in 2001. A larger-than-life fiberglass Holstein cow with golden wings, dubbed "Holy Cow," stands at the castle entrance.

State-sponsored memorials represent another family of roadside attractions and include important historic sites such as Civil War battlefields and house museums where noted public figures lived. An example of the state-sponsored roadside attraction is Cyrus McCormick's "farmstead" near Steeles Tavern at the Augusta and Rockbridge county line. Here, a short distance off U.S. 11, a small collection of replica farm buildings stands at the place where McCormick built his grain reaper in 1831. The five-acre national historic landmark is part of a Virginia Tech agricultural experiment station and is maintained by the university. As a roadside attraction, the place bears the signature landscape attributes of a publicly owned park; the log buildings are well-maintained reconstructions, and the grounds are groomed with mowers and weed trimmers. No garish billboards hail the site from U.S. 11, only a modest historic plaque and an official state highway sign designate the turnoff from the main highway.

The 220-acre Frontier Culture Museum near Staunton is a much larger state-sponsored roadside attraction. Though positioned near the intersection of Interstates 81 and 64, the museum is only about a mile from U.S. 11. Created in the spirit of European rural folkways outdoor museums, the place commemorates the main European groups whose culture lent distinctive character to the Virginia frontier. Farmstead building clusters transplanted from their original sites represent German, Ulster, and English traditions, and an American farmstead represents the amalgamation of New World cultural traits. As with the McCormick site, this museum controls maintenance and signage. Although it attracts many thousands of visitors each year, the access road is not lined with motels, souvenir shops, or other manufactured attractions.

Traveling in Class

The road and the roadside structures that people build are material attributes of the larger cultural milieu within which people conduct their lives. Built structures are also the product of many interrelated and interconnected social processes associated with living and making a living. Some processes operate locally, others regionally, nationally, and even internationally. Temporally, all such processes have an initiation, a continuation, and a termination — inflection points of change that may or may not be objectively identifiable by time or date. Some social processes grow out of prior conditions or situations; others seem to have been invented and implemented as original ideas. People who build and maintain roads operate within a context of science and engineering principles. Those who travel upon roads, be it for business or leisure, operate within a context of traditional cultural habits and social mores. People create most American landscapes, including roads and roadsides, piecemeal according to conventions that value liberal individualism, laissez-faire capitalism, and political democracy. More explicitly, a transcendent theme of the American cultural system is the establishment and protection of property rights and freehold land tenure.[61] People who purchase and develop roadside property expect to be able to work their will upon it, largely sheltered from outside regulation or opinion. Building roads according to scientific principles and engineering best practices required a sea change in political temperament and state and federal legislation that removed the road surface and right-of-way from the traditions of private property and subjected them to the new disciplines of public law and regulation. In this way, the beginning of the automobile era initiated rather drastic changes in traditional political and social practice, and underwrote the creation of new kinds of places. People nevertheless adjusted to the new discipline of highway travel, and travelers soon came to accept the new road form and the evolving roadside, what might be collectively termed a "vernacular landscape," as natural, ordinary, and beyond question — as "the way it should be."[62]

Yet, while road travel has democratic qualities, the actual travel process and operation of roadside businesses are largely idiosyncratic, individualized activities. That is, one's educational background, profession or occupation, socioeconomic standing, class, and even cultural milieu all provide a personal context for interacting with the road and roadside. Though subtle, it is important to recognize this context and to comment briefly upon it for three reasons. First, cultural background, and the tastes and habits that spring from it, relate to how people conceive of themselves and how they prefer to represent themselves to others through what they build, wear, and drive, as well as where they choose or choose not to go.[63] Second, people read and react to road and roadside representations in importantly different ways. Women see the road and roadside differently from men, and African Americans and other minorities see and relate to these places differently from whites.[64] The stereotypic three-year-old child can recognize the McDonald's Golden Arches from a car's back seat at a considerable distance but is not likely concerned about the differences between Mobil and Shell gas stations. Upper-class drivers of expensive European luxury cars are not likely to stop for fuel at an ill-maintained independent gas station frequented by heavily tattooed motorcyclists or people whose smoke-belching, twenty-five-year-old cars have peeling paint and are driving on one half-size spare tire. By association, people would assume that such establishments likely had wretched restrooms and offered the potential of an awkward personal confrontation. And third, the manner in which people choose to represent themselves on the road or through their roadside buildings changes as other aspects of society and technology change. Higher-quality automobiles became more accessible to a broader socioeconomic spectrum of people after 1908, when the assembly-line Model T Ford became widely available. Changes in technology have created succeeding generations of cars and trucks whose style, comfort, size, safety, cost of operation, and other attributes are assessed differently by different people. In 2008, a century after Ford's inaugural assembly line opened, gasoline prices soared to four dollars per gallon. Those who had long driven small economy cars viewed as shortsighted people who drove gas-guzzling sport utility vehicles. At roadside, construction materials changed through time; log and hewn timber-frame buildings gave way to sawn-wood, balloon-framed buildings. Later, concrete-block structures became popular but were subsequently replaced by newer steel-frame and sheet-metal materials. Roadside merchants adopted marketing strategies developed by market research firms that included innovations in advertising signs and building design. All of this also changes through time. Therefore, the road and roadside are in continual flux, both in the objective sense of building materials, structure design, signs, and other artifacts, and in the subjective sense of how personal perception changes through time, from place to place, and from one socioeconomic group to another.

One of the automobile's unanticipated attributes, increasingly manipulated by advertising firms, was the association of the car owner's self-image with their car's image — its nameplate and exterior countenance. Americans generally, be they car owners or pedestrians, came to associate one's social station, economic success, and class with the type of car they owned. In 1924, driving a large, powerful new Packard, for example, might symbolize to some a life of influence, good taste, and discretion in the same way that driving a used and well-worn 1915 Model T represented its driver as hardscrabble, unskilled, and with limited prospects.[65] Just so, people who erected businesses at roadside or structures that were intended to be accessible by road also became aware that their building's façade and general appearance became the business's representation to passersby. A structure's design, style, color, building materials, and condition in aggregate symbolized larger values that the public understood — hospitality and reliability, for example, or carelessness and indifference.

Those roadside establishments that sold services or products to the traveling public soon found that to compete successfully with other businesses their buildings had to attract and please passersby. Such considerations were a substantial departure from decisions to construct industrial or inner-city business buildings based upon plans by an architect whose charge was to create a signature company structure or an austere though internally functional commercial building. The quest for roadside identity and visibility led directly to the creation of landscapes where nothing was consistent over time or in scale or form because each business generation created new constructions, many that transformed traditional scale into outsized structures and signs.[66] Business signs, for example, following principles worked out by Las Vegas casinos, began to climb tall poles with information bracketed into three distinct sections. The design of each sign section was predicated upon anticipated visibility relative to the speed, distance, and viewing angle of auto-borne readers. The top of the sign was reserved for business heraldry, an oversized identity icon intended to be seen from a distance as a locational announcement — a kind of landmark. Below the heraldry, a second section offered generic information in intermediate-sized lettering — restaurant, motel, gas — intended to be read from an intermediate distance. Below that, a third section with small lettering intended to be read from close proximity included specific information — restaurant specials or motel or gas prices.[67] Howard Johnson's mid-1950s signs, for example, included a large neon "Simple Simon and the Pie Man" logo atop a trapezoidal sign that, in turn, stood atop a large arrow of flashing light bulbs. The sign read "Howard Johnson's, Ice Cream, 28 Flavors." The small sign at the bottom read "Restaurant," or, on older signs, this section listed special menu information — "Fried Clams," "Salads & Sandwiches," and "Special Daily Luncheon." New roadside businesses embraced the three-part sign, and one can find recent iterations at each section of U.S. 11 where the road links to the interstate at an interchange. North of Lexington, for example, the Red Oak Inn motel draws travelers off the road with a three-part sign on forty-foot stilts. Thus, auto-related behavior and roadside architecture tended to become "other-directed," or designed to please and attract consumers, instead of "self-directed," or intended to function in certain desirable ways or to please the tastes and whims of the owner and the builder.[68]

Roadside representation was not simply a matter of placing symbolic garnish atop a building's roof or turning one's building into a sign — although this became a standard practice among those small businesses that seemingly give little thought to the process of self-representation. Rather, as J. B. Jackson has argued, a business building was most successful if it offered the traveler the opportunity to transmogrify vicariously into a world of higher class. Americans had long admired, if not coveted, the social and economic advantages enjoyed by the upper class.[69] Preferences and tastes associated with the upper class — be it in art, architecture, music, sport, or lifestyle — came to folk in the middle classes from many sources: best-selling books, mass-circulation magazines, popular movies, advertising copy of all sorts, and perhaps even personal observation.

Thanks to Henry Ford's five-dollar-per-day wage for auto assembly-line workers and active labor unions, the chasm between rich and poor narrowed dramatically between 1910 and 1929, expanding the middle class and enabling laborers to become active customers for services and the products that they manufactured. And increasingly, subjective evaluations of taste and fashion steered product and service sales. The century from the 1820s — Andrew Jackson's presidential inauguration — through the Roaring 1920s was, in Russell Lynes's estimation, the beginning of the Age of Public Taste, a period during which the middle-class public's consciousness of matters relating to class and taste "became everybody's business and not just the business of the cultured few."[70] Entrepreneurs, abetted by market researchers and architects, created an "architecture of persuasion" that, as applied to roadside buildings, promised customers a transcendent experience whereby their leisure and holiday activities could be imitations of the everyday activities of a superior social group, the so-called leisure class.[71] Gas station designers shunned the pump-and-grease-pit image in favor of revival-style cottages with Spanish, Colonial, or Moderne overtones. Restaurants outfitted in polished dark wood ornamentation, brass fixtures and fittings, and cloth-covered chairs drew clientele with more buying power than the spartan greasy spoon diner equipped with a smoky iron grill, tables covered with frayed oilcloths, and begrimed linoleum floors. Howard Johnson's 1930s roadside restaurants took on a colonial flavor, resembling a fine New England home, albeit brightly colored. A few observers, writing in the national media, embraced the emerging American roadside and its commercial and aesthetic experimentation as a "commercial, exuberant, and unpredictable burst of construction" that permitted the traveler to discover that "the character of the country actually changes from one region to another" and that the roadside was "still under the firm control of the thousands of individualists who live along it."[72]

In 1931, billboard advertisers organized their research and lobbying efforts as Outdoor Advertising Incorporated, which, together with other advertising interests, supported research at Harvard University directed toward establishing a science-based method for evaluating the effectiveness of outdoor advertising. Soon thereafter, in 1933, advertisers established the Traffic Audit Bureau, which initiated traffic counts at key highway and city street sites nationwide to provide outdoor advertisers a quantitative basis for expending advertising funds on billboards at the most desirable high-traffic locations. Market research confirmed that outdoor advertising placed on billboards along well-traveled city streets was the most effective way of presenting information about products and services to those in the upper socioeconomic groups who drove to work.[73] Advertising signs sprouted from roadside prominences and many buildings with roadside exposure. Given the speed of passing automobiles and the narrowing effect that increasing speed had on a passenger's viewing angle, roadside signs by necessity became large enough to be read from 220 yards or more.[74]

Roadside signs and the businesses that paid for them drew harsh criticism from elite, professional-class planners and critics, whose essays in national magazines castigated local businesspeople for creating "an interminable monotony of signs, billboards and ugly roadside slums," and a "scorching ugliness of badly planned and laid out concrete roads peppered with impudent billboards" where traffic had become "a snarl and a nuisance."[75] Few examples of roadside billboard advertising remain along U.S. 11, in part because in 1958 Virginia joined with twenty-five other states to participate in a federal voluntary program to control roadside billboard advertising, an effort strengthened by the National Highway Beautification Act of 1965. Furthermore, roadside billboards are now less effective because the old highway has a higher volume of local traffic than of interstate travelers, who tend to prefer nearby I-81. Most old billboards that stood on private property along U.S. 11 have been removed, although a few empty 1930s Art Deco billboard frames still stand. At some U.S. 11 roadside locations where I-81 lies in close proximity, old businesses may erect "interstate signs" in addition to their U.S. 11 frontage signs. To announce their presence to interstate travelers, business owners may erect large signs with oversized letters and primary colors on rooftops or stilts that are plainly visible from the interstate but, ironically, may be too high or angled the wrong way to be seen readily from U.S. 11 (see fig. 8.17). The 1960s Budget Motel on Winchester's south side, for example, though fronting on U.S. 11, has affixed signs five feet high running the full length of the roof gable, over one hundred feet of total sign length, to signal its presence to interstate travelers a quarter mile away.

Although professional-class critics found discomfiture in the roadside architecture of consumer persuasion, one encounters no critiques by mainstream folk of those roadside structures that members of high society built or supported by their business — country clubs and private golf courses, boarding schools, prestige colleges, or exclusive spas and resorts. Such places are most often couched in subtle representational understatement because their operation is not dependent upon patronage by the middle-class masses and drop-in travelers. Their grounds more often than not resemble parks or exclusive estates. Examples abound: In

Fig. 8.16. (*Top*) Reflecting the diminished traffic on U.S. 11, an empty billboard, now partially screened by a mature tree, stands along the highway at the northern gateway to Harrisonburg. A mini-van and a lawn mower are offered for sale in front of the sign. (Scott Jost 2003)

Fig. 8.17. (*Bottom*) The owners of a gas station facing U.S. 11 north of Natural Bridge in Rockbridge County installed an "interstate sign" on a high bank behind the building, intending to inform drivers on Interstate 81, about a quarter mile away, that gas and groceries are available at this interchange. (Scott Jost 2004)

Lexington, U.S. 11 fronts the Virginia Military Institute and Washington and Lee University, and in Staunton, Mary Baldwin College stands at the roadside. Nineteenth-century professional-class people often built their Victorian mansions along the road near the edge of town.[76] Of those mansions that still stand, some remain private residences, others are funeral homes, and a few have been refit as bed-and-breakfast operations where a room for the night is often sufficiently expensive to ward off the middle-class traveler.

Post-Interstate Road and Roadside

After World War II, especially after the construction of local bypasses and Interstate 81 in the 1960s, the old U.S. 11 roadside began to change rapidly and radically. I-81 siphoned off regional traffic that had used U.S. 11 to move between the mid-Atlantic states and the southern mountains. From 1948 to the eve of the interstate, traffic on U.S. 11 increased steadily (see figs. 8.18 and 8.19). Traffic counts in each of the Virginia Shenandoah Valley counties revealed that between 1948 — after war rationing was lifted and fuel, tires, and new cars were increasingly available — and 1958, U.S. 11 traffic increased dramatically, more than doubling along some road segments. By 1968, however, the new interstate's siphoning effect was already pronounced. With one exception, traffic on all U.S. 11 road segments declined, some precipitously, after the interstate opened. In Botetourt County, 1968 traffic was only 39 percent of that in 1958, for example. Only in Frederick County at Winchester did post-interstate traffic actually increase, nearly doubling to 9,125 vehicles per day. Given that the highway section sampled there included a segment between a new interstate interchange and the central city, this count could have included all those vehicles making interchange connections.

By 1978, the old road had regained the total traffic counts of twenty years earlier but with a difference. U.S. 11 traffic was now largely local — people commuting to work from distant rural subdivisions or towns where unemployment remained high, or people using the road as they always had, for access to local businesses. From 1978 to 2001, traffic in most counties increased at a more gradual rate with the exception of Augusta County. The traffic count section of U.S. 11 ran south of Staunton to Greenville. Within the section, east–west I-64 intersects north–south I-81, and three interchanges link U.S. 11 traffic with the interstates. One of the interchanges became a node for light manufacturing. Other traffic generators include the Frontier Culture Museum, which is sited in the angle of land

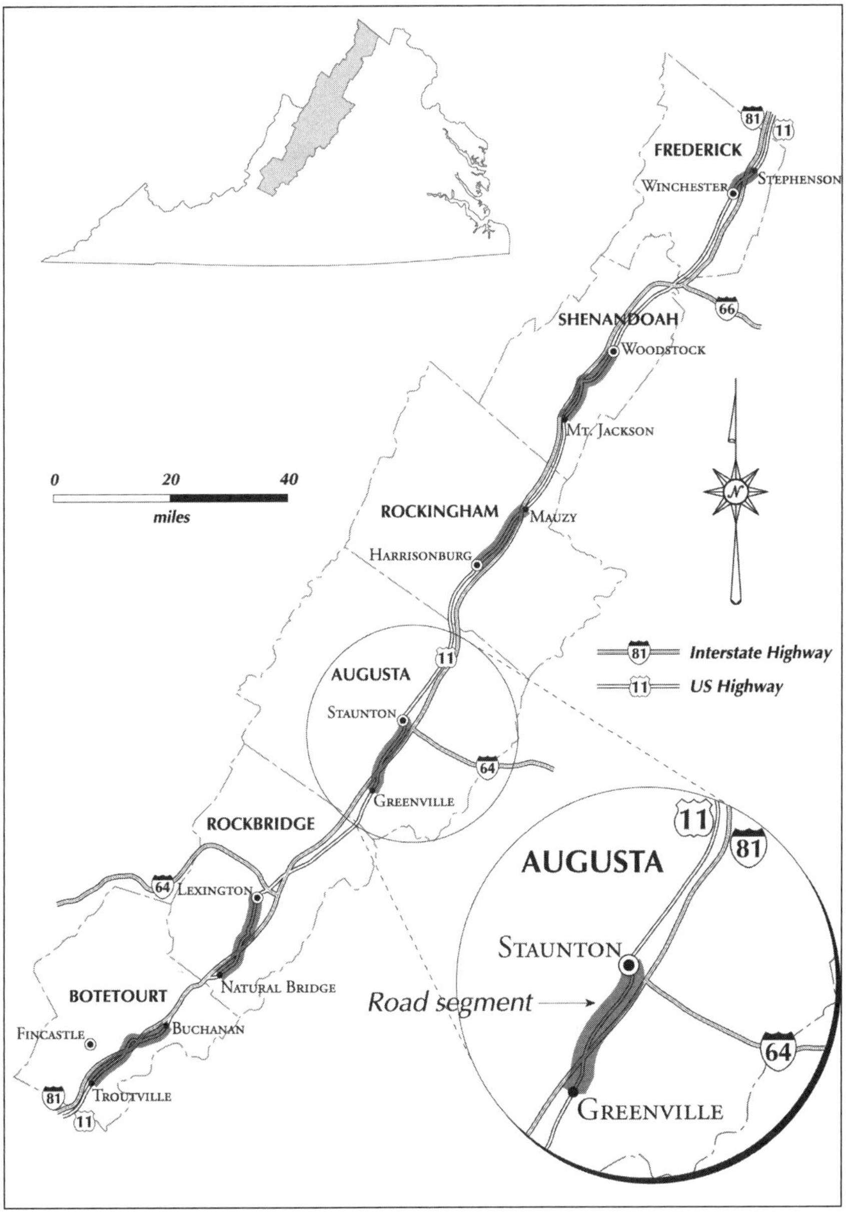

Fig. 8.18. U.S. 11 traffic count road segments, 1938–2001. (Gyula Pauer Cartography Lab, University of Kentucky)

between the interstates and U.S. 11 near Staunton, and its seasonal traffic may inflate this section's aggregate traffic flow.

After World War II, as franchise businesses increased in towns and at interstate interchanges, the through traffic draw-off from U.S. 11 accelerated, exacting ferocious costs from longtime roadside businesses and altering the relationship between road traffic and those making a living at roadside. As traffic declined, the traditional symmetrical relationship

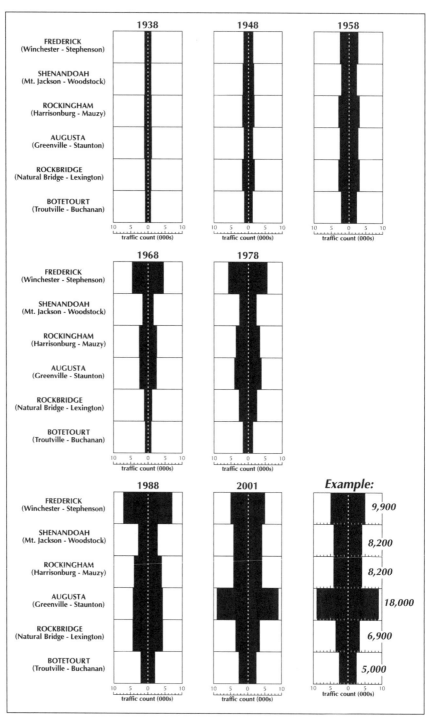

Fig. 8.19. U.S. 11 traffic count, 1938–2001, showing the average total number of vehicles per day. (Gyula Pauer Cartography Lab, University of Kentucky)

between travelers and roadside businesses faltered and then began to fade. Financial solvency evaporated for gas stations, motels, and roadside restaurants, all businesses that had catered to travelers, as they experienced precipitous declines in business when traffic moved to the new roadways. Other retail businesses that had occupied small, town's-edge strip shopping centers also vacated their stores as soon as the owners could find alternative accommodations near an interstate interchange, or on the road that linked the interchange to a city business district. A new, asymmetrical relationship between the roadside and road begin to emerge wherein new kinds of businesses that did not directly serve road travelers or depend necessarily upon road traffic volume for financial success reoccupied vacated roadside structures. Though the process was spatially ragged and temporally idiosyncratic, it was roughly akin to a rotation or cycling that might be termed the "clientele transition."[77]

As applied to U.S. 11, the clientele transition meant that sites that had been occupied by businesses that had directly served truckers and automobile-borne travelers were either leased or sold to new occupants whose business was incidental to highway access, or the buildings were closed and stood empty. Should the second business fail, the building might be reoccupied by another business even further removed from direct dependence upon highway traffic. In abstract form, the roadside clientele transition might read as follows:

Primary Clientele — Roadside buildings are occupied by businesses that are directly dependent upon selling products or services to road traffic, such as gas stations, restaurants, and motels. Land values and rents are high.

Secondary Clientele — Buildings sold or leased to businesses that are indirectly related to road traffic. Examples include a gas station that becomes a used-car lot, a nationally franchised restaurant that becomes a locally owned mom-and-pop restaurant, or a motel that is converted into apartments or a retirement home. In each case, the new building use relates more or less directly to the qualities and plan of the original building. A used-car lot can make use of the recycled gas station service bays for reconditioning, servicing, and washing used cars, just as motel rooms with bathroom facilities can be readily converted into small apartments that rent by the week. Land values stagnate or decline, and rents are substantially reduced.

Tertiary Clientele — Buildings resold or leased to new businesses that relate to the road only in the sense that the road, as with any other road or street, provides access to customers. The gas station that became a used-car lot is sold and becomes a florist shop or horticultural nursery. The original gas station space and facilities now relate to its occupying business only in that it offers sheltered interior space. Some roadside structures, especially those in small towns or open country, may cycle directly from primary to tertiary uses without passing through the intermediate stage of the transition. Land values are stable, responding to general inflation in the land market, but rents or lease costs remain reduced.

The clientele transition in roadside businesses may be accompanied by a change in the class or socioeconomic status of the people who utilize the recycled structures. Roadside motels, for example, catered to mainstream middle-class travelers.[78] When recycled into apartments or "weeklies," however, the motel's clientele will likely change to the economically marginalized. Motel apartment residents may not be able to afford the high monthly house or apartment rents demanded in county seat towns because they are underemployed, or are subsisting on government payments for disability or child care. The clues to permanent motel apartment residence include signs that advertise "rent by the week or month," children's toys scattered about, and charcoal grills and patio furniture near the unit doors.

In the automobile era's early decades, roadside buildings erected by local people with limited training in business or building design were often improvisational — people built according to other businesses that they saw, or they recognized the need to increase their visibility and invented ways of representing their businesses through signs and symbols. Proliferating businesses segmented roadside real estate into a concourse of small properties, each uniquely detailed and configured.[79] Such nonstandard building design waned with the 1930s–1950s boom in franchising, when standardized formulaic buildings began to shoulder out the older vernacular structures at roadside.

When the interstate began to siphon away U.S. 11 traffic in the 1960s, improvisation returned to the roadside, not in building design but in the types of businesses that reoccupied closed properties. Along the road in open country, ten miles south of Staunton at Poor Creek Lane, stands a 1930s cabin court, the twenty-unit Sleepy Hollo Motel ("Hollo" rather than "Hollow"). Though a considerable distance from the nearest sizable town, the rationale for this motel's location seems clear because across the highway, no more than two miles to the east, the Blue Ridge presents its superlative western face to those who might appreciate the view. The motel's office and restaurant building are closed, sealed against antique poachers and vandals. A hand-lettered "For Rent" sign is nailed to the out-

Fig. 8.20. A U.S. 11 commercial strip south of Staunton. Business cycling and redevelopment are suggested by the Mexican restaurant that occupies a building that formerly housed a local restaurant and by a quick-lube business that has supplanted the full-service gas station. (Scott Jost 2004)

side wall. All of the cabins, now nearly seventy years old, are occupied by long-term residents who rent by the week. This is the most common secondary use of recycled motels along the old highway. The antique motel sign out front is heavily weathered; jagged pieces of neon light tubes still cling to their mounting brackets. The painted words "Tile Baths," "Radiant Heat," and "AAA Approved" are still legible.

Farther north, at Staunton's south side, just south of the railroad viaduct, a 1950s–1960s strip lies less than a mile from the I-81 interchange. Intensive development around the interchange is anchored by new four-story motels, auto dealerships, the Staunton Colonial Mall, and big-box stores that strive to capture the region's business. Destabilized first by the interstate and now by interchange development, the old strip is fully engaged in the clientele transition process. An old Kentucky Fried Chicken restaurant became an ice cream parlor, which then moved out, replaced by a quick loan business that caters to migrant workers and others who need bridge loans between paychecks. A full-service gas station has been refit as a convenience store. A classic 1950s drive-in restaurant became, in turn, a Mexican restaurant, two different Chinese restaurants, and an Asian restaurant.

Another dimension of the roadside transition relates to the comparative value of roadside land after the interstate was completed in the early

Fig. 8.21. The Harrisonburg Motor Express Company parks truck tractors along U.S. 11 north of Harrisonburg. This site adjoins a road with direct access to an Interstate 81 interchange about one mile to the east. Sleeper units the size of small camping trailers are accessible from the truck cab and suggest that "over-the-road" truckers no longer patronize roadside motels but can reduce operating costs by overnighting at interstate highway roadside rests. (Scott Jost 2004)

1960s. Land values along the old federal highway stagnated while land costs close to interstate interchanges rapidly increased, especially at those select locations that linked directly to county seat towns and major east–west federal highways.[80] The land price differential was critical to space-intensive businesses such as mobile home and manufactured housing sales, new and used truck and car sales, truck and trailer repair, farm machinery dealers, and landscape nurseries. The five-to-ten-acre sites these businesses required to display or store merchandise became prohibitively expensive if located in proximity to interstate interchanges. Instead, these businesses chose selected sites along U.S. 11 that were close enough to an interstate access point to serve auto-borne customers but sufficiently far away that land costs were not prohibitive. At Harrisonburg, the old U.S. 11 strip south of town — once the exclusive site of the Belle Meade Motel and drive-in restaurants — is now lined with four manufactured housing sales businesses, a Mack Truck sales and service center, several auto dealers, and a big-box lumber store.

The complex, multilayered process of land use change and build-

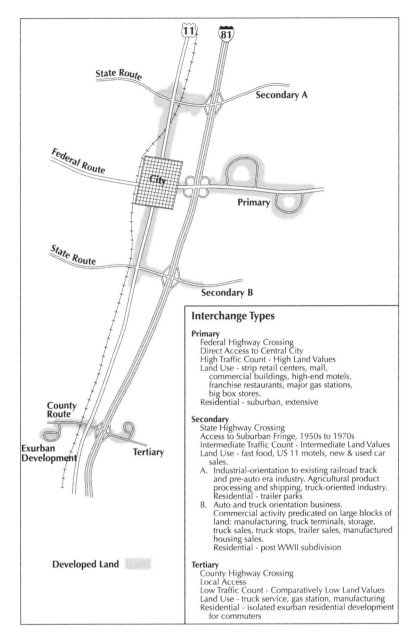

Fig. 8.22. U.S. 11 and I-81 interchange types. (Gyula Pauer Cartography Lab, University of Kentucky)

Interchange Types

Primary
  Federal Highway Crossing
  Direct Access to Central City
  High Traffic Count - High Land Values
  Land Use - strip retail centers, mall,
      commercial buildings, high-end motels,
      franchise restaurants, major gas stations,
      big box stores.
  Residential - suburban, extensive

Secondary
  State Highway Crossing
  Access to Suburban Fringe, 1950s to 1970s
  Intermediate Traffic Count - Intermediate Land Values
  Land Use - fast food, US 11 motels, new & used car
      sales.
  A. Industrial-orientation to existing railroad track
      and pre-auto era industry. Agricultural product
      processing and shipping, truck-oriented industry.
      Residential - trailer parks
  B. Auto and truck orientation business.
      Commercial activity predicated on large blocks of
      land: manufacturing, truck terminals, storage,
      truck sales, truck stops, trailer sales, manufactured
      housing sales.
      Residential - post WWII subdivision

Tertiary
  County Highway Crossing
  Local Access
  Low Traffic Count - Comparatively Low Land Values
  Land Use - truck service, gas station, manufacturing
  Residential - isolated exurban residential development
      for commuters

ing transition along U.S. 11 and its umbilical links to the interstate can be summarized diagrammatically (see fig. 8.22). Most Valley county seat towns also became important crossroads for federal highways such as the junction of U.S. 50 and U.S. 11 in Winchester, and U.S. 60 with U.S. 11 in central Lexington. State highways and county routes also intersected with U.S. 11 but often on the periphery or in small villages some distance from larger urban places. When the interstate opened beside U.S. 11 in the 1960s, the effects were multidimensional. As the interstate siphoned traffic away from U.S. 11, established roadside businesses faltered and failed, setting the clientele transition process in motion. As demand for interchange land increased, land values soared at the primary interchange that linked the interstate with the old federal cross highway. Those businesses that depended upon high traffic counts erected new structures at these primary interchanges. Secondary interchanges, on the edge of town or where state highway routes crossed, were less attractive for these businesses but offered cheaper accessible property to businesses that required land in large blocks. Where railroad tracks crossed U.S. 11, existing industry and related truck traffic created a nuisance landscape that discouraged investment in high-quality residential projects so those places tended to remain in industry and related land uses.

Finally, the tertiary interstate interchanges a mile or more beyond the town's suburban fringe, often intersecting a small county road and crossroads village, attracted a mix of traditional roadside businesses and became places for speculative exurban residential developments built for people seeking cheap homesites but willing to commute to work via the interstate. Of all land use changes along U.S. 11 or at I-81 interchanges, new residential developments are the least ambiguous visually, are contributing to highway traffic, and are creating profound social and economic changes in the traditional roadside communities where they are sited. Many new suburban or exurban residential developments have sprouted in the Valley's north end, now an hour's commute from Washington, D.C., via I-66, in response to high land and housing costs in the nation's capital. But local economic growth and the Valley's attraction to new businesses and retirees also stimulate rapid conversion of farmland into tract housing and apartment construction.

Since 1994, when the North American Free Trade Agreement (NAFTA) went into effect, the flow of consumer goods via truck between Canada, the United States, and Mexico has increased sharply. Heavy truck traffic in the Megalopolis corridor from Boston to Richmond, especially on I-81, aggravated congestion and compromised safety on the four-lane roadway. Two large construction consortiums, STAR (Safer Transport and Roadways) Solutions, and Fluor Virginia, Inc., have presented to state and federal transportation officials competing plans to upgrade I-81. The STAR plan would increase the present four-lane interstate to eight lanes, cost over $13 billion to complete, and impose a toll on trucks. The Fluor plan would add one additional lane to each side of the interstate, cost about $7 billion, and be paid for in part by tolls on both cars and trucks. Both plans met with considerable local resistance. Just as the initial construction of

I-81 created a sea change in U.S. 11 usage and roadside landscapes, so will a large-scale expansion of the existing in-state highway result in unintended consequences for the Valley communities that lie in its proximity.[81]

Coda

Reconstructing the old Valley Road into U.S. 11 evoked the disciplines of engineering and state and federal regulations that configured highway use in systematic ways. By the 1930s, road construction had become a formal engineering enterprise, sufficiently expensive that even minor roadwork required considerable legal work, surveying, and engineering preparation. The engineered road was broad, low gradient, and of consistent dimensions, and road surface quality differed little from one mile to the next. Subject to federal and state standards, the managed road included uniform signage that proclaimed speed limits and directed drivers' attention to railroad crossings and highway junctions. Centerline strips divided lanes, and highway patrol and ambulance services enforced regulations or attended to those injured in traffic accidents. Regulation and regimen-

Fig. 8.24. Traffic stopped for a vehicular accident on southbound I-81 near Fairfield in Rockbridge County. (Scott Jost 2004)

tation made the new hard-surface highway a highly predictable place — a boon to drivers and an invitation to roadside entrepreneurs to divine ways to serve travelers' needs and to exploit the golden stream of money that passed along the corridor.

The U.S. 11 roadside became a stage for local occupants who erected all manner of idiosyncratic vernacular buildings and businesses that represented themselves to the traveling public through new signs and symbols. The roadside became a trial ground of experimentation in vernacular business rather than a product of proven moneymaking models as taught in professional business schools. Franchise gasoline stations in the 1920s and 1930s and, later, franchise restaurants and motels displaced the vernacular roadside in favor of structures based upon calculated corporate decisions that produced standardization and predictability. But the U.S. 11 roadside never became fully franchised as locally owned businesses, especially in small towns, continued to serve local markets as well as inquisitive travelers. By the mid-1960s when I-81 opened, the roadside was a polymorphous agglomeration of vernacular and franchise businesses, manufactured tourist attractions, private residences, farmsteads, and a broad assortment of other land uses. Some structures dating from the 1920s and 1930s — gas stations and cabin camps — had been abandoned or recycled into other uses. Opening the interstate siphoned off a large proportion of the old highway's regional traffic, and with that the sustaining income that provided the solvency for many U.S. 11 roadside businesses.

From its inception as an automobile highway in the 1920s, the roadside building ensemble has never been stable but has cycled and recycled, first in localized vernacular modes, then to franchise standardization, followed by a revernacularization of structures and businesses when travelers fled to the interstate. The result is a federal highway roadside of fragments representing different eras, technologies, and business philosophies. Some long-abandoned structures are in ruins; others retain their outward shape and configuration even as their interiors serve other uses. Now disconnected from the historic contexts from which they sprang, these old structures are neutralized in the sense that they no longer directly embody the ideas that provided their original reason-for-being as functioning sites. Nevertheless, the contemporary U.S. 11 traveler, if inquisitive and thoughtful, may assemble a montage of historic building and landscape images that, through imagination and allegory, will suggest or imply the ideas and ideals that roadside businesses embodied when they were being used according to the builder's original intentions. The U.S. 11 roadside, as with other major federal highway routes, promoted the freedom of movement that auto drivers embraced by adopting new forms of travel accommodations, assuring reliability of the transport medium, and providing a sense of security. In this manner, roadside businesses extended the "comforts of home" along the road.[82]

A considerable irony can be distilled from the very complex process of roadside transition and recycling — the interstate highway has bolstered the old U.S. highway landscape even as it replaced the old road as the primary regional thoroughfare. The geographic shift of business away from U.S. 11 highway road frontage to interstate interchanges also removed the rationale for tearing down outdated roadside buildings to replace them with new structures conforming to formulaic franchise requirements. At some future date, communities along U.S. 11 may recognize that although considerable automobile-era roadside building stock remains, awaiting reuse or restoration, it is also in need of some form of stabilization and preservation. While preservation of old roadside structures will most likely be idiosyncratic to community motivation and sensibilities, however it is undertaken, substantive preservation programs must transcend mere antiquarianism to incorporate more compelling rationales. For example, representations of the past can offer an "escape" or an alternative to an unacceptable present, as well as providing a basis for rendering the present familiar.[83] What would be more reasonable than trying to understand the profound consumerist magnets that interstate interchanges have become — infusing into the travel experience a repetition of interchangeable experiences at nationally franchised chain gas stations, motels, restaurants, malls, auto dealerships, and the rest — by experiencing these same activities in a 1950s context?

Having observed the roadside clientele transition in operation, however, one must also voice concern that an extensive preservation program could disturb the new social dynamics of roadside occupancy. Refurbishing roadside structures could disable the social transition process and displace those people who utilize foregone structures as their entry point into a new entrepreneurial life or as a last defense against homelessness. The road and the roadside must not be viewed in a detached, mechanistic way predicated in the basic economics of profit or loss, use or abandonment. Rather, we must recognize that the road and roadside have become inextricably interwoven with the larger social and political processes that operate in each community. Much more than an objective nexus of asphalt highway and concrete block buildings, the road and the roadside are mutually contingent, mutually contextual, and are together embedded in a community's cultural geographies.

Notes

The quotation by John Brinkerhoff Jackson that serves as this chapter's epigraph is from Helen Lefkowitz Horowitz, ed., *Landscape in Sight, Looking at America* (New Haven: Yale University Press, 1997).

1. Warren R. Hofstra, "Private Dwellings, Public Ways, and the Landscape of Early Rural Capitalism in Virginia's Shenandoah Valley," in Elizabeth Collins Cromley and Carter L. Hudgins, eds., *Gender, Class, and Shelter,* Perspectives in Vernacular Architecture no. 5 (Knoxville: University of Tennessee Press, 1995), 219.

2. N. S. Shaler, *American Highways: A Popular Account of Their Conditions and of the Means by Which They May Be Bettered* (New York: Century, 1896), 26.

3. Ibid., 193.

4. Malcolm M. Willey and Stuart A. Rice, *Communication Agencies and Social Life* (New York: McGraw-Hill, 1933), 47–48.

5. Corey T. Lesseig, *Automobility: Social Changes in the American South, 1909–1939* (New York: Routledge, 2001), 95.

6. David L. Cohn, *Combustion on Wheels: An Informal History of the Automobile Age* (Boston: Houghton Mifflin, 1944), 177–81.

7. Joseph B. Earle et al., "Automobiles for Physicians' Use," *Journal of the American Medical Association* 46, no. 16 (1906): 1117–207.

8. Albert W. Coates Jr., ed., *. . . the most convenient wayes . . . A Story of Roads in Virginia* (Richmond: Virginia Department of Transportation, 1973), 12.

9. Wilbur Zelinsky, "The Pennsylvania Town: An Overdue Geographical Account," *Geographical Review* 67, no. 2 (1977): 127–47; Richard Pillsbury, "The Urban Street Pattern as a Cultural Indicator: Pennsylvania, 1682–1815," *Annals of the Association of American Geographers* 60, no. 3 (1970): 428–46.

10. Joseph Barnett, "The Highway in Urban and Suburban Areas," in Jean Labatut and Wheaton J. Lane, eds., *Highways in Our National Life: A Symposium* (Princeton, N.J.: Princeton University Press, 1950), 151–53.

11. Bruce E. Seely, *Building the American Highway System: Engineers as Policy Makers* (Philadelphia: Temple University Press, 1987), 25.

12. Willey and Rice, *Communication Agencies and Social Life*, 45.

13. Jean Gottmann, *Virginia in Our Century* (Charlottesville: University Press of Virginia, 1955), 136.

14. Coates, *A Story of Roads in Virginia*, 12.

15. Federal Highway Administration, *America's Highways — 1776–1976: A History of the Federal-Aid Program* (Washington, D.C.: U.S. Government Printing Office, 1976), 86.

16. Ibid., 86–87.

17. Ibid., 108.

18. Howard L. Preston, *Dirt Roads to Dixie: Accessibility and Modernization in the South, 1885–1935* (Knoxville: University of Tennessee Press, 1991), 50.

19. John A. Jakle, "Pioneer Roads: America's Early Twentieth-Century Named Highways," *Material Culture* 32, no. 2 (2000): 2.

20. Susie C. Palmer, "The Development of Virginia Highways" (master's thesis, University of Virginia, 1930), 39; Richard F. Weingroff, "Dr. S. M. Johnson, A Dreamer of Dreams," http://www.fhwa.dot.gov/infrastructure/johnson.htm.

21. Federal Highway Administration, *America's Highways — 1776–1976*, 110; "Standard Signs Adopted for Federal Highways," *American City Magazine* 33 (October 1925): 412–13.

22. John W. Wayland, *The Valley Turnpike Winchester to Staunton, And Other Roads* (Winchester, Va.: Winchester-Frederick County Historical Society, 1967), 28.

23. Stanley Willis, "'To Lead Virginia out of the Mud': Financing the Old Dominion's Public Roads, 1922–1924," *Virginia Magazine of History and Biography* 94, no. 4 (1986): 427; Gottmann, *Virginia in Our Century*, 136.

24. Coates, *A Story of Roads in Virginia*, 18.

25. Palmer, "The Development of Virginia Highways," 41.

26. Seely, *Building the American Highway System*, 72–77.

27. A. G. Bruce and R. D. Brown, "The Trend of Highway Design," *Public Roads* 8, no. 1 (1927): 7, 12, table 1.

28. Ibid, 8–9.

29. David R. Levin, "Highway Right-Of-Way Problems," *American Highways* 27, no. 1 (1948): 9–10.

30. Wayland, *The Valley Turnpike Winchester to Staunton*, 17.

31. Bruce and Brown, "The Trend of Highway Design," 14.

32. Wayland, *The Valley Turnpike Winchester to Staunton*, 76.

33. Ibid., 95.

34. Ibid., 90–91.

35. Gerald Carson, *The Old Country Store* (New York: Oxford University Press, 1954), 280–82.

36. This trend was not restricted to Valley residents and institutions but oc-

curred nationally (see Lesseig, *Automobility*, 99–102; and Catherine M. Stock, *Main Street in Crisis: The Great Depression and the Old Middle Class on the Northern Plains* [Chapel Hill: University of North Carolina Press, 1992], 114–16).

37. William O. Stevens, *The Shenandoah and Its Byways* (New York: Dodd, Mead, 1941), 76.

38. John A. Jakle, "The American Gasoline Station, 1920–1970," *Journal of American Culture* 1, no. 3 (1978): 522–24.

39. R. James Claus and Walter G. Hardwick, *The Mobile Consumer: Automobile-Oriented Retailing and Site Selection* (Don Mills, Ontario: Collier-Macmillan Canada, 1972), 64–65.

40. Jakle, "The American Gasoline Station," 524–29.

41. David E. Kyvig, *Daily Life in the United States, 1920–1939: Decades of Promise and Pain* (Westport, Conn.: Greenwood Press, 2002), 38–39.

42. "Gasoline: Mr. Jenkins and Sir Henri," *Fortune* 6, no. 4 (1932): 34–35, 104.

43. Jakle, "The American Gasoline Station," 529–32.

44. John A. Jakle and Keith A. Sculle, *The Gas Station in America* (Baltimore: Johns Hopkins University Press, 1994), 72.

45. Ibid, 154.

46. Beckie Kelly, "To Co-brand or Not to Co-brand," *National Petroleum News* (July 1998), http://www.petroretail.net/npn/archives/0798/798cstre.asp.

47. Stevens, *The Shenandoah and Its Byways*, 71.

48. Willey and Rice, *Communication Agencies and Social Life*, 69.

49. Norman Hayner, "The Auto Camp as a New Type of Hotel," *Sociology and Social Research* 15, no. 4 (1931): 370–71.

50. Ibid., 66–67; Rolland S. Wallis, "Auto-Tourist Camps," *National Municipal Review* 12, no. 4 (1923): 180–81.

51. Wayland, *The Valley Turnpike Winchester to Staunton*, 79.

52. The material on auto courts and motels was drawn from John A. Jakle, "Motel by the Roadside: America's Room for the Night," *Journal of Cultural Geography* 1, no. 1 (1980): 34–49. See also John A. Jakle, Keith A. Sculle, and Jefferson S. Rogers, *The Motel in America* (Baltimore: John Hopkins University Press, 1996).

53. American Hotel Association Directory Corporation (AHADC), *The Official Hotel Red Book and Directory, 1950–1951*, 65th ed. (New York: AHADC, 1950), 978, 982.

54. Chester H. Liebs, *Main Street to Miracle Mile: American Roadside Architecture* (Boston: Little, Brown), 187.

55. James Agee, "The Great American Roadside," *Fortune* 10, no. 3 (1934): 174.

56. Karl Raitz, ed. *The National Road* (Baltimore: Johns Hopkins University Press, 1996), 303.

57. Richard L. Nelson, *The Selection of Retail Locations* (New York: F. W. Dodge, 1958), 66–78.

58. John A. Jakle, "Roadside Restaurants and Place-Product-Packaging," *Journal of Cultural Geography* 3, no. 1 (1982): 80–82.

59. John Durant, "The Movies Take to the Pastures," *Saturday Evening Post* 233 (1950): 24.

60. Duncan Hines, *Duncan Hines "Food Odyssey"* (New York: Thomas Y. Crowell, 1955), 26–27.

61. Richard H. Schein, "The Place of Landscape: A Conceptual Framework for an American Scene," *Annals of the Association of American Geographers* 87, no. 4 (1997): 663.

62. Ibid.

63. Erving Goffman, *The Presentation of Self in Everyday Life* (New York: Doubleday, 1959), 22–30.

64. Karen Fields, *Lemon Swamp and Other Places: A Carolina Memoir* (New York: Free Press, 1983), 43; Clay McShane, *Down the Asphalt Path: The Automobile and the American City* (New York: Columbia University Press, 1994), 227–28.

65. David Gartman, *Auto Opium* (London: Routledge, 1994), 53–54.

66. Phil Patton, *Open Road: A Celebration of the American Highway* (New York: Simon and Schuster, 1986), 159.

67. Robert Venturi, Denise Scott Brown, and Steven Izenour, *Learning from Las Vegas: The Forgotten Symbolism of Architectural Form* (Cambridge: MIT Press, 1972), 51–67.

68. J. B. Jackson, "Other-Directed Houses," in Helen Lefkowitz Horowitz, ed., *Landscape in Sight: Looking at America* (New Haven: Yale University Press, 1997), 190–91.

69. Dixon Wechter, *The Saga of American Society: A Record of Social Aspiration, 1607–1937* (New York: Charles Scribner's Sons, 1937), 1–7.

70. Russell Lynes, *The Tastemakers* (New York: Harper and Brothers, 1955), 5.

71. Jackson, "Other-Directed Houses," 190–91; Robert Venturi and Denise Scott Brown, "A Significance for A&P Parking Lots," *Architectural Forum* 128, no. 2 (1968): 38. See also Reyner Banham, *Los Angeles: The Architecture of Four Ecologies* (New York: Penguin Books, 1973), 121.

72. Mr. Harper, "American Landscape I," *Harper's Magazine* 200, no. 1196 (1950): 101.

73. Phillip Tocker, "Standardized Outdoor Advertising: History, Economics, and Self-Regulation," in John W. Houck, ed. *Outdoor Advertising: History and Regulation* (Notre Dame, Ind.: University of Notre Dame Press, 1969), 35, 45.

74. William R. Ewald, *Street Graphics* (McLean, Va.: Landscape Architecture Foundation, 1977), 15–24.

75. Elizabeth B. and Walter L. Lawton, "The Story of a Highway," *Nature Magazine* 34, no. 5 (1941): 262; Benton Mackaye and Lewis Mumford, "Townless Highways for the Motorist," *Harper's Magazine* 163, no. 8 (1931): 347. See also Walter B. Pitkin, "The American: How He Lives," in Fred J. Ringel, ed., *America as Americans See It* (New York: Literary Guild, 1932), 202.

76. William K. Wyckoff, "Landscapes of Private Power and Wealth," in Michael P. Conzen, ed., *The Making of the American Landscape* (Boston: Unwin Hyman, 1990), 349–50.

77. James Darlington, "Landscape, Image, and Social Change: The Catskill Resort Region, 1820–1940," manuscript, 1995.

78. Travelers have long sorted themselves by class in their choice of roadside

accommodations (see, for example, J. Winston Coleman Jr. *Stage-Coach Days in the Bluegrass* [Lexington: University Press of Kentucky, 1935; repr., 1995], 163). Automobile manufacturers pitched their products to class-conscious buyers. A 1925 General Motors advertising slogan was, "A car for every purse and purpose," referring to their full-spectrum line of vehicles — Chevrolet, Oldsmobile, Buick, Cadillac, Oakland, and GM trucks (William Leach, *Land of Desire: Merchants, Power, and the Rise of a New American Culture* [New York: Pantheon Books, 1993], 341).

79. Karl Raitz, "American Roads, Roadside America," *Geographical Review* 88, no. 3 (1998): 385.

80. Rudolf Hess, "Land Values Before and After Freeway Development," *American City* 67 (October 1952): 117.

81. See, for example, http://www.dnronline.com/archives2004/1-24-04/story1 .asp.

82. Susan Buck-Morss, *The Dialects of Seeing: Walter Benjamin and the Arcades Project* (Cambridge: MIT Press, 1989), 164–65.

83. David Lowenthal, *The Past Is a Foreign Country* (Cambridge: Cambridge University Press, 1985), 36–50.

CONTRIBUTORS

James K. Bryant II is Associate Professor and former Chair of the Department of History at Shenandoah University in Winchester, Virginia. His areas of specialization take into account nineteenth- and twentieth-century American history, African American history, U.S. military history, Civil War history, the American South, the Atlantic slave trade, comparative slavery, and oral history. His publications include "'... That Sable Hero': African-Americans in the Fredericksburg–Area Battlefields" for the *Fredericksburg Historical Journal,* and *Chancellorsville Campaign: The Nation's High Water Mark,* and he is revising a manuscript tentatively entitled "'A Model Regiment': The 36th U.S. Colored Infantry in Slavery and Freedom," focusing on former slaves–turned soldiers and their families in eastern North Carolina and southeastern Virginia. He has also completed chapters covering antebellum compromises and Reconstruction state governments for upcoming volumes of *Conflicts in American History* to be published by Facts on File.

Warren R. Hofstra is Stewart Bell Professor of History at Shenandoah University. In addition to teaching in the fields of American social and cultural history and directing the Community History Project of Shenandoah University, he has written or edited books on various aspects of American regional history including *The Planting of New Virginia: Settlement and Landscape in the Shenandoah Valley* (2004); *A Separate Place: The Formation of Clarke County, Virginia* (1986, 1999); *George Washington and the Virginia Backcountry* (1998); *After the Backcountry: Rural Life in the Great Valley of Virginia, 1800–1900* (2000); *Virginia Reconsidered: New Histories of the Old Dominion* (2003); and *Cultures in Conflict: The Seven Years' War in North America* (2007).

Kenneth W. Keller is Professor of History at Mary Baldwin College. His monograph *Rural Politics and the Collapse of Pennsylvania Federalism* (1982) was published by the American Philosophical Society. He has also published numerous articles in a variety of scholarly journals, encyclopedias, and essay collections concerning the frontier and Virginia, Pennsylvania, Missouri, and New Jersey history.

Geraldine Wojno Kiefer is Associate Professor of Art History and Studio Art at Shenandoah University. She teaches art appreciation, modern and American art history, history of photography, and a two-semester foundational course in drawing. Her academic interests include European and American art, photography, and critical theory, with a particular interest in cultural and feminist interpretations from about 1850 to the present. She has written book and exhibition reviews, scholarly articles, and exhibition catalogues as well as published a monograph on the photographer Alfred Stieglitz. Her art has been exhibited in solo and group exhibitions, invitational and juried, in Ohio, Georgia, Virginia, Maryland, and Hawaii.

Gabrielle M. Lanier is Associate Professor of History at James Madison University, where she directs the Public History program and the Center for Valley and Regional Studies. She is the author of *The Delaware Valley in the Early Republic: Architecture, Landscape, and Regional Identity* (2005), and *Everyday Architecture of the Mid-Atlantic: Looking at Buildings and Landscapes* (1997, with Bernard L. Herman), which won the Fred Kniffen Prize for the best book in material culture for 1999. She has published, presented papers, or lectured on topics including the building process in the early national period, the intersection of legend and regional identity in the built environment, ethnicity and the early American landscape, architectural documentation, the reconstitution of the early American landscape using the 1798 Federal Direct Tax, and interpretation issues at museums and historic sites. Her fieldwork, which has ranged from southern Maine to coastal South Carolina and central Kentucky, has concentrated on the architectural and cultural landscapes of the mid-Atlantic region.

Ann McCleary is Professor of History and Director of the Center for Public History at the University of West Georgia. Her research for this chapter draws on her experience as an architectural historian for the Virginia Department of Historic Resources, where she researched buildings and communities in Augusta and Rockingham counties. She has published several articles on vernacular architecture in the Shenandoah Valley and has spent the last twenty-five years documenting the history and material culture not only of the Shenandoah Valley but also in Georgia, where she now lives and works.

Michael N. McConnell is Associate Professor of History at the University of Alabama at Birmingham, where he teaches early American history. He has published two books, *A Country Between: The Upper Ohio Valley and Its Peoples, 1724–1774* (1992) and *Army and Empire: British Soldiers on the American Frontier* (2004). He has also published in scholarly journals and essay collections.

Karl Raitz is Arts & Sciences Distinguished Professor at the University of Kentucky. His research and teaching interests include cultural and historical geography emphasizing American landscapes, visual and qualitative methods, and regional studies in the United States, especially the upland South. His research on roads includes editing the two-volume work *The National Road* and *A Guide to the National Road* (1996). His research has been supported by the National Endowment for the Humanities, the Pioneer America Society, the Kentucky Transportation Cabinet, and other agencies.

INDEX

—